Monographs of the
Hebrew Union College
Number 24

———

To Reveal Our Hearts:
Jewish Women Writers
in Tsarist Russia

An I. Edward Kiev
Library Foundation Book

Monographs of the Hebrew Union College

1. Lewis M. Barth, *An Analysis of Vatican 30*
2. Samson H. Levey, *The Messiah: An Aramaic Interpretation*
3. Ben Zion Wacholder, *Eupolemus: A Study of Judaeo-Greek Literature*
4. Richard Victor Bergren, *The Prophets and the Law*
5. Benny Kraut, *From Reform Judaism to Ethical Culture: The Religious Evolution of Felix Adler*
6. David B. Ruderman, *The World of a Renaissance Jew: The Life and Thought of Abraham ben Mordecai Farrisol*
7. Alan Mendelson, *Secular Education in Philo of Alexandria*
8. Ben Zion Wacholder, *The Dawn of Qumran: the Sectarian Torah and the Teacher of Righteousness*
9. Stephen M. Passamaneck, *The Traditional Jewish Law of Sale: Shulḥan Arukh, Ḥoshen Mishpat, Chapters 189-240*
10. Yael S. Feldman, *Modernism and Cultural Transfer: Gabriel Preil and the Tradition of Jewish Literary Bilingualism*
11. Raphael Jospe, *Torah and Sophia: The Life and Thought of Shem Tov ibn Falaquera*
12. Richard Kalmin, *The Redaction of the Babylonian Talmud: Amoraic or Saboraic?*
13. Shuly Rubin Schwartz, *The Emergence of Jewish Scholarship in America: The Publication of the Jewish Encyclopedia*
14. John C. Reeves, *Jewish Lore in Manichaean Cosmogony: Studies in the Book of Giants Traditions*
15. Robert Kirschner, *Baraita De Melekhet Ha-Mishkan: A Critical Edition with Introduction and Translation*
16. Philip E. Miller, *Karaite Separatism in Nineteenth-Century Russia: Joseph Solomon Lutski's Epistle of Israel's Deliverance*
17. Warren Bargad, *"To Write the Lips of Sleepers": The Poetry of Amir Gilboa*
18. Marc Saperstein, *"Your Voice Like a Ram's Horn": Themes and Texts in Traditional Jewish Preaching*
19. Emanuel Melzer, *No Way Out: The Politics of Polish Jewry, 1935-1939*
20. Eric L. Friedland, *"Were Our Mouths Filled With Song": Studies in Liberal Jewish Liturgy*
21. Edward Fram, *Ideals Face Reality: Jewish Law and Life in Poland 1550-1655*
22. Ruth Langer, *To Worship God Properly: Tensions Between Liturgical Custom and Halakhah in Judaism*
23. Nili Sacher Fox, *In the Service of the King: Officialdom in Ancient Israel and Judah*
24. Carole B. Balin, *To Reveal Our Hearts: Jewish Women Writers in Tsarist Russia*

To Reveal Our Hearts

Jewish Women Writers
in Tsarist Russia

————

CAROLE B. BALIN

HEBREW UNION COLLEGE PRESS
CINCINNATI

Carole B. Balin and the Hebrew Union College Press gratefully acknowledge a generous grant from the Koret Jewish Studies Publications Program in support of the publication of this book.

Library of Congress Cataloging-in-Publication Data
Balin, Carole B.
    [Jewish women writers in Tsarist Russia]
    To Reveal our hearts : Jewish women writers in Tsarist Russia / Carole B. Balin.
        p. cm. —(Monographs of the Hebrew Union College ; no. 24)
    Rev. ed. of author's dissertation (Ph.D., Columbia University, 1998) issued as Jewish women writers in Tsarist Russia.
    Includes bibliographical references and index.
    ISBN 0-87820-423-7 (cloth)
    1. Russian literature—Jewish authors—History and criticism. 2. Russian literature—Women authors—History and criticism. 3. Jewish women—Russia—Intellectual life. 4. Russian literature—19th century—History and criticism. 5. Women and literature—Russia—History—19th century. I. Title. II. Series.

    PG2998.J4 B35 2000
    891.709'9287'089924—dc21   00-039545

Printed on acid free paper in the United States of America
Distributed by Wayne State University Press
4809 Woodward Avenue, Detroit, MI 48201

"To me, pen and ink are like good and trustworthy friends because they allow us to reveal our hearts and lighten our burdens . . . "

Twenty-two-year-old Hava Shapiro in her diary, August 2, 1900

The I. Edward Kiev Library Foundation

In September 1976 the family and friends of Dr. I. Edward Kiev, distinguished Rabbi, Chaplain, and Librarian of the Hebrew Union College-Jewish Institute of Religion in New York, established a Library Foundation in his memory to support and encourage the knowledge, understanding, and appreciation of scholarship in Judaica and Hebraica. In cooperation with the Hebrew Union College Press, the Foundation offers this work by Carole B. Balin as an I. Edward Kiev Library Foundation Book.

Contents

Acknowledgments   ix

Introduction
Neither Balabustes Nor Revolutionaries:
The Search for Jewish Women Writers in Tsarist Russia   1

1. The Makings of a Maskilah
      Miriam Markel-Mosessohn (1839–1920)   13

2. The Female Experience in Hebrew Literature
      Hava Shapiro (1878–1943)   51

3. Insider-Outsider Among the Russian Cultural Elite
      Rashel' Mironovna Khin (1861–1928)   84

4. A Jewish Life Behind the Scenes
      Feiga Izrailevna Kogan (1891–1974)   124

5. Blending Bread and Matzah
      Sofiia Dubnova-Erlikh (1885–1986)   156

Conclusion
A Composite Biography   195

Notes   203

Bibliographies of the Writers   243

Bibliography   251

Index   263

Acknowledgments

As a child, I intuitively looked to girls and women in print as models for myself. What began as enthusiasm for series like L. M. Montgomery's *Anne of Green Gables* blossomed into a mature interest in literature and history by and about women. So it is perhaps no coincidence that after completing my graduate comprehensive examinations in Jewish and nineteenth-century Russian history six years ago, I should have proposed a dissertation on the undiscovered writings of Jewish women of Tsarist Russia.

By that time, I had had the benefit of studying American women's history at Wellesley College with Jacqueline Jones, whose own elegant writing has become the measuring stick for my own compositions. I had also—like the women in these pages—come under the influence of scholarly men. Since my earliest association with Hebrew Union College-Jewish Institute of Religion a decade and a half ago, its entire faculty has been unstintingly supportive. Martin Cohen, Norman Cohen, Lawrence Hoffman, and Michael Meyer deserve special mention, as do my students, men and women alike. At Columbia University, Michael Stanislawski enabled me to find my own niche in the field of Eastern European Jewish history, and Yosef Yerushalmi's example continues to compel me to think harder and express myself ever more accurately.

I am grateful as well to Tovah Cohen, Shmuel Feiner, Menuhah Gilboa, Nurit Govrin, Erich Haberer, Marion Kaplan, John Klier, Shulamit Magnes, Shimon Markish, Alice Nakhimovsky, Lawrence Rosenwald, and Rochelle Ruthchild for responding to my inquiries for the names of Jewish women writers. Moreover, Naomi Caruso, Barbara Engel, Kristi Groberg, and Alexander Leyfell made the results of their research available to me. And Charlotte Rosenthal, from the beginning, took a special interest in my work and reassured me that this subject of study is a viable one.

Librarians and archivists have given generously of their time and knowledge. I would not have located the hidden documents that proved essential to my work without the assistance of Carol Katz and Claire Stern at the Montreal Jewish Library, Nadia Kahan and Adina Feldstern at HUC-JIR in Jerusalem, Philip Miller at HUC-JIR in New York, Gita Moiseevna Lipson at the Russian State Historical Archive, Viktor Kel'ner at the St. Petersburg Public Library, and archivists at the Russian State Archive of Literature and Art. Lena Schwartz and Vladimir Esicman were instrumental in securing much-needed materials in Moscow, and Victor Erlich graciously lent me photographs of his mother.

The Mellon Foundation in the Humanities provided me with a grant, while the World Union for Progressive Judaism dispensed funds that enabled me to travel and live for extended periods of time within Russia.

I am grateful to the following kind individuals who, over the years, read entire drafts or sections of this work and offered crucial suggestions: Maria Baader, Marcia Balin, Rebecca Balmas, Lisa Epstein, Victor Erlich, Marina Ledkovsky, Anne Lapidus Lerner, Stanley Nash, Benjamin Nathans, Gabriella Safran, and Richard Wortman, as well as members of the Jewish Feminist Research Group at Ma'ayan. Felice Batlan brought her wisdom to every page of a draft. Yuliya Viseyskaya helped me decipher nearly-illegible Russian manuscripts, and Olga Lokshin proofread Russian transliterations with care. Marjorie Lehman and Andrea Weiss encouraged me at every turn.

Barbara Selya at the Hebrew Union College Press has nurtured this book as if it were her own.

My four parents Marcia and Ted Balin and Gloria and Arthur Gertzman, my husband Michael Gertzman, and my children Nathaniel and Eve have all known and lovingly tolerated my passion as a student. I thank God for their presence in my life.

July 27, 2000
24 Tammuz 5760

Introduction

Neither *Balebustes* Nor Revolutionaries

The Search for Jewish Women Writers in Tsarist Russia

Sentimental images depicting the shtetl of Eastern Europe float across the Jewish psyche like so many figures suspended on a Chagall canvas. The glow of *shabbes* candles. Thatched roofs and dirt roads. Children at ḥeder. All evoke a life of simple piety in the small towns of mythic proportions that dotted the landscape of the Pale of Settlement—a vast area comprising central Poland, Ukraine, Byelorussia, and Lithuania, occupied by Russia in the eighteenth century. The anthropological study *Life is with People*, which came to influence the producers of Broadway's "Fiddler on the Roof," popularized the shtetl for all time as a locus of cozy, reassuring joys of family and community.[1] There, men and women knew what was expected of them and rarely ventured beyond the pale—geographically or otherwise. They willingly conformed to the strict rabbinic code of conduct that dictated instructions for daily living.

For a woman this meant maintaining a household, bearing and raising children, and earning a livelihood. For such a woman, education was a frivolity. After all, learning was considered marginal to her primary activities, while it was her husband's major occupation and objective. The Jewish woman spoke Yiddish and enough Russian or Polish to barter in the market place. She observed every precept of religious practice and was responsible for safeguarding and transmitting Jewish tradition to future generations. In a word, she was a *balebuste*, a housewife par excellence.

The *balebuste* stereotype stands in sharp contrast to a second image attributed to the Jewish woman in late nineteenth-century Russia: the rev-

1

olutionary. By most accounts, this female rebel was seduced by political ideologies that promised independence from the restrictions of traditional Jewish life and a new relationship between the sexes. Breaking with her ancestral roots, she ran headlong toward immersion in the greater society. She yearned for its secular offerings and gladly rejected or suppressed all associations with her former community—save perhaps the Yiddish language—to obtain them. The Eastern-European born revolutionaries Rosa Luxemburg and Emma Goldman, the most famous examples, marched onto the pages of radical history and represented a new kind of Jewish woman, at odds with the *balebuste* of old.[2]

In the absence of a comprehensive history on the subject, it is this pair of conflicting images—the *balebuste* and the revolutionary—that have come to define the entirety of Jewish women's experience in the Russian Empire. Such stereotypes obscure the diversity of behavior and the nuances of identity that surely existed among the millions of women in question. History thrives on specificity. It seeks to record and analyze facts as a way of differentiating one experience from another. A lack of details levels the past and silences the historian.

So where might one search for details to begin writing a history of Tsarist Russia's Jewish women? Until recently, it was assumed that the specifics were irretrievable, aside from mostly passing references to women in writings by men, including autobiography, fiction, and the corpus of legal texts of the period.[3] While memoirs and literature by women were available, most appeared after the Russian Revolution of 1917 and the Tsar's demise. The most famous exception is *Memoiren einer Grossmutter* (Memoirs of a Grandmother), composed by Pauline Wengeroff (1833–1916) in the last decade of the nineteenth century.[4] One of only a handful of women to appear in every significant Jewish encyclopedia, Wengeroff gained recognition among English readers when the historian Lucy Dawidowicz included a translated excerpt from her memoirs in the classic source book *The Golden Tradition: Jewish Life and Thought in Eastern Europe.*

Few realize that Wengeroff's actual literary debut predated the publication of her memoirs by six years. In the fall of 1902, an excerpt from her reminiscences appeared in *Voskhod* (Sunrise), the most important Russian-Jewish periodical of the era.[5] Published in St. Petersburg from 1881 to 1906, *Voskhod* boasted a readership of five thousand at the turn of the century. Fashioned after thick journals whose literary and political contents were then attracting a following among the Russian-reading public, *Voskhod* served as a mouthpiece for those advocating that Jews both preserve their national-religious values and gain familiarity with Russian language and culture.

Wengeroff's translation attracted my attention and inspired me to search the pages of *Voskhod* for additional female authors.[6] To my happy amazement, I discovered that Wengeroff was one of nearly thirty women whose translations or original works graced the journal's pages. Beginning in 1881, *Voskhod* became the first journal of the Russian-Jewish press to present a significant number of Jewish women's compositions. Prior to that date, only traces of writings by Jewish women were evident in publications geared toward a Jewish audience. The earliest example of a published piece by a Jewish woman is a Hebrew letter appearing in 1853 in *Kokhvei yitzhak* (Isaac's Stars), an annual that appeared in Vienna from 1845 to 1873.[7]

If *Voskhod* had capitalized on the literary talents of female Jews, I reasoned, so, too, did other organs of the Russian-Jewish press. Thus I searched the main publications—whether in Russian, Hebrew, or Yiddish—for female contributors, realizing, of course, that because of masculine pen names, it was impossible to account for all women writers. Simultaneously, I attempted to recover details of the writers' biographies, though most proved elusive. One Elena Berdieva, for example, penned half a dozen short stories for *Voskhod* throughout the 1880s and 90s, but nothing more is known of her. Female authors of some literary stature did, however, contribute to *Voskhod*, and more is known about them. Pauline Wengeroff's daughter Zinaida Vengerova (1867–1941), who later became the editor of the important Russian journal *Severnyi vestnik* (Northern Herald), wrote for *Voskhod*, as did Maria Saker, a participant in the Odessa literary circle that also included the essayist Ahad Ha'am and the historian Simon Dubnov. Saker also happens to be the Jewish woman credited with the first published work in the Russian-Jewish press, appearing as it did in 1869.[8]

The coincidence of two events allowed me to gain access to information invaluable to my search. The first was the publication of *the Dictionary of Russian Women Writers*, a major collaborative effort that provides biographical details on over five hundred female authors. In what might best be termed a "backdoor approach," I scoured the dictionary and others like it for Jewishly-recognizable names, hoping either to match entries with the writers I had already discovered or to augment my growing list. While I did the same for Jewish resources, searching for female names in such works as the 16-volume *Evreiskaia entsiklopediia* (Jewish Encyclopedia), my labors proved far less fruitful. The second event was the opening, and openness, of archives in the successor states of the Soviet Union. Materials from Russian archives have been supplemented by unpublished papers found in Canada and Israel.

All told, I retrieved the names of sixty-seven Jewish women who from 1869 either wrote for the Russian-Jewish press in the Russian Empire or published separate volumes of literature, poetry, history, or biography. (Several fall into both categories.) Forty-four wrote in Russian, seventeen in Hebrew, and six in Yiddish. In the pages that follow, I introduce readers to dozens of those Jewish women writers and focus on five who not only were the most prolific of the lot but also bequeathed personal information in the form of memoirs, correspondence, autobiographies, or diaries found in archives. The reader will note that because of the relative scarcity of known archival sources for non-émigré Jewish women writers of Yiddish, I focused exclusively on writers of Russian or Hebrew. Moreover, I selected women who spent the bulk of their lives in the Russian Empire and whose cultural creativity emerged out of the Russian milieu prior to the Revolution. Consequently, those who immigrated during their formative years to the land of Israel or the United States are beyond the scope of this book, as are women who came of age after 1917. Finally, I concentrated on women who were born Jews and who understood themselves as such throughout their lives. The selection is not intended to be representative in a historical sense or aesthetically definitive. I hope that my judgments about inclusion will have the positive effect of stimulating serious consideration of those whom I have excluded.

It is obvious that the extraordinary Jewish women discussed in these pages do not typify society at large. Writers tend by nature to be more reflective, more observant and thus, arguably, more removed from the mainstream. Moreover, by the very act of writing, female authors of Jewish descent trespassed the millenia-old literary domain of men and defied age-old stereotypes in the process. Nevertheless, published literary works are often all that we have to piece together a history. Moreover, as cultural historians have argued, in the context of nineteenth-century Russia, secular literature functioned as a "teacher of life" (*uchitel' zhizni*).[9] If so, for Jews seeking integration into Russian society, secular literature came to replace the internal Jewish texts that served for centuries as the exclusive guide for Jewish living. Therefore, secular works by Jews matter; they offer evidence of evolving identity among writers and readers, women and men.

In this volume, each of five Jewish women writers forms the subject of five largely self-contained chapters. In fact, each chapter might be read independently. None of these women regarded herself as part of a continuum of Jewish women writers, as no such continuum existed. Unlike typical histories of literature, in which a linear and progressive development can be discerned from one generation to the next, the Jewish woman writer constructed herself anew in each generation. She neither reacted to nor stood on the shoulders of those who came before her. Unlike her male counterpart, she neither fraternized nor corresponded with others of her sex. She instead attached herself to literary men who were participating in the flurry of cultural activities proliferating among Russians and Jews alike.

This book then is not a history of Jewish women writing. Rather, it is an introduction to five literary women whose lives and works tell a larger story of Jewish cultural history in the Russian Empire. Thus each chapters opens by situating the writer in her own cultural context. In the five chapters that follow, readers will meet

- Miriam Markel-Mosessohn (1839–1920), who became a foreign correspondent for a Hebrew newspaper at the age of forty-eight and settled in Vienna in her early fifties. Tutored in Hebrew as a young girl in the Pale, she came to translate German works into the ancient tongue and tried her hand at poetry as well. For most of her life, she toiled to advance the goals of the Jewish Enlightenment movement in Russia along with her friends Yehudah Leib Gordon, Moses Leib Lilienblum, and Avraham Mapu. Markel-Mosessohn married a man who considered his wife his equal, and she remained childless.
- Hava Shapiro (1879–1943), who used the pseudonym *em kol ḥai*

(mother of all life) and published short stories and newspaper articles in Hebrew over the course of her thirty-four year career. Born in the Pale to a scion of a printing and paper-manufacturing company and a mother fluent in Hebrew, she received a doctorate at the University of Berne and participated in the writing circle convened at the Warsaw home of Y.L. Peretz. Unhappy in her marriage, she carried on a clandestine affair with the writer Reuven Brainin and eventually divorced her husband and temporarily left her only son in his father's care.

- Rashel' Mironovna Khin (1861–1928), who wrote in Russian numerous short stories and plays, two of which were staged at Moscow's Malyi Theater. Although she spent the first several years of her life in the Pale, her father's merchant status landed Khin's family in Moscow, where she received a gymnasium education and came to hobnob with members of Russia's cultural elite, including Ivan Turgenev. Khin attended the Women's Medical Courses in St. Petersburg and took classes at the Sorbonne. She was twice married, once divorced, and had a son.

- Feiga Izrailevna Kogan (1891–1974), who composed books of Symbolist poetry in Russian while harboring a love of the Hebrew language. Born and raised in Moscow, her first volume of poems appeared in 1912 when she was just twenty-one. Four years later, she enrolled in a two-year course offered by the Society for Lovers of the Hebrew Language and studied with Menahem Gnessin. Teacher and student became pioneers in the Hebrew theater troupe known as *Habimah*, which became associated with Konstantin Stanislavskii's Moscow Art Academic Theater. Kogan remained single all her life.

- Sofiia Dubnova-Erlikh (1885–1986), typically remembered as the daughter of the renowned historian Simon Dubnov and the wife of the socialist Genrikh Erlikh, but who was an accomplished poet, essayist, biographer, and political activist in her own right. Born in the Pale, she moved to Odessa, where she received daily lessons from her father until the age of fourteen when she entered a local gymnasium, followed by study at the Bestuzhev Higher Courses for women in St. Petersburg. Dubnova-Erlikh had two sons, who

inspired her cycle of Russian poems on motherhood and with
whom she eventually migrated to America.

Even these brief biographical sketches, which will be elaborated upon in
the pages to come, demonstrate that Jewish women did indeed venture
beyond the Pale. They physically moved to Russia's interior, including
Moscow and St. Petersburg, or outside the Tsarist Empire altogether. But
more than that, they graduated from secular schools and universities,
even earning a doctorate in one instance. They received, in some cases,
an extensive Jewish education, consisting of thorough grounding in Hebrew grammar and literature. They flouted Jewish convention by remaining single and childless or divorcing their husbands. And, at times, they
earned a living through the pen. These Jewish women writers do not
conform to the accepted stereotypes of Jewish women in Tsarist Russia.
Neither *balebustes* nor revolutionaries, they resemble their Western European sisters far more than their cousins in the romanticized Pale.

Jewish historians have long assumed a dichotomy between Western
and Eastern Jewries. Because of different environments and circumstances, each population developed a distinct type of Jewish identity and
relationship to the larger society. Feminist historians have recently presented as well the varying ways that the West and the East constructed
gender roles.[10] The "Western model" refers to those nations who offered
some degree of civic equality to their Jewish populations. By the last
third of the nineteenth century, as a result of cultural integration and upward social mobility, these relatively small Jewish communities were defined primarily by their middle-class characteristics. Consequently, Jewish women of the West took their cues from the bourgeois ideology that
restricted women's access to the public realm and regarded religiosity as
a feminine attribute. This model relegated the transmission of Jewish
knowledge and identity to the domestic realm and thus to Jewish
women, while Jewish men pursued success in the worlds of commerce
and civic affairs and assumed leadership positions in public Jewish life.

In contrast, the "Eastern model" sprang from the political milieu of
multi-national territories that rejected Western-derived notions of civic
equality. These empires contained relatively large, and overwhelmingly
non-middle-class, numbers of Jews who were allowed to, and did, retain
such significant markers of distinctiveness as the Yiddish language and

observance of traditional Jewish practice. It has been argued that those Jewish women of Eastern Europe who chafed under the gender division and consequent educational restrictions of traditional Jewish society found secular culture and political activism particularly alluring. It has been argued further that women's entrance into secular culture and politics was largely facilitated by a work ethic among the traditional Jewish community that legitimated female financial support of the scholar's family, as well as indifference to and thus tacit permission for Jewish women to engage in secular learning. In sum, scholars contend there was a strong tendency toward preservation of Jewish culture among Jewish women of the West, while secularization held sway over a significant segment of their Eastern European sisters.

Jewish women writers of Tsarist Russia offer a unique perspective, fitting neatly into neither the Western nor the Eastern model. For they adopted the behavioral patterns and educational norms associated with the West while remaining in the East. The so-called *balabatishe* Jews—the merchants or professionals—in both the East and the West aspired to send their daughters to gymnasia and university to acquire expertise in European languages and literature, along with lady-like talents such as needlepoint, piano playing, and the like. These efforts to mold Jewish girls into educated ladies of the middle class received a boon in the wake of the public discussion of the 1860s known as the "Woman Question," which centered on the proper role and status of the female sex in the Russian Empire. Opportunities for educating girls and women soared in Russia as girls' gymnasia tripled in number from 1865 to 1883, and women came to have greater access to physicians' training and university-level courses than anywhere in Europe.[11] With the infamous university quotas for Jews years away, Jewish women, too, became the beneficiaries of such educational opportunities.[12] They formed part of a wider phenomenon—Russian women stepping out of subservient roles to prove their mettle in the intellectual arena.

A Brief Cultural History of Jewry in the Russian Empire

Despite the appearance of the *balabatishe* Jews in the East, most of Russian Jewry followed a trajectory unlike that of Western Europe in the nineteenth century. Largely concentrated in the Pale of Settlement and sustained by a way of life typically depicted as far more removed from that of the surrounding population than was the case for Jews of Western Europe, Russian Jewry possessed a culture honed by studying past generations' legal discussions that both guided the community's contemporary life and perpetuated its distinctiveness. The majority of Jews living in the Russian Empire in 1897 declared Yiddish to be their native tongue, reserving Hebrew for holy works and scripted liturgical events. In that Empire, with its authoritarian regime and its overwhelmingly peasant society, conditions appeared inimical to emancipation, assimilation, and modernity in general. But the dissolution of Jewish autonomy and the effects of contacts between Jews and European society began to wear away the centuries-old texture of Jewish culture.

In the absence of emancipation (which arrived in 1917 for the Jews, as for all the Tsar's subjects), some Jews found refuge in the new secular Jewish culture imported from the West. From the beginning of the eighteenth century, men had appeared within German Jewry who cultivated the German language, secular studies, and European manners while attacking traditional Jewish life and thought in accordance with the ideals of the burgeoning Enlightenment. By mid-century this trend had crystallized into a movement known as the *Haskalah* (Hebrew for Enlightenment). Pedagogic in character and optimistic in tone, the Haskalah was characterized by an acceptance of the authority of non-Jewish ideas and mores as at least equal to traditional Jewish teachings and behavior. Over a half century after its birth, the movement spread through the German principalities into the Austrian Empire and finally into Russia, where it permeated and transformed the thinking of a tiny group of Jewish intellectuals emerging during the reign of Nicholas I (1825–55). This small cluster of its adherents, the *maskilim*, regarded the government as a seat of beneficence and progress, which, they presumed, shared their own dreams of modernization and ultimate emancipation of Russian Jewry. Solidifying their alliance with and dependence on the government, the Russian maskilim gradually converted their loosely-organized coterie into a coherent movement through a network of educational institutions.

The maskilim's hopes for obtaining their objectives soared as Alexander II succeeded to the throne (1855–1881). In the aftermath of the Russian defeat in the Crimean War that had exposed his empire's backwardness, the new Tsar instituted the "great reforms" of the 1860s, including emancipation of the serfs, which sanguine Jews interpreted as a sign of the imminent emancipation of Jewry, especially in light of the emancipation already granted to the majority of European Jewry. Indeed, there was cause for optimism. Alexander removed obstacles to Jewish economic development and Jewish entry to institutions of higher learning, while his attitude of openness led to the appearance of a steady stream of essays, belles lettres, and poetry in the pages of the mushrooming Jewish press. The Haskalah reached its zenith in the Russian Empire as Hebrew, Yiddish, and Russian literature became vehicles for a secular culture of Jewish self-expression of a new order and of permanent import.

Attempting to meet European standards, Jewish writers exerted tremendous efforts to develop and enrich the Jews' internal languages of Hebrew and Yiddish, all the while combating unfavorable ideas about each. Yiddish was a living language at the time, but even its leading writers Sholem Aleichem and Y.L. Peretz dubbed it *jargon* (slang).[13] Hebrew, for its part, was considered a dead tongue in need of massive revision. Both languages were invigorated by the extensive enterprise of translation and the expansion of Jewish writing to areas like politics, art, and sciences, which, with rare exception, were not previously found within either canon. In fact, Hebrew and Yiddish writers were regularly compelled to develop the instruments of their craft during the very act of creating—manipulating grammatical forms to fit new genres and deriving usable terminology from old lexicons.

These Hebrew and Yiddish writers shared an interest in opposing the antiquated ways of the Jewish community. But their new-found secular culture was far from monolithic. Two marked trends, fractured for the most part along a linguistic fault, began to take shape: one called for intensive association with Russians and their culture and regarded Hebrew and Yiddish as merely temporary instruments for spreading enlightenment among the masses; the other called for fostering Hebrew and loyalty to the Jews as a nation. These ideological differences surfaced as early as the 1870s and intensified in the aftermath of Alexander II's assassination in 1881, when powerful anti-Jewish sentiments emerged—in both written and violent form—within the Russian Empire.[14] In reaction, some Jews continued to place their faith in progress, which, they presumed, would eventually succeed in bringing about the anticipated emancipation of Russian Jewry. Others were drawn to national movements such as nascent Zionism, which saw the solution to the Jewish problem in emigration of Jews to the land of Israel, or Autonomism, which sought a solution in a self-governed Jewish community expressing its unique culture among any number of other autonomous minorities within one extensive, multi-national Russian Empire. A considerable number of Jews joined the Russian revolutionary movements, hopeful that the overthrow of the Tsarist regime would eliminate all restrictions, and that Jews would then be absorbed into a reconfigured Russian society. As is well known in American Jewish history, large numbers chose to leave the Russian Empire altogether, heading for the shores of the *goldene medine* (golden land).

While internal Jewish cultural productivity continued apace, a small segment of the Jewish population considered itself an integral part of Russian society, and thus entitled to participate in or benefit from the cultural efflorescence of Russia at large. Accustomed to speaking and reading Russian and European languages, they were graduates of Russian or Western European gymnasia and universities, where they acquired a modern education and the necessary accoutrements to function properly among the Russian intellectual elite. For the most part, they pursued careers in the wider circles of imperial society, especially as lawyers and physicians, and made their homes within Russia's interior. Typically throughout the nineteenth century, they ignored both their ties to the Jewish community and its problems, a negligible number even converting to Russian Orthodoxy and other faiths in order to advance their careers. Many, however, gradually "returned" to the Jewish community as they witnessed the worsening plight of their fellow Jews as famine and pogroms spread across the Russian Empire. Following the dictates of heightened Jewish conscience and consciousness, this group of integrated and privileged Jews began, in large measure, to enter the struggle for Jewish rights by the beginning of the twentieth century.

* * * * *

"You're writing about *what*?" interested but incredulous people would respond when I told them the subject of this book. "Jewish *women* writers in Tsarist Russia? You discovered nearly *seventy* published female authors, poets, and translators?" Such encounters have underscored for me the prevalence and intractability of the image of the *balebuste* or revolutionary to describe nineteenth-century Jewish women in Russia. To imagine that a Jewish woman functioned in the Tsarist Empire as an author or a poet—especially in a "foreign tongue" like Russian—seems nearly inconceivable. So the contents of this book may shock some readers, I suppose, and even subvert their "received traditions."

I am indeed treading on new scholarly territory here. And I have allowed the writers to chart the journey for me. Yet many questions have emerged along the way—the answers to which lie in the specific lives and works of the writers themselves. First of all, can we create a composite biography of Jewish women writers in Tsarist Russia based on what compelled them to write, how they attained access to the literary arena, and once having taken up the pen, how their personal lives were affected? Second, in exploring the contents of their writing, are there common or repeated themes that reveal a discrete female or Jewish consciousness emerging in the latter half of the nineteenth century? Certainly, I am hopeful that my documenting of Jewish women's literary productivity in Tsarist Russia will form a cornerstone for building a comprehensive history of Jewish women in Tsarist Russia. But the book is not simply intended as an idiosyncratic history of women writers alongside that of men.

It is also meant to teach more broadly about the invention of different cultures, in different languages, among Jews in Russia at the time. Thus, I ask, what were the cultural reference groups that produced these writers and received their works? What were the critical standards by which they were judged? What role did language play in their writings? Were there impediments barring women in a particular language and inducements to write in another? What do the extent of these writers' success reveal about each culture as it developed?

The works and lives of these extraordinary writers will tell us much about Jewish women's experience in Tsarist Russia as well as the extraordinary cultural context that they inhabited.

1

The Makings of a *Maskilah*

Miriam Markel-Mosessohn (1839–1920)

Women and the Jewish Enlightenment Movement

"I am attempting to enter the sanctuary of your honor."[1] In this way did Miriam Markel-Mosessohn express her desire to penetrate the world of Hebrew letters—a world created and inhabited by and for men in a language traditionally restricted to that sex. In 1868, when she penned these words, Markel-Mosessohn was among a handful of unknown women struggling to make their voices heard by those who might appreciate their Hebrew craftsmanship. That she, as a female Hebraist, might be trespassing sacred ground remained uppermost in her mind. She feared that a "woman [like me] who boldly enters her head among those mountains [will] surely be stoned [to death]."[2]

Markel-Mosessohn had good reason to fear. Access to Hebrew—or the *leshon ha-kodesh* (holy tongue), as it was known—had for centuries been limited to one segment of the Jewish population, namely men. Jewish law required them to study their people's legal legacy, which ordinarily meant learning the Torah and Talmud by rote during boyhood and thus acquiring proficiency in Hebrew, if at all, only as a byproduct of mastering the classical Jewish texts. While a number of frameworks existed in which girls could, and did, learn, there was no standard pattern for girls' education as there was for boys'.[3] Moreover, famous talmudic dicta such as that comparing the teaching of Torah to daughters with exposing them to lechery (Sotah 20a) had for over a millenium served to bar most of the female population from traditional Jewish text study. As a result, Hebrew was generally considered the province of men and became associated with the male scholarly elite, in contrast to Yiddish, which became linked with women, common folk, and daily routine.[4]

Except for use in study and worship, Hebrew had remained a dormant language until the late eighteenth century, when it underwent a very slow resurrection and transformation into an instrument of, initially, literary discourse, and, much later, everyday conversation.[5] The story of the rebirth of Hebrew as a modern language lags behind that of the Jewish Enlightenment movement (Haskalah) by a few decades, but the latter is inextricably bound to the former. In nineteenth-century Prussia, adherents of the Haskalah (maskilim) attempted to purify the Judaism that, to their minds, had been corrupted by centuries of antiquated medievalism. In so doing, they began to rationalize the Jewish educational process and adapt their ancestral tongue to modernity. For these early writers, Hebrew meant biblical Hebrew. They regarded the Bible as the quintessential and unadulterated Jewish text. Thus they set about cleansing the Hebrew of their day of the layers of dross caked on by centuries of Jewish education concentrated exclusively on the Talmud. Despite their efforts, their writing was often clumsy, biblical Hebrew being ill-suited to the rhythms of their contemporary speech and literature. It took nearly one hundred years and a move eastward to the Russian Empire for a secular, Hebrew culture of Jewish self-expression to emerge. Throughout the second half of the nineteenth century, culturally and nationally minded Russian Jews sowed the seeds planted a century earlier by fashioning Hebrew literature in every conceivable genre. Poets, novelists, journalists, and critics rose to the challenge of reviving the ancient tongue as the Hebrew press flourished with dozens of newspapers and journals and several printing presses active throughout the Pale of Settlement and the Empire's capitals.

It was into this sanctuary of Hebrew letters that Miriam Markel-Mosessohn sought entry. And the maskilim did their part by warmly welcoming her and her qualified sisters into its innermost sanctum. Among her admirers was none other than Yehudah Leib Gordon (1830–1895), the foremost Hebrew poet of nineteenth-century Russia, whose epic poem "Kotzo shel yud" (The Tip of the [letter] Yud) established him as an advocate for women after its publication in 1875. This poem about the travails of an agunah quickly became a cause célèbre in the Hebrew press, eliciting a flood of praise and protest in its wake.[6] At once a tirade against the oppressive hegemony of Jewish law and an argument for the emancipation of the Jewish woman, the verses weave a tale of Batsheva, whose bill of divorce is deemed invalid by a court of rabbis on account of a minuscule error that renders the spelling of her husband's name incorrect. Without a kosher document, she is prohibited from marrying her true love—a maskil, of course—and is forced to eke out a meager existence for herself and her two children.[7] The hoopla surrounding "The Tip of the Yud" led to two interdependent results: the identification of its author for all time with the plight of the Jewish woman and the flow of compliments by a number of female correspondents to Gordon's mail box.

All but one of the six women who initiated contact with Gordon did so after his poem appeared in print.[8] The exception was Miriam Markel-Mosessohn. Her first letter arrived seven years prior to the writing of "The Tip of the Yud" and resulted in a twenty-year correspondence between the two. That first letter contained a request for advice on whether or not she should pursue the task of translating works from German into Hebrew. Gordon's response was overwhelmingly favorable: "When I received your treasured letter . . . my heart rejoiced to see in these days and at this time one of the daughters of Jerusalem so eager to speak lucidly in the language of our ancestors. . . . [There is such] joy in my heart [over the fact] that the language of Judaism, which has been forgotten by so many of her sons, has now found enlightened female readers who study it and strengthen it."[9] Gordon was among several maskilim who actively sought female participation in their efforts to increase their Hebrew reading audience.

They succeeded to a limited degree by the 1870s, when Markel-Mosessohn was joined by a small circle of women attracted to Hebrew literature. One eighteen-year-old by the name of Sarah Novinsky, for instance—who had already mastered Russian, Polish, German, French, and Italian—claimed that she had ultimately come to "seek refuge under the shadow of the Hebrew language." There, she argued in an 1876 letter, Jewish women rightfully belonged along with men, to "raise the banner of the [resurrected] tongue."[10] The Israeli scholar Iris Parush explains the curious phenomenon of a female Hebrew readership as a byproduct of the maskilim's efforts not only to increase the number of readers of Hebrew literature but also to infuse the language with "feminine" qualities, in order to animate it with a broader range of feeling so that it could compete in the marketplace of modern languages.[11] With other supporters of the Enlightenment, the maskilim subscribed to the belief that women were more in communion with nature than men and graced from birth with emotion and aesthetic refinement.[12] Thus, they argued, women ought also to write in Hebrew so as to bring "warmth, softness, flexibility, subtle, delicate and shifting hues into the dead, forgotten, old, dry, and hard Hebrew language."[13] In a letter of 1881 addressed to Sheine Wolf of Grodno (in modern-day Belarus), Gordon indicated the advantages of incorporating the female sex into the coterie of Hebrew readers and writers:

> . . . receiving a letter in the holy tongue from a Jewish woman is to me like receiving manna from heaven. . . . All the writings in the holy tongue composed by women that I chance to read are better in style and purer in language than many of those by men. The woman writes with the pen of a bird and the man with the pen of iron and lead. . . . The reason for this is, in my opinion, because the minds of women were not ruined in their youth in the death chambers of the *ḥadarim* [Jewish primary schools], and their common sense was not distorted with *drashot* [pontificating] and *pilpulim* [aimless argumentation].[14]

Ironically, according to the maskilim, because of the lack of standard Jewish education for girls, women's minds remained free of the plagues that traditional Jewish institutions and methods of learning visited upon boys.

In the maskilim's general war on traditional Judaism, practices involving women became part of the ammunition in their arsenal. This battle took place against the backdrop of and was influenced by the controversy over the proper education and role of women in the family and society raging in general in Russian intellectual circles in the 1860s and 70s.[15] Specifically, the maskilim attacked traditional Jewish marriage and family patterns where matchmaking and early betrothal were de rigueur. Instead, they sought a relationship between husband and wife founded on romantic love and meaningful emotional and spiritual affinity. To further their cause, maskilim engaged in a number of activities: composing literature critical of the inferior status ascribed to women by Jewish tradition,[16] promoting modern education for Jewish children of both sexes,[17] making independent female protagonists a mainstay of their fiction and poetry,[18] and emboldening female authors in letters exuding abundant praise.[19]

Rarely, however, did the maskilim regard educating women as a good in and of itself, or as a necessary means to female self-fulfillment. Instead, their seemingly progressive activities on behalf of women's emancipation were informed by the ideas of the so-called "enlightened" philosophers who idealized the nuclear family and motherhood, thereby reinforcing differences between the sexes and the appropriateness of an exclusively domestic role for women. Only the woman who had received an excellent education and who had fully developed her intellectual potential could properly fulfill her roles of wife and mother.[20] This middle-class cult of domesticity, which came to prevail among Jews and gentiles of the bourgeoisie in Western countries by the second half of the nineteenth century, was imported into the Russian Empire and gained momentum among its middle class.[21] The movement encouraged women to acquire the standard accoutrements of a bourgeoise to prepare her for her role as an enlightened mother to her children and a desirable companion for her enlightened husband. The hope was that daughters of the middle class would similarly help to transform the traditional Jewish household into a font of enlightened belief and action.

It was those maskilim most closely associated with raising the level of Jewish women's knowledge, like Gordon and David Frischmann (1859–1922), who were most vocal in articulating the ultimate end of such pursuits. In a letter of January 3, 1886, Gordon advised sixteen-year-old Nehamah Feinstein—who would become Nehamah Pohazhavski (1869–1934), the published author of short stories in Hebrew—that "just as you are a good student, so, too, will you become . . . a good mother."[22] A year later, Frischmann rhetorically asked: "Of what does our literature stand in need if not the hands of delicate and tender women who see to the upbringing of our children?"[23]

In effect, maskilim were upholding the gender division etched by centuries of Jewish law and custom but rationalizing it anew with ideas and vocabulary culled from the "modern" cult of domesticity. The laws of rabbinic Judaism, which had held sway over most Jewish communities until the modern era, were rigid in the separations they ordained between male and female roles and the status pertaining to each sex. In this patriarchal system women were seen as connected to the realm of nature, as opposed to culture, and their activities, ideally, were confined to the private sphere of the home, husband, and children. In theory then, the roles of men and women being proposed by the maskilim resembled those designed by the Rabbis of old.

Recent scholarship generated in history and literature departments in Israeli and American universities has begun to confirm that maskilim did not, in fact, wholeheartedly accept the Enlightenment's every principle.[24] The Israeli historian Shmuel Feiner persuasively argues that the maskilim accompanied their calls for change and refinement within the Jewish community with warnings against the dangers of progress, stressing the need for a moderate and (maskilic-) controlled process of modernization vis-à-vis women. Antedating Feiner by seven years and two years respectively, Ben Ami Feingold and David Biale draw similar conclusions.

In the end, the maskilim failed to overturn or even revamp the educational system for the majority of Jewish women in the Russian Empire. However, through their efforts a notable and singular phenomenon resulted: a cohort of women reading and writing in Hebrew. Throughout the Pale of Settlement—from Riga to Lvov to Kishinev to Grodno—women became proficient in the language of their ancestors. Unlike the maskilim who corresponded among themselves with great regularity and used the pages of the Hebrew press as a link to kindred spirits, the female Hebraists did not band together in any sort of network, male- or female-dominated, written or otherwise oriented.[25] With so few women writers being published, they had no forum for becoming acquainted with other female Hebraists within the Russian Empire with whom they could potentially correspond.[26] Nor, at the same time, did they have the freedom to relocate to centers of maskilic activity, like their male analogues. Rather, female Hebrew readers and writers were isolated individuals who remained alone among their families, venturing forth from their birthplaces only for the sake of marriage. At the same time, the correspondence and literary activities of certain female Hebraists reveal regular, avid, and often successful attempts to connect to the maskilim and to contribute to their publications.

For all these efforts, however, the connections forged between maskilim and female Hebraists neither elevated any single woman writer of

Hebrew to the vanguard of the Haskalah nor defined her as a *maskilah*. In fact, the designations used by the maskilim for a woman writing in Hebrew may be revealing. As in other patriarchal structures, masculinity was conflated with the universal and the unmarked, while femininity attracted ambivalence and attention as the "other."[27] A woman writing in Hebrew received the appellation *almah maskilah* (enlightened maiden), *bat maskelet* (enlightened daughter), or *ishah maskelet* (enlightened woman). That is, an adjectival form (*maskelet*) was employed rather than the corresponding feminine noun for maskil—*maskilah*.

Dubbing a woman a "maskelet" did not, however, necessarily mean that she endorsed or lived according to the tenets of the Haskalah. But she assuredly became cognizant of the ideology of the Jewish Enlightenment by reading the only works available in modern Hebrew: fiction and non-fiction that maskilim churned out in the Hebrew press and in separately published volumes. The writings of these women and their male associates attest to the fact that they were familiar with the standard-bearers of the Haskalah. To take but one example, several female Hebraists admired the novels of Abraham Mapu (1808–1867), the individual credited with originating this genre in modern Hebrew. According to his well-known autobiography *Ḥata'ot ne'urim* (Sins of Youth), Moses Leib Lilienblum read Mapu's *Ahavat Zion* (The Love of Zion) aloud to his admirer Feiga Novakhovitz in the summer of 1869 at her request.[28] And, more significantly, Devorah Ephrati of Kalvirija (Lithuania), who became Devorah Zabludovskii of Bialystok after marriage, read the entire manuscript of *The Love of Zion* in 1852, a year before it appeared in print. Mapu sent her the manuscript with the hope that she would critique it from her female perspective. Drawing on her instincts and insights, she readily complied, offering suggestions intended to improve the characterizations of heroines in the historical novel set in the time of the kings of Judah. As she expressed in a letter to Mapu: "As a young woman, I must remark on the matter of Tamar. [You wrote:] 'She threw a wreath of flowers to the bank of the second river.' [But] there is no way a meek young woman would [be able to] throw such a distance."[29]

Besides advice, female Hebraists contributed the works of their own hands to the maskilic enterprise. Sarah Shapira of Duenaburg (modern-day Daugavpils, Latvia), for instance, sent Gordon copies of her verse for his perusal in 1891, a full four years after her first and only poem appeared in print.[30] Shapira could be called a third-generation maskilah, for both her grandfather Rabbi Isaiah Meir Kahanah (1828–1887) and father David passed their interest in secular and Jewish studies on to their female offspring. Isaiah, who was said to have been immersed in all the Jewish holy works by the age of thirteen, turned four years later to the study of philosophy, math, and astronomy; while David, who studied Talmud and science in his father's house, visited Prussia as a young man, became a physician at the Duenaburg hospital, and composed Hebrew poetry.[31] In 1886, he defended Gordon after a fiery onslaught launched by Lilienblum, and, one might surmise, consequently advised his precocious daughter that Gordon might be willing to peruse her poetry in return for the favor.[32]

Having been instructed in the ancient tongue as a child and absorbed the ideas of the Ḥibbat Zion movement (Lovers of Zion) as a teenager, Shapira began to compose verse extolling the virtues of the land of Israel.[33] Her single extant poem with its telling, if unoriginal, title "Zion" is a patriotic hymn in the tradition of the Zionist and subsequent national anthem of the State of Israel "Ha-tikvah" (The Hope) by Naphtali Herz Imber (1859–1909). Indeed it emerged out of the same historical and geographic context: late nineteenth-century Galicia. Shapira's images, culled from nature, link the yearning of the people Israel to the land of Israel and its climate. It reads in its entirety:[34]

Not dew and not rain[35]—[but] my tears moisten Zion's mountains!
Not fire and sun—[but] my blood reddens Zion's sky.

And the mist rises from the tears of my eyes
And is the rain of the sky.
And the waters of rest calm our spirit,
the spirit of the mourners of Jerusalem![36]

The shedding of tears are comfort for the soul
and healing for the broken spirit.
Hands strengthen the miseries of the heart
and improve the stormy soul!

Neither as developed or as captivating as Imber's, Shapira's ode to Zion at the least demonstrates that Jewish women in pre-turn-of-the-century Russia were penning Hebrew compositions worthy of attention and, even, publication.

Shapira's Hebraic skills tantalized Gordon. In the first of four responses to her letters, he characterized her as an "enlightened maiden," applauded her work by citing the Book of Proverbs' statement "many daughters have done valiantly!" (31:29), and requested that she send writing samples.[37] The young bard complied by sending two poems. To the first, which appears from his remarks to be her "Zion," he offered unstinting censure; to the second, mild approbation. While acknowledging in a letter of January 2, 1891 that "Zion" "conveys well the love of the land of our ancestors and the desire to return to it. Its style and words," he continued bluntly, "are not beautiful."[38] He then enumerated six specific grammatical errors that corrupted her verse and closed with an apology for his inability to refrain from giving criticism that he felt would ultimately help her. Undeterred, Shapira thanked Gordon for his "letter of love" and demonstrated her appreciation of his careful reading by sending him a hand-crafted picture frame, which he prized until his death.[39]

Gordon matched his private criticism of Shapira's writings with public accolades in the form of poetry to or about her.[40] On December 31, 1891, just two days before sending the scathing review described above, he composed "Aharon aharon haviv" (Last but not Least), a rhymed apotheosis that he forwarded to her along with his book *Kol kitvei Yehudah Leib Gordon* (The Complete Works of Yehudah Leib Gordon). Offering a stark contrast to the harsh words that issued forth from his pen a mere forty-eight hours earlier, the poem reads in its entirety:[41]

To my sister the dear daughter of Zion
my companion in the temple of poetry
a beautiful and pure maiden
[who] during her youth
accumulated knowledge and clarity
with motherly wisdom and honesty
This is her name and her association: S a r a h[42]
the fruit of the tree of the Hadar:[43] S h a p i ra[44]

This book is sent as a remembrance
from the pen of one who loves and cherishes her.

A complete reversal in attitude is apparent here, especially in Gordon's embrace of Shapira as "my companion in the temple of poetry." This commendation comes close to full acceptance of a *maskelet* into the rarefied ranks of maskilim. Three others poetic tributes to Shapira followed, each restoring to her some of the dignity stripped by the severe evaluation addressed to her only in confidence. That Gordon should reveal his misgivings about Shapira's compositions only privately while heaping on praise publicly indicates his steadfast commitment to encouraging female Hebraists, whatever the extent of their talents. Doing so in public made sense on two fronts: it might have inspired reticent women to join Shapira, and it might have provided men with a model to emulate so that they, too, could foster Hebrew proficiency among their female kin.

An additional recipient of Gordon's praise was Sarah Feiga Meinkin (1855–1936), the first woman to compose a novel in Hebrew. The five-line entry on Meinkin in *Evreiskaia entsiklopediia* (Jewish Encyclopedia, in Russian) offers few facts about her life; we learn simply that she was born in Riga and that her two-volume novel *Ahavat yesharim o ha-mishpaḥot ha-murdafot* (Love of the Honest, or The Persecuted Families) was published in the early 1880s.[45] Yet in the foreword to part one of her magnum opus—a love story set in Western Europe about the descendants of the expelled Jews of the Iberian Peninsula (the "persecuted families" of the title)—Meinkin reveals her maskilic colors. She shared, for instance, the maskilim's optimism in the political changes occurring in the Russian Empire, invigorated as they were by the great reforms of Alexander II (1855–1881). By the time Meinkin turned novelist, the progressive tsar had already implemented policies removing obstacles to Jewish economic development and entry of Jews to the universities. Thus she favorably described the Russian Empire in her preface to *Love of the Honest* as the "blessed land where every man goes forth with confidence and [where] there are no distinctions between nations." For Meinkin, "knowledge and truth [would] destroy and shatter the fortresses that the hands of [ignorance] and foolishness built."

In a letter of April 22, 1881 Gordon acknowledged (to an anonymous friend) that he had examined Sarah Feiga Meinkin's novel and that his

Russian-language review of the book was due to appear in the forthcoming issue of *Voskhod*. Though he would divulge no details regarding his assessment, Gordon elliptically noted in the same letter that "God remembered Sarah Feiga and caused her to give birth to her book."[46] Readers of this witty allusion to Genesis 21:1–2, in which it is told that the biblical matriarch Sarah was blessed at the age of ninety-nine with a first child, might assume that Gordon regarded the writing of a novel in Hebrew by a woman as nothing short of a miracle. And indeed, Gordon emphasized the marvelous aspects of such an act in his review but not without criticizing Meinkin's unrealistic characterizations of children and poor Hebrew syntax. Nevertheless, he advised her to persevere in her literary pursuits because "she has indubitable talent which, with appropriate treatment and preparation, could yield good and abundant fruit [like the biblical matriarch]." More notably, Gordon used the appearance of Meinkin's novel as an opportunity, once again, to extol the virtues of the female sex's acquiring expertise in Hebrew. He welcomed the "revolution in the education of the Jewish woman, who is liberating the Torah from anathema and seizing her Talmud."[47] Two months later David Frischmann followed in Gordon's footsteps with a review displaying similar sentiments.[48] After first praising Meinkin's attention to emotion and spirit of adventure, which he likened to that of the author of "Ali Baba and the Forty Thieves," he turned his mostly negative critique of Meinkin's novel—which targeted especially her defective Hebrew—into an apologia of sorts for the Jewish woman. According to Frischmann, Meinkin and other Jewish women lacked Hebrew skills through no fault of their own. Rather, he exhorted the members of his own sex to take full responsibility for female incompetence, admonishing them to "teach every single young woman all that there is to learn."

Among all the female Hebraists, there was one whom maskilim agreed was beyond reproach: this was Miriam Markel-Mosessohn. Though similar to the others, she excelled in every instance. Like Devorah Ephrati, Sheine Wolf, and Nehamah Feinstein, Markel-Mosessohn corresponded with major players in the Russian Haskalah, who complimented her writing style and techniques. But unlike them, she interacted over the years with not one but three maskilim: Gordon, Lilienblum, and Mapu. Moreover, her correspondence with Gordon is by far the most extensive in both size and length of any known letters between a maskil and a maskelet, and, therefore, the most revealing. Like Sarah Shapira, Markel-Mosessohn received the honor of Gordon dedicating a poem to her. But the chosen poem was to become Gordon's famous aforementioned paean to the modern Jewish woman, "The Tip of the Yud." And while little is known as yet about Meinkin, we know that Markel-Mosessohn's literary career was marked by some longevity as she initially translated German works into Hebrew to great acclaim, then composed original yet unpublished poetry, and finally turned to journalism.

Most significantly, Markel-Mosessohn was unique among the female Hebraists in that she was responsible for upsetting the male-master-and-female-disciple relationship. For while she initially sought the maskilim's opinion on the worthiness of her Hebrew writings, they—primarily and especially Gordon—eventually began to regard her as a confidante. Additionally, she began as well to act as assistant to Gordon and others, translating their works from foreign tongues into Hebrew, providing them with books and journals that were, because of geography or expense, inaccessible, and later acting as a foreign correspondent for the Hebrew journals they edited.

The details of her life, to be discussed in the remainder of this chapter, show that Markel-Mosessohn was eminently qualified to enter the rarefied world of Hebrew letters inhabited by men. That she had the makings of a maskilah will be proven on the basis of her literary remains, which contain her correspondence, manuscripts, and sundry official documents such as travel permits. The forewords and dedications of her two published volumes are also useful sources, albeit in a limited way, as are the extant letters to her from various maskilim. These materials aid in reconstructing Markel-Mosessohn's journey from precocious youth to accomplished Hebraist. Her life trajectory, as will be shown, looked very different from those of her male contemporaries. As the details of her extraordinary life reveal, being female proved at times a help and at times a hindrance to Markel-Mosessohn.

An Enlightened Daughter

Miriam Markel-Mosessohn's[49] birthplace of Volkovyshki (modern-day Vilkaviskis, Lithuania) proved to be an ideal setting for a maskelet-

Miriam Markel-Mosessohn
From the collection of the Jewish National and University Library, Jerusalem

in-the-making. Despite a Jewish population of 4,417 out of 5,251 total inhabitants at mid-nineteenth century and a high concentration of men involved in commerce, Volkovyshki's proximity to the Prussian border meant that modern influences penetrated its bulwark of tradition.[50] Its bustling Jewish school system, for instance, included not only a secular Hebrew secondary school but a vocational school as well. Indeed, a segment of Volkovyshki's Jewish population sought to update what it regarded as antiquated approaches to Jewish learning and to "productivize" the community by offering training in crafts and agriculture, occupations considered worthier than trade and commerce.

Among the spokesmen for modernization in Volkovyshki was Shimon Wierzbolowski.[51] A well-to-do and well-traveled Jewish merchant, Wierzbolowski was no stranger to the transformation that had overtaken the Jews of nearby Prussia.[52] In 1750, King Frederick II of Prussia (1712–1786) had issued a charter that dissolved the former Jewish autonomy and brought the Jews closer to the state economically, politically, and culturally By century's end, Frederick's policy of enlightened absolutism had enabled a small group of Jews to gain access to Christian society and interact on neutral ground and at intellectual parity.[53] By 1850, when the Jews of Prussia in their entirety were emancipated, the ideological undergirding for that act—the Enlightenment—had already crossed the border into the northern part of the Russian Empire via Koenigsberg (modern-day Kaliningrad). The capital of Eastern Prussia, Koenigsberg was, along with Berlin, one of the two centers of Jewish Enlightenment in that Empire, and with its own Hebrew printing press published the important organ of the Haskalah, *Ha-meassef*. The Jews of Volkovyshki, located one hundred miles due east of Koenigsberg, indubitably fell under the influence of their neighbor—Shimon Wierzbolowski included.

Shimon and his wife Hayah welcomed a daughter into their family in 1839, whom they named Miriam.[54] Like her biblical namesake, the girl had two brothers, Yosef and Shmuel (though she also had a sister Devorah), and by life's end gained some prominence among her people for her unusual talents.[55] Miriam Markel-Mosessohn's limited reputation would be made through her superior ability to write in Hebrew, a language her parents introduced early on in their daughter's life. Of one mind when it came to the education of their children, Hayah and Shimon agreed that both their sons and daughters would attend the local Jewish school in

Volkovyshki. Markel-Mosessohn described her parents and matriculation
as such:

> My father is of the remnants of those who study Torah and wisdom.
> He is a respected merchant who is cognizant of the [ways of the]
> world, . . . my mother is a good and compassionate and wise
> woman. When I was seven years old, my mother sent me to the
> local Jewish school [*beit sefer*] to study there how to read and write
> Hebrew. Boys and girls studied together as was the custom in small
> cities. From my youth, there awakened within me a strong yearning
> to study and to understand, and I became envious of the young
> boys who were in "*ḥeder*" [her quotations—traditional Jewish pri-
> mary school], who studied "*ḥumash*" [her quotations—the first five
> books of the Hebrew Bible], and wrote Hebrew. So my father hired
> a tutor so I, too, who thirsted for the font of the Torah [could
> learn]. And [the tutor] instructed me in understanding the scrip-
> ture.[56]

This short excerpt from a letter drafted by Markel-Mosessohn at the
age of thirty-six contains several striking revelations that dispel some of
the myths about Jewish education for girls in nineteenth-century Russia.[57] First, it challenges the commonly accepted notion that girls were
altogether excluded from Jewish study. Findings by scholars as diverse as
Dan Miron, Emanuel Etkes, and Dov Sdan confirm that Markel-Mosessohn was not unique, and that by 1846, under ordinary circumstances,
some girls studied the rudiments of Hebrew alongside boys.[58] On the
other hand, of course, Markel-Mosessohn mentions being barred from
attending the traditional Jewish institution known as the *ḥeder*. However,
Shaul Stampfer has documented that parents did indeed enroll their girls
at *ḥadarim*, basing that decision on convenience and cost. A *ḥeder* was, as
Stampfer explains, less expensive than a tutor.[59] Secondly, the passage indicates that the mixing of the sexes for study was not considered anathema. Although perhaps not ideal, pragmatics dictated coeducation as a
less costly venture, especially for smaller locales, as Markel-
Mosessohn notes. Thirdly, the excerpt shows that the Wierzbolowski
family challenged the traditional balance of power between fathers and
mothers insofar as the education of their children was concerned. Jewish

legal strictures enjoin fathers to assume full responsibility for their sons' courses of study; while women are required only to encourage and enable their sons' scholarly pursuits.[60] About daughters, no direction is given. But here it is Markel-Mosessohn's mother who sends her daughter to school, evidence perhaps of women's expanding role in the training of their children or of women's already constant role in that venture. That Markel-Mosessohn, in the same letter, characterized her mother as "wise," an adjective typically reserved for men of that generation, might be a further sign of cooperation and perhaps even intellectual parity between mother and father.[61] Models such as these explain the growth of Markel-Mosessohn's "yearning to study and understand," which matured as did she.

In 1851, the Wierzbolowski family moved to Suvalk (modern-day Suwalki, Poland) perhaps owing to its pecuniary advantages, it being a lively center of trade. Under Prussian rule since the eighteenth century, following the Congress of Vienna in 1815 Suvalk and much of the surrounding area were annexed to the Russian Empire as the semi-autonomous Kingdom of Poland, also known as Congress Poland. The kingdom constituted the core of ethnic Poland, the center of Polish politics and culture, and an economic area of importance. It can be distinguished from Austrian Poland (Galicia), Prussian Poland (Poznan, Silesia, and Pomerania), and the Russian northwestern region known as Lithuania-Byelorussia, of which Volkovyshki was a part. While only fifty miles south of Volkovyshki, Suvalk was worlds away in terms of the character of its Jewish population. The Jews in Congress Poland were mostly urban and middle class, had a long-standing tradition of what might be called a "Polish orientation," and were therefore far more acculturated than their coreligionists in Galicia or in multi-national Lithuania-Belorussia. To this bastion of Polish-Jewish fraternization and cooperation the Wierzbolowskis arrived with their twelve-year-old daughter Miriam.

Not neglecting his daughter's penchant for Hebraic study even in this Polish-ly charged environment, Shimon Werzbolowski searched for an "enlightened and God-fearing teacher" and secured the services of Yehudah Leib Paradiesthal.[62] He instructed Markel-Mosessohn for two and a half years in Hebrew, along with the main works of German and a little French. When he left the Wierzbolowskis to become a tutor to a wealthy family in Warsaw, Markel-Mosessohn abandoned formal study of the ancient tongue. Her interest piqued and her skills honed, she continued her studies independently, "acquir[ing] scraps upon scraps of Hebrew writing, which [she] read two and three times over." Jubilant about her progress, reading Hebrew "became a daily pleasure for [her]," and she eventually "obtained many books by Hebrew authors."[63] So by her late teens, Markel-Mosessohn was imbibing the classics of the Jewish cultural revival.

It is important to note that Markel-Mosessohn followed a course of Hebrew study far different than that of her male peers. As has been well-documented by their pens, as well as those of historians, maskilim were generally the offspring of families whose observance of Jewish law was axiomatic and who considered acquisition of a Jewish education an essential feature of childhood. For them then exposure to Hebrew came only as a byproduct of immersion in the sacred texts, including the Torah and Talmud. Training consisted of a standard, if unsystematic, curriculum whereby boys were first introduced to the Torah's text by inferring its contents through classical biblical commentaries in Hebrew. Once mastered, they became eligible to study the Talmud, voluminous tracts of Jewish law and lore written for the most part in Aramaic and not Hebrew. The learning was mostly by rote and neglected the essential keys to mastering a language: grammar and syntax. Consequently, would-be male authors and poets of Hebrew began their writing careers at a disadvantage, to which their often awkward, early attempts testify. At the same time, of course, reading works beyond the prescribed curriculum was considered an unnecessary diversion from "real" study, and so male adolescents began surreptitiously to sample the forbidden fruits, under the influence usually of an indoctrinated older sibling or acquaintance.[64] They turned first to Hebrew works of philosophy and moral guidance firmly ensconced within the parameters of traditional Jewish culture, then to the staples of the Hebrew Enlightenment literature of the day, and finally to literature written in non-Jewish languages.

By her own account, Markel-Mosessohn's educational experience offers a stark contrast. Though raised as well in a traditional Jewish household, as a girl she would be expected to master only the limited core of customs and law necessary to allow her to function as wife and mother in the daily life of a Jewish family. Immersion in sacred texts was an indulgence few fathers afforded their daughters, and the minority of women who came to acquire more than perfunctory acquaintance with Hebrew did so usually by observing the lessons of their brothers.[65] But through a combination of daring, self-motivation, and a father who sought to "guide his daughter on the path of understanding," Markel-Mosessohn engaged in a very serious course of Jewish study, with an emphasis on acquisition of Hebraic skills.[66] In a strange irony, because she was a girl and thus not forced to suffer the traditional Jewish curriculum, she had greater access to Hebrew qua Hebrew and was free to pick up the rudiments of the language with the help of tutors secured for that very purpose. Likewise, as her skills developed, she was given the freedom to read the secular publications of Hebrew authors and poets beginning to appear with greater frequency. Moreover, it is likely that because of her socio-economic background, she received a thorough grounding in secular subjects. As one example, like other daughters of the Jewish merchantry living in the Russian Empire in the first half of the nineteenth century—especially those at the western-most reaches of the Empire and thus closest to the modernizing influences of Prussia—she was versed in both German and French.[67] Indeed, Markel-Mosessohn's eclectic training laid the foundation for her subsequent literary achievements.

The Influence of Men

That she was exceptionally well-prepared for the task of writing in Hebrew is borne out by the fleeting correspondence of Markel-Mosessohn and the Hebrew novelist Avraham Mapu (1808–1867). The handful of letters that passed between the two in 1861 and 1862 testifies that Markel-Mosessohn's unconventional education provided her with a felicitous style that garnered her lavish praise from one of the greats of Hebrew literature.[68] At the age of twenty-one, Markel-Mosessohn mustered the courage to reach out to one of the authors she so admired. Clearly daunted by his talents and influence, rough drafts of letters addressed to him show how she painstakingly crafted her words, attempting repeatedly to frame the correct greeting for her idol: "respected sage" is scribbled out and replaced by "the wondrous rhetorician," which is followed by the "precious man of pure spirit and knowledge." Markel-Mosessohn may have elected to write first to Mapu because of all the Hebrew authors, he lived within closest geographic proximity. Mapu was then residing in

Kovno (modern-day Kaunas, Lithuania), where he had lived off and on since the age of seventeen. With its sizable population of Jews—16,540 in 1864—the town was a center of Jewish cultural activity not seventy-five miles from the Wierzbolowksi residence in Suvalk. Markel-Mosessohn sent her initial letter to Mapu, along with an original piece, which does not survive, on the love in a woman's heart. He replied with many thanks and compliments to the "maskelet, who speaks so lucidly."[69] Four additional letters changed hands before the correspondence terminated. Their contents echoed that of the first exchange: admiration on the part of each for the other, peppered with the following witty play on their biblical namesakes. Mapu urged the young Miriam to "take a drum in [her] hand and raise [her] poetic voice because it is lovely . . . so that [she would become] an inspiration to the daughters of Judah."[70] She returned the compliment, saying: "With your writing to me, the gates of heaven have opened for me, and I have seen the Garden of Eden. . . . For you are Avraham the Hebrew, the first father of the Jews."[71]

Markel-Mosessohn and Mapu came to know each other not only in print, but in person as well.[72] The first meeting took place in 1861; the second in 1866 or 1867. Both were brief encounters at Mapu's home in Kovno. Although neither was apparently eventful, they do reveal both Mapu's willingness to greet aspiring authors—even unknown female ones—and Markel-Mosessohn's strenuous efforts to seek out men—even prominent ones—who would support her endeavor to write in Hebrew.

Markel-Mosessohn's practice of soliciting support from men who sought to revive the Hebrew language is reflected in her choice of mate as well. Miriam Wierzbolowski of Suvalk wed Anshel Markel-Mosessohn of Kovno (1844–1903) in 1863, when the bride was twenty-four and the groom was nineteen.[73] Their marriage appears to represent the ideal of conjugal bliss then being promoted by maskilim: a relationship based on companionship, love, and intellectual equality rather than the traditional arranged matches made during adolescence that in short order were often reduced to housekeeping and childrearing. In a letter to her husband of one year, Markel-Mosessohn's effusive affection is much in evidence: "I smell your love in the fragrance of beautiful flowers . . . If you were to penetrate my heart, you would find no thoughts, only true love. Even death will not separate us!"[74] Eleven days later, she expressed to him her hope that their future would be "lived in fellowship and friendship."[75]

Common intellectual interests were a mainstay of the Markel-Mosessohn marriage. As the bride of five years revealed to Yehudah Leib Gordon: "I have nothing to complain about . . . [my husband] is pure and a lover of knowledge. His thoughts are like my own thoughts."[76] The couple shared an abiding love for the ancient tongue and its revival. Notably, they penned letters to each other in Hebrew, and each engaged in a separate correspondence with Gordon.[77] Anshel supported his wife's calling, assisting her with and listening attentively to the details regarding her compositions.[78] He granted her as well freedom and presumably financial backing to travel to important centers of publishing to inquire about the feasibility of printing her works.[79] In return, she took a lively interest in his business dealings and fielded questions from business associates in his absence.[80]

Married for forty years, the couple never had children. Gauging Markel-Mosessohn's reaction to this fact is difficult in light of the slender available evidence. Yet given the typical expectations for women of her day, one might reasonably assume that her lack of offspring caused her considerable anguish. Her archives do reveal that she maintained close contact with her siblings' children through the years, freely dispensing advice to her nephews.[81] In the late summer of 1869, when she was already thirty years old, Gordon closed a letter to her by expressing his hope that "God will bless you in the forthcoming [Jewish] new year and remember you as He remembered Sarah [with the child Isaac]."[82] Besides underscoring the intimacy of their relationship, his words suggest that she suffered from infertility. Two decades later, Markel-Mosessohn would tersely inform Gordon that the biographical entry on her in a recently published book on Jewish women by Meyer Kayserling was riddled with errors, including the note that she had ceased writing because of child-rearing responsibilities.[83] In fact, the opposite was true. A home free of children left Markel-Mosessohn time and energy to pursue her literary ambitions.

Turning to Translation

Like the earliest women writers in the Russian language, initially Markel-Mosessohn turned with gusto to the act of translation, leaving for the most part the creation of original literature to the pens of men of her generation.[84] Since, as professors of Russian literature have suggested, fluency in European languages was the hallmark of the educated women of the bourgeoisie, many often broke into print as translators.[85] The same can be said of Markel-Mosessohn, who already in her late adolescence had "little by little, . . . tried translating from [a foreign] language to [the Hebrew] language, and . . . edited works in Hebrew."[86] A letter to her father indicates that by 1863, male authors of lengthy manuscripts and speeches were enlisting her assistance by commissioning her to translate over thirty of their works.[87] In addition, she completed a full Hebrew draft of *Der Flüchtling aus Jerusalem* (The Fugitive from Jerusalem), a history by Ludwig Philippson (1811–1889), who achieved renown as the founder and editor of the periodical *Allgemeine Zeitung des Judentums*.[88]

By the end of the 1860s, Markel-Mosessohn fixed on translation as a route to publication. Surely she knew that since the beginnings of the Jewish Enlightenment movement, the two-pronged goal of the maskilim was to enliven Hebrew with works that originated in foreign languages and in disciplines and genres never before expressed in the ancient tongue, while introducing their readership to new areas of knowledge. In 1868, Markel-Mosessohn contacted Yehudah Leib Gordon, seeking his advice on the viability of joining their extensive enterprise of translation. Along with her humble letter requesting his counsel, she sent her translation of the first part of Eugen Rispart's *Die Juden und die Kreuzfahrer unter Richard Löwenherz* (The Jews and the Crusades under Richard the Lionhearted) (Leipzig, 1842). Rispart was the pseudonym of Isaac Asher Francolm (1788–1849), an interesting man in his own right. Francolm had arrived in Koenigsberg—a city familiar to Markel-Mosessohn, given its proximity to her hometown—in 1820 as a religious teacher and a preacher. An advocate of reforming Judaism, he established a school in the town, but the traditional majority of the community, who resented his holding a confirmation ceremony for boys and girls, protested to the local authorities. Suspicious of all innovation, they prohibited him from opening the institution. So Francolm fled Koenigsberg for Breslau, presumably a more agreeable environment for him, given its equally active and powerful liberal and traditional populations. There he set about writing a chronicle of Jewish life in England during the time of the Crusades.

Significantly, in both instances where Markel-Mosessohn undertook full book translations, she selected historical works. Since the time of Moses Mendelssohn, when secular culture and philosophy began to be accepted as a central value among Jews, an interest in Jewish history had taken root as well. Serious and scientific research into the Jewish past on a wide scale emerged, however, after 1819 with the founding of the *Verein für Cultur und Wissenschaft der Juden*. Equipped with the idealistic conceptual apparatus of Hegel, this association of young Jewish intellectuals understood Jewish history as a progressive unfolding of the idea of Judaism resulting from natural historical factors rather than acts of Providence. The emergence of historical consciousness, coupled with critical methodology, supplanted traditional views on the fate of Israel and shattered restrictive norms by embracing the varieties of experience gleaned from the past. Thus modern Jewish historiography became a component of Haskalah ideology, an attempt to use the past as validation for changes being undertaken in the present.[89]

Markel-Mosessohn was infused with the new historical spirit of her day. An avid reader of the newly-flourishing genre, she especially admired Heinrich Graetz (1817–1891), whose *Geschichte der Juden* (History of the Jews) became one of the most widely read Jewish books in Germany, as well as the basis for the study of Jewish history for generations to come. The Hebrew adaptation-translation exerted much influence among the Hebrew-reading public of Eastern European Jewry, including Markel-Mosessohn. When the eleventh volume of the *History* appeared, she wrote her brother:

I'm yearning to see this precious book because the great sage Graetz [describes] the present era in his latest book. [We live in an] excellent and free time . . . , a time in which the sun shines tolerance down upon us. The Inquisition has ceased, as have the blood libel accusations, and the Jews are designated "human being" by many people. All the gates of wisdom and every occupation that was closed for many generations now have been opened wide to us . . . and [Jews] have entered the houses of wisdom and knowledge . . . and are loyal and worthy citizens of the lands of their birth. [her quotation marks][90]

Markel-Mosessohn's Hegelian optimism could hardly be contained. For her, history was on a forward march, with the Jews in lock step with their neighbors toward equality and fraternity. Studying degradations such as the Crusades served as proof to contemporary Jews and gentiles that progress indeed accrues with time. And translating historical works into Hebrew provided the additional benefit of elevating the ancient tongue to a vehicle for secular and scientific expression.

Gordon reacted quite favorably to Markel-Mosessohn's translation of *The Jews and the Crusades under Richard the Lionhearted.* Sharing both her sanguine outlook and devotion to the Hebrew revival, he enthusiastically replied within a matter of days, saying: "I read the first part of your translation . . . . The version is very, very good. The style is light and beautiful and easy to understand. I'm certain that it is worthy of publication. And I'll surely help you put it into print."[91] True to his word, with Gordon's assistance, the first part of the book appeared a year later as *Ha-yehudim be-Angliyah* (The Jews in England).[92] Two hundred forty-three pages long, she dedicated the volume to her parents and husband.

Gordon publicly offered his stamp of approval to *Ha-Yehudim be-Angliyah* by contributing a glowing preface, which is a partial reproduction of a letter addressed to Markel-Mosessohn for this purpose.[93] Laudatory in the extreme, he signed it, "Your friend who knows your soul and recognizes your worth." Markel-Mosessohn had different ideas than Gordon about the "worth" of women writers and deliberately kept the full contents of the letter hidden from public view. She omitted a passage in which Gordon defended the Jewish woman against those who claimed that her place is in the home. "Every day," he argued, "this assertion is being challenged by the women of our people. . . . The only difference between the sexes is physical. The spirit operates [equally] among male and female." Markel-Mosessohn feared that including Gordon's defense in her book might aggravate what she perceived as her already-tenuous, budding reputation as a *woman* writer. As she explained in a letter to her friend Moshe Hacohen Prozer:[94] "I will not announce the hidden objects of my heart in the streets and within earshot of all. I will not open the eyes of the blind . . . for not everything said between a man and his friend ought to be a matter of public record!"[95] Specifically, Markel-Mosessohn dreaded exposing and highlighting what she perceived as "my sin against the laws [observed by] valorous women."[96] Making a reference to the biblical injunction of Deuteronomy 22:5, that a "woman shall not wear that which pertains to a man, neither shall a man put on a woman's garment," she explained in an earlier letter to Gordon: "Tradition dictates that women support the household and raise children. . . . They may read good books, but they may not write and publish them. I have violated the law by dressing like a man. Who knows whether a crowd of people will gather and strip this garment from me. And then what will be the fate of my work?"[97]

Markel-Mosessohn was one of many women whose fear of disapprobation caused her to consider withdrawing from the official literary scene.[98] Yet, despite her anxieties about publicity for herself, Markel-Mosessohn privately supported the notion of female advancement. She urged young women to educate themselves and even to find gainful employment. As she wrote to her friend Prozer concerning his daughters: "[They] ought to finish gymnasium and then find paths for themselves [that will allow them to continue] to study and . . . to find a job. . . ."[99]

Markel-Mosessohn's own success continued to hinge partly on the unwavering enthusiasm of powerful literary men. Besides Gordon, others wrote to congratulate her on the masterful translation of *The Jews of England*. The Hebrew scholar Senior Sachs (1815–1892), who was a friend of Mapu, offered his kudos to the growing mountain of praise. Additionally, he suggested that he might be able to persuade his employer, the wealthy financier Baron Gunzburg, to subsidize the publication of part two of the translation of Francolm's book.[100] Moses Leib Lilienblum echoed Sachs's sentiments, exclaiming: "My heart jumped for joy when I received [Markel-Mosessohn's] book."[101] And his correspondence indicates ongoing support of her endeavors.[102]

However, the true object of Lilienblum's admiration was Feige Novakhovitz, whom he met in Vilkomir (modern-day Ukmerge, Lithuania) in May, 1869.[103] Impressed from the start by her intelligence, Lilienblum took to reading Mapu's Hebrew novels aloud to Novakhovitz on summer evenings.[104] Within a month, he confessed in his diary that he was in love with the young woman, and the affection he felt for her contrasted sharply with his feelings for his wife of ten years. These conflicting sentiments found expression in a poem entitled "Enkat asir" (Shackled Prisoner), which Lilienblum composed and which Novakhovitz promptly translated into German.[105] Late that summer, Lilienblum left for Kovno, though their "vicarious love affair" persisted for the next twenty-six years through words alone, including a torrential exchange of letters and Lilienblum's dedication in verse to "F.N." of his pseudonymously published autobiography *Hata'ot ne'urim* (Sins of Youth).[106]

Though similar to Lilienblum and Novakhovitz in that letter-writing acted as the primary vehicle of communication between the two, an altogether different sort of rapport existed between Markel-Mosessohn and Gordon. Theirs began exclusively as a working relationship that blossomed over time into a platonic friendship of interdependence. Though the two never met, Gordon acted throughout their twenty-year correspondence as a goad urging her on to further literary production. Early on, Gordon prodded her to translate additional works into Hebrew, even inquiring if she would like to finish his Hebrew translation of the novel *Vale of Cedars* by the Jewish-English writer Grace Aguilar (1816–1847).[107] While other offers followed, Markel-Mosessohn mysteriously dropped out of the translation loop for nearly two decades; no works would be published under her name between the years 1869 and 1887.[108]

A Changed Relationship

Meanwhile, however, the pair's relationship flourished, though in an altered state. For over time, Gordon came to lean increasingly on Markel-Mosessohn as the balance of power between the two shifted from one-sided dependence on her part to mutual reliance. He came to discover that she could be of use to him in a variety of ways. As early as two months into their correspondence, for instance, she was regularly sending him articles and books that he could not obtain otherwise.[109] Living in Kovno—and thus close to the site of a major Hebrew printing press in Koenigsberg—gave Markel-Mosessohn easy access to the works Gordon sought. Likewise, her husband's itinerant business patterns, which brought him and his wife to other printing centers like Warsaw and Vilna, enabled Markel-Mosessohn to visit booksellers on Gordon's behalf.[110] Of his twenty-eight letters to her, nearly half contain requests or appreciation for supplying him with Hebrew works. Markel-Mosessohn even began to act as intermediary between Gordon and Peretz Smolenskin (1840/2–1885), whose Vilna journal *Ha-shahar* (The Dawn) Gordon was unable to secure on his own but which published his articles and poetry.[111]

Besides business matters, the letters reveal a growing intimacy between the two, with discussions ranging from family matters to personal health. Gordon, whose wife Bellah could barely speak Russian and who remained completely disconnected from his literature, turned to Markel-Mosessohn for advice on educating his two daughters.[112] At several junctures he asked if she knew of an "enlightened woman" in Kovno available to tutor his children since, as he put it, "my daughters' development depends on it."[113] A year later, he even inquired if she might be willing to offer room and board to his ten-year-old daughter while she attended a school in Kovno. Markel-Mosessohn replied in the negative on account of her failing and unpredictable health.[114]

Illness, in fact, featured prominently in their correspondence. Both complained of exhaustion that forced them to curtail their activities in some measure. This was especially true of Markel-Mosessohn, who was afflicted on and off, and occasionally for several months at a time, with an apparently undiagnosable ailment.[115] The primary symptom was fatigue, such that when she was not bedridden, she often had to lie down and rest throughout the day. The spring of 1871 found her in Koenigsberg sapped of her strength and spirit. As she disclosed to Gordon: "I'm here to convalesce and am embarrassed to show my face among my friends. Everyone toils under the sun to make every second of life pleasant . . . but what about me? . . . I haven't accomplished a thing. I've lost my strength. . . . I'm no longer capable of doing good. I'll never be able to feel at peace again because hope is so distant from me. . . . The doctor promises that salvation is near, but I don't feel it."[116] It is risky indeed to diagnose an illness that occurred over a century ago and about which there are no extant medical records. But factors come together to aid in answering the challenging question of why a thirty-two-year-old woman (who was to live until age eighty-one) would sound such a note of despair. Perhaps Markel-Mosessohn had absorbed into a guilt-ridden corner of her being the Jewish community's distrust of a woman who took to writing and who at the same time was childless. One might employ the phrase "severe identity crisis" to describe the terrible period she was passing through.

Misfortune continued to plague Markel-Mosessohn. While sickness consumed her in the early 1870s, the latter part of the decade found her "honor turned into shame."[117] After a six-year break in communication, she renewed contact with Gordon to inform him that her husband, Anshel, had engaged in shady financial dealings that resulted in his imprisonment and that had thrown their reputation and fiscal well-being into jeopardy. She solicited Gordon's emotional support, "put[ting] [her] trust in the fact that [one who] composed verse like 'Bi-metzulot yam' and 'Bein shinei arayot'" (In the Depths of the Sea and Between the Lions' Teeth) would surely be capable of "knowing and feeling [her] emotions."[118] These two poems, along with "Ha-isha vi-yladeha" (The Woman and her Sons), form a metaphysical triptych of sorts that explores the philosophical meaning of existence in general and Jewish existence in particular.[119] The beleaguered wife asked specifically that the compassionate poet act as a character witness for Anshel and use his influence to secure his release.[120] Whether Gordon consented is left a mystery, for none of his letters to her on this matter survive.

Yet it is clear that Markel-Mosessohn did not stray far from Gordon's thoughts. In 1875, he dedicated his poem "Kotzo shel yud" (The Tip of the Yud) to her. Already by 1870 Gordon relayed to Markel-Mosessohn that he had attended a friend's wedding that, at the last hour, did not take place because of a conflict over the bride's ketubah (marriage contract).[121] He set about almost immediately composing a poem with this episode at its center, transforming the unfortunate circumstance into a satire-in-verse critiquing the obscurantism of traditional Jewish law, which could render a bride unmarriageable on account of a minute grammatical error that invalidated her ketubah. Though it was not published until 1875, from the outset Gordon determined to pen the poem in Markel-Mosessohn's honor.[122] And two years after it appeared, she acknowledged his kindness in the same letter detailing her husband's calamity.

After 1877, the Gordon-Markel-Mosessohn correspondence flagged once again but was revived after a decade's hiatus in much the same way in which it had been initiated. That is, Markel-Mosessohn wrote informing Gordon that she had completed a Hebrew translation of the second part of Rispart's *The Jews and the Crusades under Richard the Lionhearted* and that it was finally ready for publication. She asked him to compose a letter to be used as a foreword to the volume.[123] As delighted with the sequel as with the original, he consented with the following message: "I would be happy to write a few lines [for your book]. After acting as the *sandak* [godfather] to your son when entering him into the covenant, why wouldn't I act as best man when entering him under the *ḥuppah* [marriage canopy] now that he is eighteen?"[124] Though we might imagine that Gordon's quip offended its childless recipient, Markel-Mosessohn herself used similar language to refer to her literary productivity. She called part one of *The Jews and the Crusades under Richard the Lion-hearted* her "firstborn" and part two her "baby." Perhaps she regarded herself as a cultural mother of sorts—reproducing writings to enlighten the next generation of women and men.[125]

A Foreign Correspondent

While their correspondence was interrupted from 1877 to 1887, Markel-Mosessohn was on the move, wandering from one European city to another—with a three-year stint in Danzig—and settling finally in Vienna in 1881.[126] The details concerning her activities during this time evade us due to lack of documentation. Letters from the period in question reveal only her heightened involvement in business affairs during her husband's incarceration. She made frequent visits to members of her immediate family as well. Once happily ensconced in Vienna, she obviously felt ready at last to take up the challenge of becoming a writer in her own right, producing original works in Hebrew.

Though the familiar doubts returned, Markel-Mosessohn reluctantly accepted Gordon's repeated invitations to become the Viennese correspondent for *Ha-melitz* (The Advocate), the newspaper he then edited. In fact, she let an entire month slip by before sending him her first completed article, fearful that it would not meet the necessary standards for publication and that her words would be judged with especial severity on account of her sex.[127] When Gordon explained to her that typically only the author's initials appeared as a byline, Markel-Mosessohn was much relieved.[128] "Your words reassured me," she replied to the editor, "for now [they] will not deem the words written by a woman as nonsense, and they won't depreciate their worth."[129]

So at the age of forty-eight Markel-Mosessohn became a published author.[130] Though far from prolific, her four articles in *Ha-melitz* were an accomplishment of significant historical and personal dimension. For the first time, Gordon had made good on his promise to advocate for women writers. While in theory he had been encouraging female Hebraists for nearly two decades, now he put the words of one on *public* display. However, although Gordon explained the use of authors' initials as standard procedure for *Ha-melitz*, skimming the newspaper's contents reveals that many (male) correspondents published under their full names. Whether Gordon concocted the initials byline for Markel-Mosessohn's peace of mind or to cloak his own editorial permissiveness in allowing a female hand to publish must remain an unanswered question.

Qualified for the task and encouraged by the titans of Hebrew literature, Markel-Mosessohn edged into the authorial role slowly, with apprehension constantly at her heels. "The writers of Israel are so wise," she had maintained at the age of thirty-six, "I tremble at the thought" of being counted among them.[131] Yet twelve years later her attitude seemed to shift. As she expressed in the introduction to part two of *The Jews and the Crusades under Richard the Lionhearted*:

> Since the time that the first part [of the book] was published [in 1869], a new generation has come of age. I brought my firstborn near only to my brothers [but] then the love for our language grew among our people . . . and it found a route into my sisters' hearts. . . . Many of the daughters of Zion have come to enjoy reading and writing Hebrew . . . I heard great fear in my own heart, [but] I praised my Lord who had not forsaken the language of Moses and the prophets, the language [also] of Miriam, Devorah, and Hannah . . . So now I bring my baby near as well to my sisters who delight in [it]. And it will be my reward if [my sisters] will lift their countenances toward me . . . and I will bless them in the Lord's name.

Thus it seems that only among other women could Markel-Mosessohn make her peace with the Hebrew language. Fearful of being alone among men, she mustered the courage to write once her sisters joined her ranks.

At the same time, it is evident that by the late 1880s, Markel-Mosessohn's motive for writing exceeded self-fulfillment. Her husband's detention and the fine exacted upon his release presumably burdened household finances to such an extent that Markel-Mosesohn was forced to secure writing assignments to supplement their income.[132] In letters to publishers—that is, potential employers—she became quite vociferous about the earnings she expected her volumes to fetch. To the Warsaw publisher Tzuckerman, she bluntly announced: "I want five hundred rubles up front and three hundred later for the first and second parts [of my book] that you will publish."[133] Moreover, she asked Gordon's advice on placing an advertisement for her book in *Ha-melitz*.[134]

Although such a notice never appeared, Markel-Mosessohn's articles reached the readers of *Ha-melitz* throughout the spring and summer of 1887. They grew progressively longer and more interesting. The first was simply a translated reiteration of news of Jewish interest published elsewhere in European newspapers, while the second was a lengthy report of graduation exercises at a Jewish school for the blind.[135] Markel-Mosessohn hit her stride with the third piece, a rendering of details regarding the emergence of political antisemitism in the latest Hungarian elections in Tiszaeszlar, where a blood libel accusation had erupted five years earlier.[136] The greatest testimony to the beauty of Markel-Mosessohn's language is her fourth and final work for *Ha-melitz*, a feuilleton about summer in the Austro-Hungarian capital that winds its way into a reminiscence of Viennese Jewry.[137] The first paragraph provides a glimpse of her elegant style, blending as it does biblical allusion and evocative impressions of a city anesthetized by the summer heat:

> Today burns like a furnace. The sun sends forth its rays and numbs the city like a drug. Her inhabitants are like glowing fire and burning sparks. All is quiet and calm abounds. No one goes out and no one is parched, for they have abandoned the city and gone to the "one thousand mountains" [Psalm 50:10] to escape the heat, to regenerate from the toil of winter and to breathe fresh air. They turn to the "one thousand mountains" and to the hills and valleys that are wrapped in rapturous growth and gardens . . . and delight in them.

The article then describes the leisure activities of those few left behind who congregate at Vienna's magnificent parks. Among them, it relates, are Jews who "participate in the life of the city—not as guests, but as [first-rate] citizens" who figure prominently among Vienna's population as lawyers, doctors, artists, and writers. These Jews are integrated into the very fabric of Viennese society. "Many"—this for the Eastern European reading audience—"are not pious . . . and keep their shops open on the [Jewish] Sabbath," taking their respite from the work week on Sundays. Here readers are tantalized by sumptuous images of the good life that exists for the entire population of Vienna, including Jews. At the same time, they are offered a very subtle defense of Jews who take advantage of such a life. This is, in other words, no apology for abandoning Jewish tradition. Rather, it seems to suggest, stripping oneself of outward religious trappings is a fair price to pay in exchange for communal acceptance and even respect. That Jews are part and parcel of Viennese society, it makes clear, is a source of great pride.

By the time the article appeared in 1887, Markel-Mosessohn had been residing in the Austro-Hungarian capital for six years and would make it her home until three years before her death, thirty-four years later. Various statistics confirm that Jews occupied a predominant place in the city's cultural elite and in its social and educational base. Viennese scientists, musicians, and writers of Jewish descent, including Freud and Mahler, achieved world fame. As the historian Steven Beller has suggested, these well-placed men can best be characterized as Jews in social rather than ethnic terms. In other words, most hailed from merchant families, who having decided to integrate into Western society, sent their children to secular schools and abandoned Jewish particularism along the way. Their tactic was to ally with the people and the ideas of the future so as to not be identified as outsiders. They acquired culture as a means of overcoming Jewishness, and culture in effect provided them with a new form of identity.[138]

Markel-Mosessohn's satisfaction with her new home is evident in a letter to Gordon composed after their friendship had been rekindled in 1887. Vienna, she wrote, is an "enlightened land [where] the people are good and happy. They don't make a distinction between people of the convenant [i.e. Jews] and those who are not. Every person who lives here is subject to one law."[139] The prevailing tolerance appealed to Markel-Mosessohn. By the time she had left the Russian Empire in the late 1870s, she had, like large numbers of the Russian-Jewish intelligentsia, begun to lose hope that the liberal, emancipationist politics of the

Haskalah would find fertile ground in the Russian Empire. Vienna offered greener pastures.

Markel-Mosessohn acknowledged that both external and internal factors conspired to keep Jews apart from their neighbors. In an undated and unpublished essay, she set about explaining the causes of hatred against Jews and Judaism and then turned a mirror on her own community to describe how its composition resulted in estrangement from the larger community.[140] In her perspicacious analysis, she employed history to show that Jew-hatred had become manifest in a variety of forms over time and place. There were those who despised Jews for "believing in the religion of their ancestors." Perpetuators of medieval blood libels, for example, "wanted [only] to draw the Jews in toward themselves [i.e. to convert them] and not to destroy them." She contrasted them with those of modern Prussia "who supposedly struggled for love of man and religion, . . . and tradition and logic, . . . but whose single desire and deliverance was 'Hep!Hep!' [the famous anti-Jewish rallying cry in the early decades of the nineteenth century]." Markel-Mosessohn was underscoring here the differences between anti-Judaism and antisemitism—the former being a desire to root out the people's religious beliefs and the latter being a wholesale attack on the people qua people.

At essay's end, Markel-Mosessohn exhorted the Jews' enemies to "plunge below the surface" in order to view the totality of the Jewish people. Rather than "envision[ing only] the remnants of the Jews who live in the streets of the ghettos," they ought to recognize that "there are other Jews who are civilized in the European fashion. . . and have succeeded greatly in every [field of] wisdom, science and craft, in literature and politics, in theory and practice. They are a great improvement . . . over the smelly jacket of the Jewish-Polish peddler." That Markel-Mosessohn belonged to and approved of the enlightened segment of the Jewish community is here beyond doubt. She blames the simple Eastern European Jew for the outsider's contempt for all Jews and serves up her own dole of disdain for her coreligionist's incorrigible backwardness.

It is thus logical that Markel-Mosessohn easily blended into the social structure of Viennese Jewry, sharing as she did its outlook, as well as its merchant origins and appreciation of secular culture and knowledge. She may, however, have found it more of an effort to reconcile her religious practice with its sub-traditional norm, having been raised in a traditional Jewish household. Clearly she was aware of the rhythms of the Jewish calendar, regularly dating her letters by it and observing the festivals with punctiliousness. She remarked at one point, for instance, that she was consumed by the cleaning rituals of Passover as she prepared her home for the approaching holiday.[141] At another point, she mentioned in passing that she must quickly close her letter on that Friday afternoon for the Sabbath was coming and she intended to attend worship services.[142] At the same time, like her idol Graetz—a well-known lover of rationalism— she harbored intense dislike for the Hasidim, members of the pietistic movement, as indicated by an anecdote she related to Gordon about her visit to Warsaw:

> The days I have spent here have been feverish. I went to the theater, to friends' homes. I walked in the streets, accompanied by my brother, meandering from one sight to another . . . mingling with the crowd that is so varied in language and dress. I would be all the more pleased if I were to happen upon a Hasidic man, dressed in rags, emerging from the mikvah [ritual bath] dripping with water . . . and upon encountering a woman, his face would become distorted [by embarrassment], convulsing into a spasm.[143]

Markel-Mosessohn's Jewish identity was from childhood most strongly expressed through her attachment to the Hebrew language. Over her long life, the cities that she called home—Volkovyshki, Suvalk, Kovno, and even Vienna—were hubs, each in its own way, of the Hebrew vivification. Volkovyshki, with it local Jewish school, ignited within her a passion for the ancient tongue. Suvalk was the stomping ground for a number of followers of the *Am olam* movement, a group committed to the Jewish national revival, which considered acquisition of modern Hebrew a critical plank of its program. Kovno was the site of a cultural revival of not insignificant proportions. And from Vienna radiated for the first time a series of articles articulating, albeit in a rather inchoate form, how the concept of modern nationalism then emerging in the Austro-Hungarian Empire might logically be applied to the Jewish condition. Peretz Smolenskin argued in the pages of *Ha-shaḥar* (The Dawn), a Viennese-based newspaper under his editorship, that while most nations are dependent on a territory and a state structure, the Jews have a national tongue in Hebrew, a constitution in the Torah, and a shared history. To preserve and advance their unity, he contended, they must put "national sentiment" at the center of their identity and rejuvenate the Jewish national spirit. There is no record to suggest that Markel-Mosessohn subscribed to Smolenskin's beliefs, though she did produce a Hebrew translation of a German short story by Theodor Herzl, the father of political Zionism. It is doubtful that Jewish nationalism played any role in her zeal for the Hebrew language.[144]

Abandoning the Cause

While belief in the centrality of Hebrew acted as an anchor of Jewish identity throughout her life, Markel-Mosessohn did not allow herself to become a full-fledged participant in its revival. After submitting the four articles to *Ha-melitz*, she abruptly renounced authorship, explaining to Gordon:

> Sin begets sin,[145] and a person who sins and does not repent immediately keeps procrastinating. I have collected sins in my soul [for] I see the shoddy writings I was submitting to *Ha-melitz*, and it has become loathsome to me. I see the works of *accomplished* writers [her emphasis] who come to you, and I want so to be like them. But my desire and ability are not one and the same . . . and [so] it is my responsibility to confess all [of this] to you. . . . Surely you will understand. . . . It is appropriate that I leave you.[146]

By this Markel-Mosessohn meant more than yielding her post as Viennese reporter. For with this letter, all communication between the long-standing correspondents ceased.

For his part, Gordon's silence can be explained by the fact that his life was on a downward spiral at the very moment that Markel-Mosessohn drafted her final letter. When he received word of her resignation in January 1888, the poet was drained both physically and emotionally, embroiled as he was in a war of words with his critics and working frenetically to churn out six issues of *Ha-melitz* a week. He was in no shape to boost his friend's confidence, feeling himself a failure in his lifelong en-

deavor to make Hebrew a focus of all Jews. By the fall of that year, he re-
signed as editor and descended precipitously into a malaise that persisted
until his death in 1892. Thus in terminating his relationship with
Markel-Mosessohn, Gordon was merely severing one more tie to the organized world of the Jewish intelligentsia.

Only a single written reference to Gordon is found among Markel-
Mosessohn's papers after 1888. She complained in 1902 that she had received absolutely no compensation from the editor of *Ha-melitz* for four
articles published years back save a volume of his poems with the inscription: "Please take my book as a remembrance, my sister Miriam.
This is for you in exchange for your precious letters. . . ."[147] Markel-
Mosessohn's tone insinuates a lingering anger at Gordon. While she was
undoubtedly cheated out of earnings she deserved, her spite may well
have stemmed from her friend's silence after twenty years of fellowship
and support, which had flowed in both directions. Moreover, as his ideological disciple, she surely felt betrayed by Gordon's actions, vanishing
from the literary scene as he did without a trace of explanation to her.

With Gordon, along with his encouragement and writing offers, expunged from her life once and for all, Markel-Mosessohn's literary career
predictably terminated. Though she never again attempted to publish
original works in Hebrew, she did endeavor to sell what she uncharacteristically praised as a translation of "very high quality" to various Hebrew
newspapers. No editor accepted. Little is known of the remaining thirty
years of Markel-Mosessohn's life. A handful of letters and miscellaneous
documents dating from the turn of the century indicate only that Anshel
died on November 18, 1903 and that she remained in Vienna until at
least 1906.[148] One scholar has it that she remained in Vienna until the
outbreak of World War I and then spent the last three years of her life in
Grajewo (modern-day Poland), ninety miles south of her birthplace,
where her brother Yosef's family lived. She died on December 18, 1920
at the age of eighty-one.[149]

* * * * *

Beyond uncovering the curiosity of a woman intimately and actively involved in the Haskalah, Markel-Mosessohn's educational trajectory and
literary accomplishments underscore how being a woman was paradoxi-
cally the very means by which she came to inhabit the world of Hebrew

letters *and* the chief impediment to her functioning in that world in the same capacity as her male peers. But it was not the mere fact of being a woman that caused Markel-Mosessohn to be both a part of and apart from the driving forces producing literature in Hebrew in nineteenth-century Russia. Rather, it was the fact of what womanhood meant within that world. Men and women were expected to play very different roles on account of the perceived differences between the two.

Markel-Mosessohn's gender was the very factor that catapulted her to the rarefied realm of the Hebrew literary world. Expectations for women acquiring Hebrew skills were very low, or did not exist whatsoever. The gendered differentiation of Jewish education, which exempted girls from Torah study, exempted Markel-Mosessohn as well and thus freed her to pursue a different course of study that provided her with far better training in Hebrew than she would have received had she been a boy with the attendant expectations. To her father, her brothers, her husband and later to players in the Haskalah, she addressed letters that testify that by young adulthood she was capably wielding the pen in this language. Moreover, as an adolescent, she was tutored by a young man she described as enlightened, while voraciously beginning to read secular works in Hebrew, whose maskilic ideas influenced her thoughts and outlook. In contrast to her male counterparts, this was an acceptable activity for Markel-Mosessohn, or at least one undeserving of notice or safeguarding against.

At the same time that Markel-Mosessohn was equipping herself with the tools for reading in her people's ancient tongue, the vanguard of the Hebrew literary world was looking to increase its audience and add female voices to its enterprise. If Hebrew was to become an authentic and respected modern language, it needed the sounds that only women could produce. Notably, the leaders of the Hebrew literary world began to subscribe to the notion that the female sex—this time as prescribed by gender standards of the Enlightenment—possessed a unique emotional tone that would enhance the quality of their resurrected language. Stereotypes aside, female Hebraists schooled in European languages and literature surely would have had belletristic know-how that could be applied to the Hebrew literary case. Moreover, given their gender-determined exteriority to the Jewish textual tradition, women were strategically positioned to assist in the revivalists' attempt to release

Hebrew from its millenium-long exclusive association with the tradition of male legalism and its outdated values. So once Markel-Mosessohn made her abilities known, the leaders of the Hebrew literary world lined up to receive from her (and her female compatriots) that which they deemed necessary for the realization of their goals.

In fact, they engaged in a publicity campaign of sorts, spotlighting the achievements of female Hebraists in an effort to boost Hebrew's status in their eyes and the public's eye. Simultaneously, of course, they were proving to themselves and the world that Jewish women were capable of playing in the literary arena, a feat that their non-Jewish sisters were already achieving. Maskilim thus began to articulate new educational expectations for the female sex in an effort to stay competitive with their non-Jewish enlightened rivals, as well as to combat what they regarded as the outmoded gender roles prescribed by their Jewish rivals, the upholders of the status quo. While they surely opened new prospects for educating Jewish women, ironically, their idealization of the bourgeois family led to an existence for women that in large part resembled that ordained by the Jewish tradition.

But for Markel-Mosessohn, the embrace by maskilim of women writers translated into an enthusiastic cheering squad for her abilities. As evidenced by her extensive correspondence, she enjoyed the mentorship of men who urged her at every turn to produce literature in Hebrew. Yet she failed to live up to their expectations, for her own were a constant hindrance to her progress. She failed to realize her potential as a writer because she was haunted by traditional Jewish expectations for women that she had come to accept and demand of herself. She maintained that publishing original works would shame her by exposing her efforts to transgress sacred male ground. Yet, despite self-doubts, Markel-Mosessohn sought to encourage other young women in their professional pursuits. In letters to maskilim, she responded to their requests for advice on how to educate their own daughters.

So much of Markel-Mosessohn's biography and worldview pivoted on a maskilic axis that it is tempting to identify her as a maskilah. Her broad education in things Jewish and secular prepared her for adopting attitudes espoused by maskilim. Her marriage, characterized as it was by true companionship, met the criteria for modern marriage ordained by maskilim. Her literary output, with its emphasis on translation, conforms to the maskilic demand for enriching Hebrew with foreign tongues and ideas. And most important, her strong links to individuals who made up the leadership of the Haskalah meant that she, too, was involved in their network and enterprise.

But she was not one of them. Their strict pronouncement and observance of gender differentiations, which Markel-Mosessohn herself accepted, precluded her from obtaining the status of maskil. And though, to the contemporary eye, she may have possessed the makings of a maskilah, no such category existed at the time. In effect, Markel-Mosessohn straddled two gender worlds, belonging to neither.

2

The Female Experience in Hebrew Literature

Hava Shapiro (1878–1943)

In 1900, twenty-two-year-old Hava Shapiro confessed to her diary: "To me, pen and ink are like good and trustworthy friends because they allow us to reveal our hearts and lighten our burdens . . . (especially) for the one whose words are burning . . . like a fire but who is unable to speak. To him, the pen and ink seem like the opening of the Garden of Eden, which was forbidden him to enter" [her parentheses].[1] For Shapiro, as for Miriam Markel-Mosessohn, Eden was the world of Hebrew learning and literature. Though generally off limits, if not forbidden, to the Jewish woman, Shapiro entered this paradise as a young girl primarily under the tutelage of her parents: her mother was herself proficient in the ancient tongue, and her father, an heir to a Hebrew printing and paper manufacturing dynasty in Slavuta, Volhynia (modern-day Ukraine), insisted that his children correspond with him only in Hebrew.[2] Her great-great grandfather Rabbi Pinhas of Koretz, a disciple of the Ba'al Shem Tov, would no doubt have disapproved of Shapiro as she broke all the conventional gender molds cast by the Jewish community.[3] Not only did she become an accomplished female Hebraist. Shapiro divorced her husband, left her son to his father's care while she pursued higher education abroad, and carried on a long-distance romance with a married admirer. Writing thus afforded Shapiro emotional solace as she shed her old identity and searched for a new one.

Shapiro did more, however, than turn to literature as a result of her dilemma: she turned her dilemma into literature. Her literary oeuvre emerged directly out of her existential turmoil. The pain of the Jewish woman alienated from Jewish society by her intellectual acumen and am-

bition reverberates throughout her compositions, as she appointed herself town crier of the female soul, exposing to all its concealed aspects.
Over her lifetime, she composed some fifty pieces of literary criticism,
fiction, or journalism appearing in over half a dozen Hebrew periodicals,
as well as a collection of short sketches and a scholarly monograph.[4] Of
those nineteenth-century women writers of Hebrew who remained in the
Diaspora, Shapiro is the most prolific—though her works have received
virutally no attention, save for a master's thesis focusing on her correspondence, a handful of reviews, and brief entries in encyclopediac
sources.[5] Her more famous Hebrew-writing sisters—including Rahel
(Bluwstein),[6] Devorah Baron, Nehamah Pohazhavski, Itta Yellin, Yehudit
Hararit, and Hemdah Ben-Yehudah[7]—followed their linguistic longing
and immigrated to the land of Israel from Eastern Europe during their
young adulthood. Despite a trip to Palestine in 1911 and repeated yearn-
ings late in her life to be among fellow lovers of the ancient tongue,
Shapiro chose to live out her days in a self-imposed exile far from even
the European centers of Hebraic literary activity and creativity.[8]

Early in her life, however, Shapiro interacted regularly with those involved in the Jewish cultural renaissance in fin-de-siècle Warsaw. The
man who stood at the center of this revival, Yitzhak Leib Peretz
(1851–1915), offered Shapiro emotional counsel and literary advice. As
Shapiro described their first meeting:

> I was just a girl of twenty when I met Peretz. I had gone to live in
> Warsaw, to tend house. Until then I had been closeted in my hid-
> ing-place, and I didn't know life . . . but I had already experienced
> pain that had expanded until it tore my heart. I began to visit his
> house and he became a friend, a brother to me. . . . [Though] he
> wasn't all that effusive, I knew and felt [his concern] for everything
> that had happened to me. . . . My life became exposed and revealed
> before him. . . . He understood me and my life more than others to
> whom it would become necessary to explain.[9]

Shapiro divulged her secret torment to Peretz when the mute pages of
her diary offered no consolation. "I'm unable to reveal it [in writing],"
she confessed to her diary, "because who would read it? Who would respond to the laments and inner pain that trouble a woman? It's impossi-

ble *to describe the things in the heart*" [her emphasis].[10] Yet describe them she did to the man whose glance, according to Shapiro, "penetrate[d] to the hidden recesses of [my] heart."[11]

Shapiro's sorrows began in 1895 when she married Limel Rosenbaum, the wealthy son of a Warsaw banker. Approximately three years after the birth of their son Pinhas in 1897, the trio moved to Rosenbaum's native city, where the couple's incompatibility intensified as she participated in the secular Hebrew cultural revival, while he engaged in financial activities among the Jewish bourgeoisie. Warsaw was in the late-nineteenth and early-twentieth centuries the third city of the Russian Empire, trailing only St. Petersburg and Moscow in size and importance. It had an ethnically-mixed population, with Poles making up a little more than half the total, and Jews thirty to forty percent. By the turn of the century, significant sections of its Jewish commuity were adopting the culture of the surrounding gentile world, and Shapiro found there a niche for her growing interest in Hebrew literature, which further deepened her estrangement from her husband.[12]

Shapiro flirted with disaster in May 1899. While taking the baths with her mother near Berlin, she met Reuven Brainin (1862–1939), who would become her mentor and lover for the next quarter century. Brainin was sixteen years her senior and well on his way to becoming an established Hebrew and Yiddish author. While their relationship became in many ways the bane of Shapiro's emotional well-being, it drove her as well to liberate herself from her claustrophobic marriage and pursue a formal education for the first time.

In the wake of their meeting, Shapiro turned to writing in the Hebrew language as a palliative for her metaphysical anguish. First, she entered into a clandestine correspondence with Brainin, punctuated by rare trysts beyond the watchful eye of his lifelong wife, whom Shapiro tagged "the policeman."[13] Of the more than two hundred Hebrew letters that survive chronicling their twenty-nine year mostly epistolary affair, only a single one bears Brainin's signature. The others, penned by Shapiro, provide a glimpse into the female correspondent's psyche in its shimmering workings, for she unbuttoned her self before Brainin and exposed her emotions and thoughts on the page. At once confidential and confessional, her revelations are of a most intimate nature, disclosing everything from

her vacillating mental and physical health to her profound spiritual attachment to Brainin and her ongoing attempts at intellectual self-im-
provement. Moreover, Shapiro began in 1899 to keep a diary, a practice
that endured virtually until her death in 1943. The extant 267-page
notebook, handwritten in a Hebrew prose that dramatically improves
with time, is a record of an unfinished journey toward self-definition—a
journey Shapiro took along with thousands of other members of the
bourgeoisie. Her family's lucrative business enabled the Shapiros to become part of the emerging middle-class in the Russian Empire, which
meant, along with financial security, a desire to replicate behavioral and
thought patterns imported from the enlightened West.

With its emphasis on the individual, the European Enlightenment
spawned a generation of men and women who set out on what the historian Peter Gay terms a "pilgrimage of the interior."[14] Both love letters and
diaries grew more common and more candid over the course of the nineteenth century; while autobiography, self-portrait, biographical history
and novels exploring character exploded into a sizable domestic industry
among the middle class. Preoccupation with the self loomed large across
Europe and even into the Russian Empire. As Pavel Yakovlevich Shubin
of Turgenev's novel *On the Eve* (1859) explains, they are "always studying
themselves in disgusting detail, feeling their pulses with every sensation
that they experience and then reporting to themselves: 'That's how I feel
and that's what I think.' What a useful, sensible sort of occupation."[15]
Stereotypes of men as reasoning and women as emotional did not govern
nineteenth-century diaries and letters. The confessional style flourished
equally among men and women.[16] Through introspective compositions
writers of both sexes sought to define themselves anew as the dizzying
changes about them chipped away at any semblance of a fixed and
knowable self.[17]

The Jewish intellectual elite of Eastern Europe was not immune to this
paradoxical need for inwardness and its simultaneous exploration
through expression. From Moses Leib Lilienblum's autobiography *Sins of
Youth* (1876) to Micah Yosef Berdischevsky's novel *A Raven Flies*
(1899–1908), the spiritually uprooted expected some form of retrospective learning or wisdom to be delivered in the course of baring their
souls.[18] Enlightened Jews redoubled their confessional literary efforts
during the final decades of the century as they experienced cognitive dis-

sonance when their supreme faith in the Haskalah conflicted with powerful anti-Jewish sentiments then emerging in the Tsarist Empire. Hopes dashed and expectations thwarted, Hebrew authors in unprecedented numbers and with unmatched intensity employed introspective writings as a means for finding, constructing, and securely establishing a new identity following the demise of a heretofore fixed Weltanschauung.

Shapiro, too, turned her love letters and diaries into repositories of her innermost life as she struggled to define her identity. Voluntarily cutting herself off from the familiar moorings of Jewish bourgeois norms by divorcing her husband and rejecting the conventional roles of wife and mother, she endeavored both to find and anchor a new self-identity in writing.

This chapter will explore how Shapiro's gender cast her as eternal outsider on two separate stages. It is obvious why a successful female Hebraist—and a divorced one at that—would be alienated from bourgeois Jewish society. As discussed in chapter one, "enlightened" standards confined middle-class women to the domestic, conjugal sphere, where they were to civilize their children and act as complementary companions to their husbands. Surely Shapiro, the Hebrew writer, had as little use for middle-class dictates as the bearers of such dictates would have for her and what they undoubtedly perceived as her hyper-talents.

But the overarching question posed by Shapiro's life and work is why a skilled female Hebraist like Shapiro had equal difficulty fitting in with the Jewish literary elite crystallizing at the turn of the century. She, like them, was busy unveiling the inner workings of her heart in the language that they, and she, agreed was the most natural and appropriate for such a pursuit. Indeed, the leaders of the Hebrew renaissance readily admitted her to their ranks, and many lavished praise upon her. A list of Shapiro's admirers reads like a "Who's Who" of the late nineteenth- and early twentieth-century Jewish nationalist corps. Besides Peretz and Brainin, there were David Frischmann, Nahum Sokolov, Micah Yosef Berdischevsky, and Hayim Nahman Bialik. Yet Shapiro, as a woman writing, held only a tenuous positon among them. As with Markel-Mosessohn, her life and work raise questions about the role gender played in the resuscitated Hebrew language and its attendant culture. Specifically, what did it mean to be a woman writer in a culture (both in its old and new manifestations) whose fundamental definitions of literary authority were covertly and overtly patriarchal? And to what extent could and would modern Hebrew, especially in its nascency, tolerate an infusion of female Hebraists whose writing grew out of their experiences as women? A detailed examination of Shapiro's fascinating life and literature will illuminate these issues.

A Descendant of the Pious

Hava Shapiro's ancestry can be traced back six generations to her fore-bear Pinhas, who made preaching to Jewish apostates his life work in the wake of the Chmielnicki massacre of 1648–49, which left the Jewish population of Poland-Lithuania as disillusioned as it was decimated. Years later, Pinhas' son Abraham Abba had a son whom he named for his father. Pinhas the Younger (1726–1791) mastered the Talmud and its commentaries along with several branches of secular knowledge before devoting himself to the study of Jewish mystical texts. Not long before his death in 1760, the Ba'al Shem Tov—the founder of Hasidism—met with Pinhas on three separate occasions, imparting to him his basic teachings.[19]

Pinhas' three sons took up residence in three different towns; his middle son, Moses Shapiro (1759–1837), settled in Slavuta, Volhynia. In 1791, the year of his father's death, Moses sought and secured permission from the local duke to establish a Hebrew printing press and a paper-manufacturing factory. Within two years, as Russia annexed Slavuta in the second Partition of Poland, the press began to prosper.[20] Under the direction of Moses' two sons, Shmuel Avraham Abba (d. 1864) and Pinhas (d. 1872), it proved extremely profitable and unrivaled among Hebrew presses in the Russian Empire. But the Shapiro brothers' printing fortune was to suffer a severe and irrevocable reversal in 1835 because of a sordid affair, which Pinhas' granddaughter Hava Shapiro was to dramatize in an essay nearly eighty years after the fact.[21]

The brothers' troubles arose in the summer of 1834 as a result of the unexplained death of a devoted bookbinder of the Shapiro printing press, whose body was found (hanged) in a local house of worship.[22] Some alleged that the brothers murdered their employee for fear that he would reveal his bosses' most coveted secret: the Shapiros were illegally printing certain books without consent of the official Russian censor. An

Hava Shapiro
From the collection of the Jewish Public Library, Montreal

investigation ensued, and according to several accounts, two enlightened Jews—apparently motivated by a desire to abolish any printing press that scrupulously abstained from publishing literature of the Haskalah—came forward to testify against the brothers.[23] The Shapiros were found guilty, and once the matter became known to the authorities in St. Petersburg, Tsar Nicholas I closed every Hebrew printing press in Volhynia and Lithuania in 1835 and sentenced the brothers of Slavuta to whippings[24] and banishment to Siberia. Upon ascending the throne in 1855, the more lenient Tsar Alexander II set the brothers free.

Shapiro's account of the brouhaha begins as a chronological overview, recounting the establishment of her family's printing press in the heyday of the Haskalah with a cast of characters drawn from her own family tree. Her opening remarks allude to the secrecy surrounding this shameful "incident," about which no one breathed a word and for which she cast about endlessly as a child searching for hints that she could piece together to form a coherent sequence of events. Shapiro's version portrays her hapless relatives as the victims of angry maskilim, who hated them for publishing Hasidic texts that prevented the reading public from drawing near to the principles of the Enlightenment. As Shapiro narrates:

> And the Haskalah was then in the land. The ruler who governed over it was Nicholas I, who allowed the Haskalah to flourish. And among the Jews then the Hasidic movement grew, which had as one of its founders Pinhas of Korez. And this movement, which was distinguished by its romanticism, was hateful to the first maskilim. . . . And the evildoers of the [Haskalah] . . . wanted to inform against Moses and his sons, saying: "See the Rav and his sons, descendants of Pinhas, who cling to the Torah of their fathers, who increase darkness among the people by continuing to publish their bad opinions and thus impede the spreading of the Haskalah."[25]

The bulk of Shapiro's account focuses on the exemplary behavior of her relatives in the face of the scourging, as well as the formidable esteem in which they were apparently held as a result. With dramatic flourish, she details the pietistic preparation undertaken to withstand their "valley of tears."[26] As the crowd gathered to watch the spectacle, she claimed that her fiercely devout relations wrapped themselves in prayer shawls and phylacteries and earnestly prayed to their God. Passing through the gauntlet, the "righteous ones" restrained from uttering so much as a sigh, as the two hundred fifty armed soldiers, arranged in double rows, whipped the exposed shoulders of the accused. Moses, by then an octogenarian, died soon after hearing the news of his sons' beatings. Shapiro concluded her tale of woe by describing the brothers' jubilant release from prison and the heroes' welcome showered upon them at each Jewish community through which they passed en route home to Slavuta. In her apocryphal tale, Shapiro struck a subtle blow to the adherents of the Haskalah, who brought misfortune to so virtuous a pair. Her version alone describes the fate of the slandererous maskilim who were forced to make financial restitution to and seek forgiveness from the honest Shapiro brothers.

By the time Shapiro tried to set the record straight in 1914 with her account of the scandal, the printing press of Slavuta was long defunct. It closed in 1835 and then reopened and relocated to Zhitomir in the 1860s. The lucrative paper factory, however, continued to flourish in Slavuta, providing a handsome income to Pinhas, whose son Ya'akov Shamai took over the family business after his father's death in 1872. Ya'akov Shamai brought his second wife, Menuhah (née Sheinberg) from Kishinev, Bessarabia to Slavuta.[27] By the end of the nineteenth century, 4,891 Jews were registered in the town (57 percent of the total population), making it a typical shtetl of the Pale of Settlement.[28] There the couple availed themselves of the bourgeois way of life: servants attended to their domestic needs, tutors provided the children with lessons in the necessary accoutrements of civility, and family excursions abroad were de rigueur.

Groomed for Eminence

On December 26, 1878 Ya'akov Shamai and Menuhah welcomed a daughter into their growing brood.[29] Whether or not they chose her name Hava (Eve) because she was the *first* girl after three sons remains a mystery.[30] What can be confirmed, however, is that Hava herself eventually played on the resonance of her biblical namesake, pseudonymously calling herself *em kol ḥai* (the mother of all life) in many of her published works.[31] As the sister of three brothers, Shapiro described in an autobiographical sketch, published in 1909 and entitled "Sanctification of the Moon," how she "regarded [herself] as one of [the] . . . boy[s]."[32] She imitated her older siblings in all things, religious and secular alike:

> At first I participated in all their games. I ran, jumped, skipped so much like a boy that all the people of the house were almost unable to distinguish between me and my brothers in every mitzvah. When they were busy building the sukkah, I, too, climbed up on the roof with my brothers and helped with everything. . . . Together with my brothers I heard lessons from the old rabbi, . . . who made an exception for me, who in his holiness [permitted me] to study Torah! My soul so desired Torah! I wanted it so much![33]

In like fashion, Shapiro revealed that when she came of age as a bat-mitzvah, the old rabbi recognized the event in a ceremony at the family home.[34]

Shapiro's complete embrace of traditional Jewish life was to be short-lived, however. Already as a young girl she recognized the "great advantages [her brothers] had over her" during times of ritual obligation, as made evident in the same sketch. Chronicling the pain caused by this growing realization, she lamented: "Not only did they deprive me of [fulfilling] the commandment of blessing the new moon, which seemed to me then such a great joy, but also my brothers warned me not even to look at their faces as they blessed . . .. They made me cover my eyes with my hands because a young girl who looks . . . will get punished in the World to Come."[35] Though increasingly distressed by the words, "If only she had been a boy! Oy, what a shame"—which appear like a refrain in "Sanctification of the Moon"—Shapiro never completely abandoned the Jewish practices she had known growing up as a child in a traditional household.

Traces of her continued attention to and awareness of religious life color her diary and letters, including continual dating by the Jewish calendar and mention of attendance at High Holiday worship and Passover seders.[36] By the age of twenty-seven, she confessed that she was no longer a "woman of faith" according to the definitions set by the pious.[37] Yet she continued to admire those of the older generation, whom, she argued, "had religion to elevate and purify and cleanse them" in contrast to the "emptiness of the heart and smallness and debasement" of her own generation.[38] Recognizing traditional Judaism's exclusion of women from the public realm, Shapiro sought spiritual sustenance in Jewish culture, finding especially in the Hebrew language a vehicle to transport her to a modern Jewish existence.

Shapiro's movement toward secular culture differed from that of male writers, such as Peretz and Brainin. They criticized Jewish life for its discrimination against women only insofar as it related to the overall purging of Judaism of obscurantism. But for Shapiro, sexism was the chief factor driving her away from traditional Jewish life and toward secular Hebrew culture. Like men, her immersion in the ancient tongue began in childhood. Encouraged by her mother, whom the daughter described as equally capable of reading Hebrew books and newspapers and of corresponding in Hebrew, Menuhah drilled her daughters in the rudiments of the ancient tongue.[39] Moreover, along with her brothers, Shapiro studied the Pentateuch and Talmud. And each Shabbat the children would gather to hear their father expound on the weekly Torah portion, in tandem with lessons drawn from *Dor dor vedorshav* (Generations and Interpretations).[40] It is notable that Ya'akov Shamai Shapiro chose selections from this particular history of Jewish law and lore, for its author, Isaac Hirsch Weiss (1815–1905), had as his chief aim the blending of talmudic study with secular culture and scientific methods. The five-volume work, which appeared over the course of two decades beginning in 1871, provided the children with an appreciation for lucid Hebrew and an approach to classical Jewish texts far removed from traditional Jewish study. The great-grandson of Rabbi Pinhas of Koretz evidently had no qualms about introducing his flock to the latest in critical scholarship, even as the family's daily activities seemed to be organized according to the principles of Jewish law.[41]

At the same time, Shapiro was drilled in modern languages, for which she developed both an affinity and a flair. In addition to her native tongue of Russian, her faulty Yiddish and perfect Hebrew, she came to know Latin, French, Polish, German, and Czech—in the former two she had at least reading capabilities, and in the latter three she was fluent. [42] But it was Hebrew alone that was to become her passion, and writing in the ancient tongue her sole ambition. Beside the solid training in classical Hebrew, which she received at the hearth as a teenager, Shapiro became connected to a circle of "lovers of the Hebrew language," which met each Saturday evening after sundown in Slavuta to recite and discuss Hebrew literature. According to a childhood friend of her son's, Shapiro gained prominence in the group and on occasion read from her works "in her husky voice."[43] Although a polyglot, throughout her life Shapiro would write only for Hebrew publications. In fact, years later, she refused to translate her Hebrew article on President Tomas Masaryk—the first president of the newly-formed republic—for the local Czech newspaper.[44] In her own words, "[Hebrew] is hidden in my soul; it is connected to my holy of holies."[45]

Constrained by Marriage

Eventually Shapiro outgrew her local literary circle, as well as the provincialism of rustic Slavuta. Some time after her sixteenth birthday, she accompanied her mother on an excursion to Kishinev, perhaps as a means of consolation for the harrowing death of her eleven-year-old sister stricken with scarlet fever.[46] Shapiro was beset by wanderlust upon her return, and it was temporarily assuaged the following year, in 1895, when she married Limel Rosenbaum, whose father's Warsaw-based financial connections meant a change of scenery for the young bride. The couple set off for the groom's hometown, and returned to Slavuta during the summers and for the birth of a son, Pinhas, in 1897.[47] Although Warsaw's intellectual and cultural offerings far surpassed Slavuta's, it became readily apparent that Shapiro was ill-suited for the role of affluent banker's wife. Though certainly accustomed to the external comforts of bourgeois life, she had neither patience nor tolerance to suffer the "idle conversations" of chatty women (and presumably men as well) who cared not at all for the life of the mind and spirit.[48] Though no records remain of the first three years of their troubled marriage, in 1899 Shapiro registered her profound dissatisfaction in her diary: "It's said that one knows emptiness only after tasting bitter despair . . . [but] I see the emptiness of life all around me. . . . The questions 'why?' and 'for which purpose?' exhaust my mind. I cannot find the answers to my questions among those around me—I want at times to be alone in my room with my thoughts. I so much want another life and different surroundings. How can I change [them]?"[49]

The impetus for change came not five years after her wedding day while Shapiro was vacationing with her mother in Francisbad, a spa near Berlin. There in May 1899, as a twenty-year-old wife and mother of a two-year-old boy, Shapiro met and fell in love with another man, who at thirty-seven was nearly twice her age. Reuven Brainin contributed to almost every Hebrew periodical of the time as either writer or editor. Moreover, as a critic of traditional rabbinic attitudes against women, he stood poised to offer Shapiro the intellectual stimulation and encouragement she desperately sought. In a letter on the heels of their meeting, Brainin complimented Shapiro for being an "impressive Hebrew writer, [who] is unique among our daughters."[50] Her linguistic talents demonstrated that "there truly are great and marvelous lady Hebraists." The flattery proved just the cure for Shapiro's flagging confidence, as she wrote eighteen months after receiving his first letter: ". . . Reuven Brainin saw in my writings 'exalted and sublime ideas' and a captivating style. He pleaded with me not to kill off my talents."[51]

But it was not only the lady's "sharp intellect" and linguistic capabilities that mesmerized the gentleman. Brainin's letter indicates a profound romantic longing for his "beloved sister," whose "modesty, innocence and purity won [his] heart and soul forever." "I would gladly give my life," Brainin wooed Shapiro, "for a brief glimpse of [your] face and a chance to talk to [you]." She had become as well a source of inspiration, "awaken[ing] all [his] dormant forces and filling [him] with new power, hope and life. . . . ." He closed with "regards to your honorable mother and a kiss for your son," and to his signature affixed the sweetheart's phrase, "I am completely yours."

While only this single letter of Brainin to Shapiro remains, it is complemented by over two hundred extant letters and postcards of Shapiro to Brainin written between 1899 and 1928. Brainin conscientiously saved every item he received from Shapiro, ignoring her repeated admonitions to destroy all evidence of their affair. Nevertheless, their correspondence remained successfully concealed from their relatives: each kept close track of the other's travel plans and arranged for the letters to be sent to the main post office or through a trusted messenger. To give but one example, in a single year (1908–9), Shapiro's letters followed Brainin from Antwerp to Paris to London, Glasgow, and Berlin.[52] After a time, Brainin was able to send his letters directly to Shapiro, while she continued to address letters to him to bogus figures like "*Kulmos*" (pen) and signed "Dr. Hayim Sheinberg" (her mother's maiden name).[53]

Their correspondence reveals the dual nature of their relationship: the pedagogical coaxing of master to disciple, and the intimacy of lover to lover. From the outset, Shapiro asked Brainin to be her mentor, an invitation he readily accepted.[54] In return she promised to be an "attentive student" and "to listen to all his advice," as well as to show him all her manuscripts before sending them off to editors for their consideration.[55] Moreover, Shapiro read and critiqued Brainin's writings, being an avid reader of the maskilic journals in which many of his works appeared, including *Ha-melitz*, *Ha-tzofeh*, *Ha-tzefirah* and *Ha-shiloaḥ*.[56] The pair also discussed foreign works, for Brainin prided himself on his knowledge of world literature, and his student immersed herself in the classics, regularly sprinkling her letters with references to Goethe, Gorkii, Chekhov, and Mill, to name but a few examples.[57]

Albeit behind a veil of Victorian modesty, Shapiro and Brainin employed the only means available to them to express their wholehearted affection and deep-seated connection. As the years passed, their feelings for each other became increasingly manifest: Shapiro's signature closing "your faithful friend" metamorphosed into "the one who loves you truly and eternally." She confessed early on only to her diary, "We're close in spirit and in soul. It's impossible to prove this. The matter is *felt*. It is . . . spiritual integration" [her emphasis].[58] Finally in 1909, she informed Brainin directly: "I am yours in spirit forever."[59] Although she occasionally threatened to end the affair, Shapiro's heart belonged to Brainin and his to her.[60]

Besides expressing their emotions, the correspondence traces the course of Shapiro's deepening despair. The day after Yom Kippur 1901, Shapiro disclosed to Brainin that the ordained ritual fasting was nothing compared to the daily torture afflicting her soul. At every moment, she added, "inner contradictions" urged her "to exclaim the truth": namely, that she was no longer able to feign being a virtuous wife and mother.[61] Even her literary debut in December 1901—a two-page allegorical work published pseudonymously in David Frischmann's *Ha-dor*—brought her no solace.[62] "I felt none of the same joy and satisfaction" that is typically conferred upon new authors. "My heart," she continued, "did not leap upon seeing my name in print. . . . I will not be satisfied until the sorrow of my heart is revealed on the page."[63]

Despite her words to the contrary, when viewed through the lens of her unhappy circumstances, Shapiro's first published work can be interpreted as self-revelation. On first blush, the allegory entitled "Hashoshanah" (The Rose) appears to be as simple as a children's story. A single rose has undergone the unfortunate experience of being plucked from the garden, placed indoors in a vase and later transplanted outdoors only to encounter a fierce windstorm. "I suffered a great deal," the rose recounts, "I saw from a distance the daughters of my kind who enjoyed the light, the air, the freedom. . . . The maidservant came and imprisoned me and strangled my soul . . . my only responsibility was to be pleasant, and my voice was not heard." By story's end, the flower turns rosier about the future, expressing the hope that "a new rose will grow in my place, . . . a free rose who will not accept your yoke or recognize the boundaries to which you want to restrict me." She closes: "I may perish, but my seed will live forever!"

Literary critics and cultural historians alike have found in this sketch a metaphor for the Jewish people as a whole as it began to return to its homeland buoyed by the nationalistic flurry of fin-de-siècle Europe.[64] Surely, the transplantation motif lends itself to such an interpretation, especially in light of the Zionistic ideology and action sprouting at the time of the appearance of "The Rose."[65]

However, from an entirely different vantage point, "The Rose" can be understood as an attempt by the author to symbolize her life experience. The fact, for instance, that Shapiro selected the rose (*shoshanah*, a female noun) as a megaphone for her own voice is neither coincidental nor incidental. *Shoshanah* "longed for open space," where her soul could roam freely. Shapiro, too, sought to extricate herself from imposed restraints that grounded her in surroundings at odds with her nature. Years later, after gaining her freedom, she would write: "I stand [now] on my own turf."[66] Once rooted in their natural soil, both the rose and Shapiro would truly blossom.

Shapiro found her "promised land" in Warsaw at the small home of Y.L. Peretz, where a circle of men assembled each evening to discuss their Hebrew works in progress. Like other inexperienced writers, Shapiro turned for inspiration to Peretz, who tried to shape literature in Hebrew (and Yiddish) into an instrument of national cohesion.[67] "[At Peretz's] I was more than ever in my element," maintained Shapiro, and she felt equally at home divulging her painful secret to her host. [68] Perhaps Peretz's own personal unhappiness—he divorced his first wife at the age of twenty-three—made him an empathic listener. Besides confidante, Peretz became Shapiro's teacher, helping her to hone her writing skills and inviting her to his literary gatherings. According to Shapiro, "he read everything" she penned, and she "visited him nearly every day" during the early 1900s.[69] Peretz applauded Shapiro's efforts, reportedly exclaiming to the eminent author Nahum Sokolov: "She knows Hebrew better than I."[70] Peretz even tried to enlist Shapiro to be his secretary, a job she subsequently turned down.

In February 1902, Shapiro found herself at a performance of *Uriel Acosta*, a five-act tragedy by the German playwright Karl Ferdinand Gutzkow (1811–1878).[71] Shapiro described the lasting impression the drama made on her in an unusually lengthy diary entry.[72] Da Costa was born into a Marrano family in Portugal in 1585 and later returned to Judaism only to be excommunicated once for criticizing the rigidity of Amsterdam's Jewish communal leaders and another time for dissuading a pair of Christians from converting to Judaism. While da Costa is generally counted among the most notorious of Jewish apostates, Gutzkow, like many artists of his time, idealized his protagonist as a victim of obscurantism and bigotry. Shapiro applauded the playwright's interpretation, identifying with the ignominious title character, who committed suicide at the age of sixty-five. She expressed her admiration for da Costa, who, despite the great rage he evoked in others and the shame he brought upon himself, "aspired to the truth and did not deny his opinions." Shapiro claimed in her diary to have understood "the troubles of his soul! . . . and the courage of his spirit!" Da Costa, it would seem, became a role model of sorts for Shapiro. Like him, she sought to follow the dictates of her soul, which were being stifled by outdated conventions imposed upon an unwilling participant. To this end, she arranged a rendezvous with Brainin the following summer—one of a handful successfully executed over the course of their twenty-odd year relationship.[73]

But a tryst with Brainin could neither extricate Shapiro from her misbegotten marriage nor cure her growing ennui. And on June 30, 1903, she informed Brainin of her momentous decision to leave her husband and son in order to start anew. "The time has come," she wrote, "to throw off the shackles that others put on me and be what I will be!" "After six years of suffering and waiting," the time had come to "go [her] own way alone, without help" from those who tried to restrain her.[74] At long last resolved, Shapiro secured promises of funds from her mother, left Warsaw for Slavuta, and turned immediately to constructing a program of formal study for herself.

While her parents and brothers reacted well to her unconventional decision, others were far from supportive. Brainin urged her to remain with her husband, and Rosenbaum himself begged her to stay. Initially he bullied her with threats, such as preventing her from ever again seeing their son Pinhas, and then he gradually came round to cajoling her with agreeable conditions, such as remaining in the marriage with freedom to study alone abroad (and visits from him) so long as she kept the Rosenbaum name.[75] Shapiro refused his offers, yet never blamed her husband. As she claimed, "[Rosenbaum] always loved me . . . more than all of [the rest of his family], he remained as he was . . . faithful to me with all his heart and soul. He was prepared to do anything for me that I asked, and he believed in me, [persuaded that] everything I did was good and beautiful."[76] The child would remain with his father in Warsaw until 1919, though Rosenbaum did arrange for Pinhas to visit with his mother on the condition that a paternal relation was always present. Once their divorce came through, however, the brokenhearted Rosenbaum took to spreading rumors about Shapiro, insinuating that *em kol ḥai* was guilty not only of abandoning her husband and child but also of apostasy.[77]

Even Shapiro became conflicted about her decision: she cherished her newly-won freedom, but lamented the separation from her son.[78] "Is it possible?" she asked in 1904, "Is it really me who lives and breathes in freedom? . . . I fear that someone will come along and snatch it all away."[79] Though her divorce was finalized in November 1907, her freedom would never be complete. It would be forever diminished by "longings for her son, the feelings of pain and the inability to care for him." Shapiro outwardly accepted the fact that "her son gr[ew] and develop[ed] under the influence of others" as she inwardly acknowledged his absence as the most searing of pains.[80]

A Doctor of Philosophy Becomes a Writer

Parting from her husband and son enabled Shapiro to pursue a formal course of study for the first time. Never having been enrolled in a religious school, a gymnasium, or even a class, Shapiro initially engaged tutors and then made her way to Vienna in 1904 to attend lectures. The following year she prepared for the entrance exams to the University of Berne, Switzerland, where, as in Germany, women were formally allowed to matriculate. After rigorously studying French, German, Latin, geography, world history, and Swiss history, Shapiro was accepted to the philosophy department and made Berne her home—where from 1906 to 1910 she lived on and off during the academic year with her brother.[81]

With its mix of gentiles and Jews, as well as men and women, student life in the university towns of Switzerland was hardly conducted without conventions and restrictions. Yet compared with the Pale, it was truly a liberated environment. Micah Yosef Berdischevsky (1865–1921), with whom Shapiro was acquainted from Peretz's literary circle, and who earned his doctorate in philosophy at the University of Berne in 1896, considered the Swiss city a break from the stranglehold of tradition.[82] There he discovered the life of feeling and set about writing some of his most famous Hebrew novels. The same cannot be said of Shapiro. Finding the people there to be "small, miniature, and uninteresting," she sought to "subdue [her] bad memories" through intensive study and generally kept to herself.[83] In five years, she managed to befriend but one classmate, Samuel Horodetzky (1871–1957), a student of mysticism who was attracted to the Haskalah. Shapiro felt a special bond with Horodetzky and even told him of her secret lover Brainin.[84]

While occupied with the writing of her thesis, Shapiro neglected her diary and correspondence; therefore, little is known of her scholarly interests and activities during this period. What is clear is that Shapiro wrote on the German philosopher Georg Christoph Lichtenberg (1742–1799), under the direction of Ludwig Stein (1859–1930), who had studied philosophy at universities in Berlin and Halle and was ordained a rabbi at the Jewish Theological Seminary of Berlin.[85] In 1909 she traveled to Goettingen to meet Professor Edmund Husserl (1859–1938), an apostate Jew and founder of phenomenological philosophy, who helped her obtain manuscripts of Lichtenberg's writings.[86]

Not a year later, in the spring of 1910, she completed her thesis and, as she put it, "came out crowned with the title 'doctor of philosophy.'" The laurels meant little to her, though, for the old ennui returned as she returned to Slavuta following the conclusion of her studies. "My self-esteem has not been elevated," she lamented, "What I was—I remain."[87] Beyond a vague desire "to become involved in a *Hebrew* newspaper because [she] so loved the language [her emphasis]," she was at thirty-two years of age unable to articulate future professional plans.[88]

By this point, Shapiro's publications included one article comparing Hebrew literature to world literature, a meditation on Rosh Hashanah, and six sketches in the spirit and style of "The Rose." The allegories, which originally appeared either in David Frischmann's *Ha-dor* or Nahum Sokolov's *Ha-olam*, were collected in 1909, along with an additional nine, and published as *Kovetz tziurim* (A Collection of Sketches). Each sketch is no more than a few pages in length and is less a story than a lengthy development of a character's internal world. With this volume, Shapiro was issuing an invitation to her sisters to join in the task of depicting women's experience fully and realistically. Conscious of her audacity in such a pursuit, she spelled out her intent in a preface, which anticipates Simone de Beauvoir by four decades. It is quoted here in its entirety:

> Our literature is lacking the participation of the second half of the human race: that is, the weaker sex.
>
> As I now enter into this alien group, my strongest hope is that many daughters of my kind will rise up to follow in my footsteps. All of those who don't take part in it will impoverish and diminish the quality of our literature.
>
> Every time that we are surprised by the great talent of the "wonder worker," who "penetrates the woman's heart," we feel a strange hand has struck us. We have our [own] world, our [own] sorrow, our [own] longings, and, at the very least, we need to take part in describing them.
>
> I know that it will be a long time before I reach the goal that I have set before the male author and the female author. This *Kovetz tziurim* is only an attempt, the beginning of the uncovering of the

strength of the female sex, the one who was forced to abandon "sadness, gladness, hope and desires" to the hands of others.

I know and also recognize the obstacles and stumbling blocks that are placed intentionally, and, on the other hand, unintentionally on the literary path in general; and I recognize the poverty and narrow-mindedness of our literature in particular. But . . . [these] will not arrest [my] strength nor distance me from my place.

Artistic fulfillment is my aspiration and ultimate goal.

And now as I publish *Kovetz tziurim* I fully trust that they will accept it as an attempt of a daring one to tread on "new territory" [her quotation marks].

While a handful of male Hebrew writers understood Shapiro's need for female self-expression, and accepted its literary byproducts into the pages of their newspapers, even they avoided evaluating its literary merit. In a so-called review of *Kovetz tziurim*, David Frischmann, turning Shapiro's reasoning back on itself, refused to critique the work until "a woman comes along to write it [first]."[89] He feared "forc[ing] [him]self into a domain that was not [his] own" and agreed with Shapiro that "only women ultimately have the key that opens the door of the Holy of Holies, of the heart of a woman." He instead used the "review" as a forum to dish out commentary on "woman's language" in general. Frischmann asserted in fact that men and women speak two separate tongues: "Man says 'yes;' the woman says 'yes,' but they may mean two different things." He illustrated his point by drawing the following domestic portrait:

"I'm sitting opposite a woman. She asks for the cup [of wine] that is close to me. I give it to her. She becomes angry. The truth is, she wanted me to say to her: 'But, Madam, why are you drinking wine now? You are blossoming like lilies without wine?' Or, 'But, Madam, surely you're tired and wine won't benefit you. You must travel a bit to the Riviera.'" His intention was not, he explained, to chastise or shame women but rather to demonstrate that the female "word is never the real content of her thought." Because of her modesty, he maintained, "in conversation, [and] . . . in writing, she covers her words in a veil."

Interestingly, Frischmann's analysis of women's language is echoed by twentieth-century literary critics. According to Sandra Gilbert and Susan Gubar in their groundbreaking analysis of nineteenth-century literature by women, female authors regularly employed symbolic language as a way of merely hinting at truths they thought better left explicitly unsaid.[90] Allegory acted as a buffer for ideas thought unduly bold or dangerous for women to discuss, such as rebellion, bitterness, and passionate sexuality. This is what Carolyn Heilbrun terms the "presence of absence" in literature by women; and the Israeli scholar Nurit Govrin has shown, by analyzing the works of Deborah Baron (1887–1956), that this phenomenon penetrated the universe of Jewish women writers as well.[91]

That the majority of the fifteen allegorical sketches in *Kovetz tziurim* are autobiographical is obvious when one considers the personal information freely dispensed in Shapiro's diary and letters. One sketch in particular—as even its title "Ketzutzat kenafayim" (Clipping of Wings) suggests—reflects Shapiro's own quest for independence. While it appeared in print for the first time in 1909, a letter to Brainin provides evidence that she had drafted the piece as early as November 1903, during the bleakest period of her marriage.[92] In the letter, however, Shapiro disavows any parallels between art and reality: " I don't intend in this sketch to describe my life. I need to deny this completely. . . . If you hear the song of my soul in these words—I am not to blame."

The sketch is an artless tale of a free bird (whom Shapiro refers to as a female) whose joyful song and dream to fly heavenward are arrested by young boys, who not only capture and trap the bird inside a beautiful gilded cage, but also clip its wings. Meanwhile, a second bird flies within sight of the silenced and imprisoned bird, and the boys kill it off and use its death to refute the unhappy bird's claim for freedom: "See, you're safe in there, out here dangers lurk." Unconsoled, the bird sings a mournful tune until the boys finally relent and set it free, whereupon it realizes that its clipped wings prevent it from flying. Unlike the rose of the first allegory, the bird here never regains its full independence. Rather, it is utterly and eternally transformed after being shorn of the very thing that defined it as a member of its species: namely, the ability to fly. Shapiro, too, in the wake of her divorce, no longer exhibited the defining characteristic of her species: namely, a woman's ability to mate with the male species and rear offspring. Her female wings had been metaphorically clipped, and she felt compelled to remake herself.[93] To this end, Shapiro fashioned new female types in her writings, eschewing regnant images penned by men that had served to "pen in" women.[94]

Shapiro began to stage her own quiet revolution in female representation in *Kovetz tziurim*. Women not only figure prominently in the sketches but assume roles hardly common to women found elsewhere in fiction. Throwing off the allegorical gauntlet seen in "The Rose" and "Clipping of Wings," Shapiro introduced the Hebrew-reading public to the female scholar (in "At the Library" and "The Tutor"), and the female dreamer (in the sketch by the same name). They stand in sharp contrast to the trio of "typical" types trotted out by Shapiro in a single satirical sketch in which she disparaged women who are "gossipy," "fickle," and "moody" (in "Types of Women").[95] As in fiction, so, too, in life, Shapiro condemned the "miserable creatures" who indulged themselves at spas with "no worry, no knowledge, no initiative" on their faces. She divulged in her diary that "they lack the spirit of desire . . . [and] worry only about their health, which is more precious to them than gold." For them, Shapiro felt only "deep loathing."[96]

Shapiro's portrayal of strong, but unlikely, heroines sets her sketches apart. They include the title character of "Old Maid"—a type who usually arouses pathos for her pitiable state of spinsterhood and childlessness but in Shapiro's hand comes to be satisfied with her lot.[97] Initially, Shapiro's depiction of the old maid appears to conform with society's usual response to the childless woman, as in the opening scene: "Every day . . . upon returning from the office, [the old maid] would enter the garden in the city, choose a spot on one of the benches and look at the children playing. Sometimes she would kiss one of them stealthily with a look of fear . . . and people would look at her with derision because of this weakness." But, in Shapiro's sketch, the old maid is not simply the object of others' ridicule; she is the central actor in a drama depicting the attempt to struggle free of unfulfilled societal expectations. As she directed others in her preface to the volume, Shapiro allows the reader to peer into the soul of her protagonist in order to glean the woman's response. "They didn't know," she wrote, "how they stung [the old maid] and caused her pain . . . and she hated them and their pity." Ultimately, the protagonist makes peace with her circumstances, though no details are provided on how that triumph comes to pass, save the concluding passage: "All her neighbors said that a change had come over the so-called old maid. She no longer despised her sorrow. Her voice reverberated with joy. She walked proudly. Her assistant came into her office once and asked [about this sudden change], and strange words issued forth from her mouth. She responded that she no longer paid attention to the law of men. The old maid prepared herself for hope in her life."

Here any pretense of literary dissimulation, like allegory, falls by the wayside. Shapiro was direct and to the point: even an old maid—the epitome of female failure—can achieve success (i.e. self-fulfillment) so long as she rejects the "law of men." The author herself had done as much. Her bold and innovative representation of an old maid confounds and supplants the masculine version of the same.

Yet female self-sufficiency appeared only to be an illusion, as the title characters of both "The Dreamer" and "The Loner" demonstrate.[98] While intellectual gifts allow the two protagonists to cross the border into male territory, they ultimately retreat to the familiar, but ill-suited, world of women. In "The Dreamer," the main character is admired by men and women alike in her youth for her dual powers of seeing the future and interpreting dreams. "It was as though," the omniscient narrator interjects, "she was simultaneously both sexes at once." She dreams that "the day will come when there will be no law that arrests the weaker sex or forces her into a restricted prison." Yet even the optimistic dreamer grows wise over time to the gendered expectations imposed by society. She eventually capitulates to them, marrying, rearing children, and decrying her earlier denial of "the real essence of women." She has feminized herself out of her former androgynous state after realizing that straddling two genders simply does not work. "Only a woman who feels miserable in the role of a woman is able to devote herself to knowledge and to aspirations," the dreamer concludes. In other words, only dissatisfied women make good men, provided they can withstand being outside their element and untrue to their nature.

"The Loner," too, initially opts out of female society but longs to return as she learns that intelligence in a woman brings on the state suggested by the sketch's title. Set in the lap of luxurious bourgeois living, the story unfolds at a ball given in honor of one twenty-eight-year-old Devorah, who squirms uncomfortably, alone, in the corner of a magnificent dance hall where "boys look . . . and girls wait to be chosen." Her physical appearance bodes ill for male companionship: "A smirk of bitterness and pain flutters across her lips. Her bright dress emphasizes her pale and colorless complexion. Her hair is cut so short that the tight curls fail to cover the wrinkles on her brow . . . 'This entire feast is for me and in my honor,' she thinks to herself, 'but I've had enough honor, I want life! life! life!'"

To Devorah, life constitutes the acquisition of knowledge. Her happiness depends on study, for which she is supremely well-suited, her dissertation being so insightful that a certain Dr. N. swears it to be the product of a male mind. For his part, though, Dr. N. prefers the company of Devorah's beautiful younger sister. Our heroine discovers this truth upon overhearing Dr. N. admonishing her sister: "There is no need for you to study like your sister. I love you the way you are. . . . You'll learn all you have to know by being in my presence." Devorah is defeated. Hearkening back to its title, the sketch concludes: "She suddenly feels lonely and forsaken . . . lonely in this house and in the world. . . . Her strength is sapped and her thoughts abandon her. . . ."

"The Loner" appears to be modeled after the author herself. Letters to Brainin reveal that Shapiro "enjoyed" similar occasions in her youth. In fact, a lengthy description of one such ball foreshadows the very style and detail of her fictional account. In March 1901, she wrote Brainin:[99]

I came to a very large dance hall—so large it was impossible to see from one side to the other. A warm and pleasurable light fell on all. Some of the young men and women went out to dance and it was as if they had forgotten the world and everything in it. I saw that some of them had no thoughts in their heads altogether. . . . I saw the lords gathered at one side. And after they prepared themselves . . . they went out to "take part" [her quotations]. I stared at them and I saw their power and lack of inhibition when they looked over the group of women. . . . Every one of them did this . . . and they weren't embarrassed at all if the women noticed. Some women didn't pay attention to this and didn't understand anything; but in their hearts they knew well and they became angry and afraid and ill-at-ease. The one who is pretty is here—her face shines with joy. And the second whose beauty is in great doubt has a sad, worried and fearful expression. And the third who has grown accustomed to this for ten years sits more peacefully . . . I despise all of these spectacles, especially those cursed men with their scornful

looks. I'm disgusted, and I'm surprised that these women don't see
it. I did not go out to dance.

Shapiro's protest against social mores took a far more potent turn than
refusing to dance. She refused as well to allow women to be bound by
representations by men and instead used the pages of *Kovetz tziurim* to
weave her singular life experiences into tales of protest.[100] Until female
authors like Shapiro appeared on the horizon, representations of women
in Hebrew literature, as in literature in general, had been generated solely
by male expectations and designs. As a result, women in print were often
reduced to extreme and oversimplified stereotypes that neither represented nor inspired a budding female author, and may instead have conflicted with her own subjectivity, autonomy, and creativity. Thus an aspiring woman writer may have first had to struggle free of the accepted
stereotypes before waging a battle for self-creation. Shapiro, too, became
conversant with the female images touted by generations of male authors, devoting three separate articles to this topic.[101]

In the fullest of the treatments, "The Female Image in Our Literature,"
Shapiro delineated three generations of authors, each of whom depicted
the weaker sex in a different way. The woman became a cause célèbre for
the earliest generation of Hebrew authors. Yehudah Leib Gordon was
joined by others such as Abraham Mapu and Peretz Smolenskin in a literary assault against the miserable fate of Jewish women.[102] According to
Shapiro, they were far more interested in attacking their enemies, the pur-
veyors of the status quo, than with ameliorating the real troubles plaguing
their female contemporaries. Shapiro took these male authors to task for
regarding women as objects rather than the masters of their destiny: "The
woman is characterized as an angel of God . . . who doesn't open her
mouth. Everything happens to her only as a consequence of the battle
waged over religion and life. She herself doesn't receive the law. They describe her life, . . . but not her internal [world] and soul, her longings and
aspirations."[103] Only the second generation, led by Mendele Mokher
Seforim and her old friend Y.L. Peretz, capably described the true nature
of the Jewish woman. From them one "learns not only [the Jewish
woman's] sadness, but also her plans . . . her attempt to widen her domain, to rule not only in her home." They were responsible for planting
"the seeds of Jewish women of the next generation."[104] But even their

efforts failed to broaden the restrictions put upon Jewish women, who, in contrast to their gentile counterparts, had no alternative but to marry. As Shapiro put it: "[A Jewish woman's] life is to marry . . . She may not seek a different life, . . . God forbid that she even think about a different life . . . she must stifle her own feelings thousands of times . . . [whereas] a gentile woman is capable of drawing near to what she loves. [The Jewish woman] must sacrifice her soul and her freedom."[105] For Shapiro, the Jewish woman was defined solely by her role as a wife; marriage became her snare, trapping any aspirations contrary to that expectation.

Shapiro accuses the third generation, including her contemporaries Micah Yosef Berdischevsky, Menahem Gnessin, and Joseph Hayim Brenner, of ignoring altogether the situation of Jewish women. In their preoccupation with conflicts faced by the *intelligent* Jew trapped between the old and new worlds, they excluded the woman, Shapiro says, because they incorrectly supposed that she was unaffected by the modern tangle. Not so. According to Shapiro, the Jewish woman's "search for light" had even predated that of the Jewish man, for while the latter was busily engaged in traditional Jewish study, the former had already been "schooled in world literature." According to Shapiro, exemption from Torah study made the Jewish woman's entrance to the world beyond things Jewish faster and easier.[106] In typical fashion, she concludes her article with the hope that female writers will yet surface to fill in the gaps of the past.

To that end, after obtaining her doctorate in 1910, Shapiro tried her hand at literary criticism as well as journalism. With Brainin's influential assistance, her articles soon began to appear with frequency in major Hebrew publications of the day. Her subjects ranged broadly from Martin Buber to Russian literature to Israelite prophecy, to name only a few. She reported on meetings of Zionist organizations and the excruciating details of life in Ukraine following World War I. Later in her life, as Czech correspondent for *Ha-olam*, Shapiro even developed an interview with the newly-elected President Tomas G. Masaryk into an article and book-length monograph. In addition, Y.L. Peretz, David Frischmann, and Reuven Brainin became the subjects of remembrances she published in a number of journals.[107]

As Shapiro's writing career flourished, her personal life waned. By 1910, any hope of being with Brainin had been dashed on the shores of North America, where he had hastily immigrated. The couple had seen each other a total of four times between 1905 and 1910, despite the fact that Shapiro was not only free of her husband but living for the most part within relative proximity to Brainin. Although their correspondence had come to a virtual standstill, they did spend two months together in Europe in 1913.[108] Shapiro continued sporadically to send letters to Brainin, especially after World War I when her family's fortune was lost, and she desperately needed his help. He did not respond. Gradually and painfully, Shapiro came to recognize the wisdom of Horodetzky's words when he had pegged her as "Brainin's sacrifice."[109] After she bumped into Brainin in Vienna at the World Zionist Congress in 1925, she acknowledged that she felt "nothing" upon seeing the arrogant man who "used to aspire to wider horizons" but now stooped to "accept[ing] smooth flattery."[110]

The tragic world events that would directly affect Shapiro and her family, along with hundreds of thousands of other Jews residing in the eroding Pale of Settlement, began to drive away fond memories of Brainin and the charmed, literary life he inspired. With the First World War and the Russian Revolution raging, Shapiro shuttled between Kiev and Slavuta, tending to her ailing mother—who dreaded her son's imminent conscription into the Red Army—and participating in revolutionary activities.[111] Initially Shapiro wrote optimistically of the transformation overtaking Russia: "There's new life in every corner, . . . which fills me with happiness, freedom, . . . and hope . . . new wings are spreading open."[112] But by the end of 1917, her early enthusiasm gave way to profound misgivings over changes being made in communal life at the expense of the individual. Shapiro continued to value the primacy of the "human 'I'" and its inner spirit, fearing that it was "meld[ing] and disappear[ing] into the great multitudes of the collective." She regretted that "there [had] been a dumbing-down of the human 'I' and that the possibilities for its development [were fading]."[113]

Leaving Slavuta

Ultimately, and sadly, Shapiro's childhood dream of abandoning provincial Slavuta altogether came true when her hometown became a battleground. With Jews "under a constant death threat," she herself was forced to hide for a week in a gentile neighbor's home.[114] While the war escalated and she became preoccupied with what she called "the trivialities of life," she wrote, "Before the angel of death there is but one concern: to save oneself in any way possible."[115] For Shapiro and her son, that meant leaving behind their native land for friendlier soil. Assisted by her father's former employee, a gentile living in the Czechoslovak Republic, and despite Hayim Nahman Bialik's invitation to her to settle in Odessa so that she might become part of the Hebrew literary circle there, Shapiro escaped with her son to Prague in the fall of 1919.[116]

As an eyewitness to the atrocities being committed against Jews in Ukraine, Shapiro fashioned herself a spokeswoman of sorts, publishing her testimony in Hebrew newspapers.[117] Her primary aim was "to blast [the evidence] until it enter[ed] the hearts of people who will listen."[118] "[N]ot only are the actions [against the Jews] not exaggerated," she argued, "but the opposite [is true]. I have seen no account that has adequately described the horrors." Thus she set about recounting the facts, detailing the annihilation of thousands of Jews of every stripe, who had been murdered "not in battle, not at the front, . . . but simply because of their . . . Judaism." She closed with an admonition to her readers: "You are forbidden to forget for even a second!"

The income from articles such as these helped to support Shapiro and her son as they attempted to make a new life for themselves in the Czechoslovak Republic, which had been established in 1918. Indeed, for the first time in her life, Shapiro was forced to write for reasons other than self-fulfillment or self-reflection. All the money she had managed to smuggle out of Slavuta was worthless in her new home. So she sent a steady stream of requests for writing assignments, and subsequently bills for wages owed, to editors of various Hebrew publications, including Brainin, who was at the time editor of *Ha-toren* in New York.[119] Her petitions were answered now and then, as evidenced by the nearly forty articles that appeared under her byline in various Hebrew newspapers during the 1920s and 30s. Her financial difficulties persisted nonetheless.

Moreover, Shapiro had deep misgivings about the changed nature of her writings. In 1927, she expressed regret about turning away from the revealing sketches that had characterized the earliest period of her writing career:

Of all the things I regret, what I regret most and now what really pains me most is: Why didn't I succeed in ink? . . . I regret and am pained because I wasn't able to express my spirit in writing . . . [I regret as well that] I didn't restrict my talent—if I had any—to one field. More precisely, I didn't continue writing more stories and sketches, as I had begun to do. . . . Now I'm sorry. Not because my name has not been established as a writer of a certain genre, perhaps also because of this—but because I wasted the strength of my soul and spirit. Why didn't I gather them into one place?[120]

By yielding to the realities of personal financial burdens, she had broken her oath to add her uniquely female spirit to the enterprise of Hebrew literature.

Relationships with men only compounded Shapiro's troubles. With her son enrolled at a polytechnical institute in Prague, Shapiro had made her way to Munkacs in October 1921. For the next several years—between travels to the twelfth and thirteenth Zionist Congresses and occasional visits to relatives and friends abroad—she remained in Munkacs, living with the gentile fellow who had aided her initial passage to Czechoslovakia. Despite his hospitality, Shapiro confided her discomfort over residing among gentiles: "I am foreign, foreign, foreign, foreign and even if I say one thousand times that they are dear and respectable, I'm alien to them. . . . my people are close to my spirit."[121] Following her instincts, Shapiro eventually left her gentile lover for Dr. J. Winternitz, whom she wed in the late 1920s. Her diary, the sole record of the couple's marriage, weaves a tale of conjugal misery as a result of her husband's mental illness.[122] Shapiro—never a discerning judge of male character—would live out her remaining years playing nursemaid to a deranged man in a strange land.

Shapiro's misfortunes multiplied as the years passed and those closest to her perished or departed. When Menuhah Shapiro died in the summer of 1922, the daughter mourned her mother's passing along with the passing of her own history. She was utterly inconsolable, grieving over "the past that [was] no more" and agonizing over the absence of like-spirited souls who could understand her. "Everything in the world is now alien," she lamented, "I stand alone in life . . . I am so lonely among these strange people, who are unlike me in spirit."[123] Similarly, when her son Pinhas immigrated to America in March 1940, the sting of separation was acute as her sole remaining blood relative was lost.[124] For over forty years, Shapiro had found relief from her emotional alienation in the pages of her diary. But it, too, was taken from her in 1941 when the Nazis deported her and Winternitz. Before departing, Shapiro managed to scribble a spontaneous paean to the one constant in her life: "For more than forty years I've written in this diary. It has become a part of my soul. . . . I am now being separated from [it] and giving it to a stranger. . . . It's very difficult to part even from a diary, even from this lifeless piece of paper that breathed the same air as I."[125] Hava Shapiro's breath was extinguished on February 28, 1943 at Theresienstadt. She was sixty-four years old.

* * * * *

Of all the languages Hava Shapiro mastered, she was naturally and understandably drawn to writing in Hebrew, being reared by parents who appreciated its learning and literature and later guided by several members of its cultural elite. First Reuven Brainin and then Y.L. Peretz took an interest in Shapiro and helped her to improve her skills. That she should engage the male contingent seemed only natural given her confluence of talents and training in Hebrew and its quest to create a nucleus of modern literature in the same. Her correspondence and diary in the ancient tongue became a springboard lifting her to the arena of published authors at a time when female bylines seldom appeared in the Hebrew press. Shapiro's debut work "The Rose," which was published in David Frischmann's *Ha-dor* in 1901, was an attempt to reveal the female experience to the reading public, albeit through a veil of allegory.[126] That she was uniquely qualified for such a task made Shapiro long for the comraderie of additional women writers, as she expressed in the preface to *Kovetz tziurim*, the 1909-volume of her collected sketches. During the first decade of the twentieth century, a handful of women who had immigrated to the land of Israel were involved in this pursuit, including Rahel (Bluwstein), Nehamah Pohazhavski, Devorah Baron, and Hemdah Ben-Yehudah. In the Diaspora, Shapiro was alone.

Indeed, a sense of estrangement loomed large in Shapiro's life trajectory. From the age of twenty, she moved regularly from city to city, neither settling permanently in any one place nor definitively settling on a new role for herself.

Like the biblical Cain, she often characterized herself as a perpetual

wanderer, eternally at odds with her environment and those who peopled it.[127] Late in her life, she claimed to have felt at home only as a
young adult in Peretz's home. There among the Hebrew literati, she had
been in her element. Yet, years later, when she had the freedom to roam
where she chose, she declined invitations to settle among like-minded
individuals, as in the land of Israel, Odessa, or even New York City. She
remained to her dying day geographically removed from the Palestine
center and even the main Eastern European peripheries of the Hebrew
literary revival.

Alienation plays like a leitmotif through Shapiro's fictional works as
well. In her quest to infuse Hebrew literature with new, more realistic, female types, she began to tell chapters of her own life story. She confessed
that ambitious and intelligent women like her frequently do not fit into
the given social structure. And she disclosed the inner turmoil and pain
that resulted among women whose hopes to transgress the "laws of men"
left them disillusioned "dreamers," odd "old maids," or pathetic "loners."
In *Confession and Community in the Novel*, Terrence Doody suggests that
the primary motive of confession in fiction is the individual's self-
conscious attempt to "explain his nature to the audience, who represents
the kind of community he needs to exist in."[128] During the earliest stages
of her career, Shapiro used fiction to explain herself as a woman to and
seek the support, if not fellowship, of Hebrew readers.

Hope of finding an audience receptive to her work was severely limited, however, by the reality of the Hebrew-reading public of the day. As
it was, Hebrew reached only a miniscule proportion of the Jewish population. For hundreds of years, it had been a segregated language, whose
readership was limited almost exclusively to men trained through study
or habit in the legal and liturgical texts of Jewish tradition. When it was
resurrected in the nineteenth century, it became the creation of a small
group of men undergoing a process of self-revelation, self-definition, and
self-confirmation quite different than Shapiro's. The biography of the typical Hebrew writer in Eastern Europe describes the young man's immersion first in traditional Jewish texts and then, on the sly, his encounter
with secular literature that causes a permanent rupture with his past.
Jewish men fashioned a secular Hebrew culture that could express their
collective story even as it undermined the old order in which Hebrew
was the exclusive provenance of Jewish worshippers and legalists. The

culture itself offered an entirely new type of Jewish identification. It provided a haven for those Jewish men caught between an unacceptable Jewish world and an inaccessible wider one.

As a woman writer of Hebrew, Shapiro's existential crisis was unlike that of her male counterparts, and that of the bulk of the female Jewish population for that matter. As a daughter of the middle class, Shapiro had ready access and permission to pursue the avenues of the larger cultural world, and pursue them she did. After mastering foreign languages and receiving a doctorate in philosophy, far geographically and metaphorically from the traditional Jewish community, she chose to return to her people to write in the language "connected to her holy of holies." In Hebrew, she maintained, she could best represent her innermost soul and that of the female sex in general, which she made her professional task, initially. Her writings show the difficult, if not impossible, position of the educated Jewish woman casting about for a foothold in modern Jewish society. Instructed to seek enlightenment, she did so, only to find that she was overqualified for the positions available to her. Shapiro knew well of what she wrote. Her fiction mirrored her life experience, but when it was reviewed even her strongest advocates proclaimed that women and men spoke a different language. Shapiro, though part of the Hebrew revival, formed a literary subculture of one—defined in relation to the "main," male-dominated literary culture—with its own distinctive goals that proved too daunting for an individual to achieve single-handedly.

So after 1909, Shapiro abandoned altogether her endeavor to represent the Jewish woman in fiction. As she wrote in her diary: "[During my] whole life I've been distant from others—in spirit and in thought. If it's impossible to express everything [of import] then there's no need to say anything [of import]."[129] Thus she turned to the straightforward and neutral ground of journalism. Here she could retreat from earlier displays of intimacy by presenting material directly without the interference of potentially threatening interpretation or hidden meaning. Mundane reports of Zionist Congresses, for example, began to pack her bibliography. In addition, Shapiro churned out literary criticism devoted usually to authors who shared her interest in the human soul (including, among others, Martin Buber, Max Brod, and Tomas Masaryk). Aside from the three aforementioned articles on female representations in Hebrew literature,

Shapiro's literary attentions to the particular concerns of her own sex dissolved. Continuing in this vein, she realized, would endear her writings to neither Hebrew readers nor editors, whose fiscal support she began to seek with an even greater vengeance than their empathy, especially following World War I and the ruin of her family's financial security. Pragmatism, it seems, won the day. And so Shapiro's hope for a revolution in female representation in Hebrew literature would await not only the participation of future generations of female Hebraists but also the full embrace of male progenitors of the Hebrew cultural renaissance.

3

Insider-Outsider Among the Russian Cultural Elite

Rashel' Mironovna Khin (1861–1928)

The Intelligentsia among Russians and Jews

Rashel' Mironovna Khin holds an exceptional place in two separate, but overlapping, spheres of late nineteenth- and early twentieth-century Russian literature.[1] On the one hand, hers is among the few female names found among Jews writing prose fiction and drama in the Russian language prior to the turn of the century. On the other, hers is among the few Jewish (and even fewer Jewish *and* female) names to be recognized by the Russian literary establishment, past and present.[2] In fact, of all the women presented in this study, she alone established herself as a Russian-language writer of any reputation among readerships both Jewish and Russian. Khin is one of a handful of women who merited inclusion in *Evreiskaia entsiklopediia* (Jewish Encyclopedia). In the mere 100-word entry, which is based on information gleaned from the work of the renowned biographer Simon Vengerov, Khin's literary achievements come readily to the fore.[3] She published a dozen short stories and novellas in the realist style for a general Russian audience in the last two decades of the nineteenth century. They appeared in popular journals such as *Russkaia mysl'* (Russian Thought), *Russkoe bogatstvo* (Russian Wealth), and *Mir bozhii* (God's World), and in publications addressed principally to Jewish readers, such as *Voskhod* (Sunrise). Khin penned as well several articles and supplied chapters on some of her acquaintances for volumes dedicated to their memory. She also translated into Russian the works of such notables as Guy de Maupassant, Emile Zola, and George Sand. Moreover, critics occasionally reviewed her literature in both the Russian press and the Russian-Jewish press. Her collected stories appeared in two volumes, and, significantly, two of her plays were staged at Moscow's celebrated Malyi Theater. Most of her belles lettres are peopled with representatives of the gentile middle- and upper-income merchant classes and intelligentsia, and she made occasional but notable attempts at portraying the particularities of Jews—both men and women—who inhabited these worlds.

Khin was eminently qualified to write about the Russian intelligentsia, being herself one of the few Jews accepted into its rarefied ranks in the 1880s until its virtual demise in 1917. Not merely intellectuals, these people devoted themselves to finding and realizing an ideal in Russia founded on consciousness, moral passion, and critical thought.[4] In Khin's day the focus of the intelligentsia—a term coined by Khin's friend, the minor novelist Petr Dmitrievich Boborykin[5]—looked very different from what it was at its conception in the 1830s and 40s, when Russians educated abroad first seized upon Western ideas and made plans to realize them in their homeland. Accepting the Romantic doctrine that every person is called upon to perform a mission beyond material existence, the newly-forming intelligentsia took upon itself the responsibility of helping the ignorant masses improve themselves and their lot. As depicted in Turgenev's defining *Fathers and Sons* (1861), by the 1860s the classical intelligentsia had divided into two conflicting segments: an older generation of philosophical idealists,whose actions were limited to education, and a younger generation of materialists and devotees of empirical science, whose pragmatism goaded them to direct interaction with the masses. The latter culminated in *narodnichestvo* (Populism), a movement whose efforts to "go to the people" to propagandize and agitate collapsed in failure by the mid-1870s. According to the historian Martin Malia, a third and final phase then emerged among the intelligentsia in the wake of Alexander II's assassination in 1881. During the reactionary reign of Alexander III (1881–1896), the "grandsons" resumed in a more moderate way the tasks of enlightening the masses and helping them in their daily lives. And for the first time, they began to identify themselves as members of political movements—they became Marxists, Socialist Revolutionaries, or Constitutional Democrats (Kadets).

As this chapter will show, Khin formed close alliances with members of the third generation of Russian intelligentsia, including especially the Kadets. She regularly played host to famous philosophers (e.g. Vladimir

Sergeevich Solov'ev) and jurists (e.g. Anatolii Federovich Koni, who presided over the trial of Vera Zasulich, and Aleksandr Ivanovich Urusov, who defended participants in the Nechaev conspiracy). Among her circle as well were prominent artists (e.g. Leopold Auer, the premier violinist of the Russian Imperial Orchestra and his wife Nadezhda Evgen'evna) and literary figures (e.g. Boborykin, Maxim Gorkii, Leonid Andreev, and the Shakespeare scholar Nikolai Ilyich' Storozhenko). Starring in the cast of characters glittering on her cultural horizon was none other than the novelist Ivan Sergeevich Turgenev, whom she met when she was a young woman studying in Paris, with whom she exchanged several letters, and to whom she dedicated her second volume of short stories and devoted two published reminiscences. Additionally, Khin's frequent travels abroad linked her to foreign literati, including the writers Emile Zola, Georg Brandes (the Danish writer), Oktave Mirbeau, and Anatole France (pseudonym of Jacques Anatole Thibault, who received the Nobel Prize in literature).[6]

While Khin hobnobbed with luminaries of the intellectual and cultural elite—some of whom were Jews themselves (Brandes) or of Jewish descent (Auer) or in sympathy with Jews (Solov'ev)—she maintained only a tangential connection to the "Russian-Jewish intelligentsia" per se. That term has been customarily employed as a catch-all for any group of Jews who adhered to values at variance with the ideological consensus of the traditional Jewish community in Eastern Europe. It surfaced in the 1860s as the Russian public began to recognize the existence of a "Jewish Question" (evreiskii vopros), discussing at length the destiny of its Jewry. Secularly-educated Jews schooled in Russian increasingly felt a need to articulate their own solutions to the "Question." Generally speaking, they first strongly championed Russification for Jews. But with the shock of the pogroms that began in the 1880s, their hope that the Jews would simply fuse with the Russian population was shattered, leading some to adopt even the cause of Jewish nationalism.

Of course, the Russian-Jewish intelligentsia, like its Russian counterpart, was not a monolith. Adopting John Klier's useful typology, at least four different ideological strains can be identified among that group.[7] At one extreme lies the "Old Maskilim," pioneers of the Jewish Enlightenment movement (Haskalah) in Russia, who raised the banner of Berlin's Moses Mendelssohn and, with the support of the Russian State, established a Jewish school system. Graduates of the state Jewish schools, especially the rabbinical institutes at Vilna and Zhitomir, constituted the second group, "Young Maskilim," who shared the traditional maskilic confidence in the good intentions of enlightened rulers toward Jews and the faith that eradicating "fanaticism" among Jews would lead directly and rather mechanically to some form of emancipation. In contrast to the Old and Young Maskilim, who were inwardly directed in their efforts for reform, the "Russian Jewish intelligentsia" (i.e. Klier's third group) considered themselves an integral part of Russian society, and thus entitled and obligated to participate in its public debate. Consisting of only a minuscule proportion of the Jewish population, they conducted themselves almost entirely in Russian before a Russian audience. Finally, Klier labels as "Total Assimilationists" the Jewish elite that had attended Russian or Western European universities and that had pursued careers in the wider circles of imperial society. Throughout the nineteenth century, most were generally indifferent to Jews and their plight, and a few even converted to Russian Orthodoxy to advance their careers. However, by the beginning of the twentieth century, with the spread of famine and pogroms, this group of integrated and privileged Jews began actively to enter the struggle for Jewish rights.

The usefulness of Klier's typology aside, I must take issue with what I consider to be a misnomer for the fourth group on his ideological spectrum (i.e. "Total Assimilationists"). *Assimilation* is a slippery term, but it ordinarily implies complete absorption into the non-Jewish culture and a disavowal of Jewish identity. Except for apostates—and even this will be shown to be questionable in some cases—those classified by Klier as "Total Assimilationists" did not necessarily regard themselves and were not necessarily regarded by others as outside the Jewish fold. As Klier's own description of this group indicates, their integration into Russian society was not absolute by any means. In fact, their Jewish sensibilities grew more powerful in direct proportion to the vicissitudes visited upon the Jewish community. A more accurate and descriptive designation for this group might be "Russified Jewish Haute Bourgeoisie."

Terminology notwithstanding, this chapter will show that Rashel' Khin belonged to the "Total Assimilationists/Russified Jewish Haute Bourgeoisie" in light of her social standing, education, philosophy, and attitudes toward Jewry. Khin's connection to Judaism and the Jews was of the most tenuous kind possible. As depicted in her voluminous diaries, her primary associations were with members of the Russian cultural elite, and she had nothing whatsoever to do with Jewish practice. She disliked what she perceived as Jewishly-familiar characteristics in others, but denounced the pogroms in Russia and contributed to several publications that supported the very Jews she found so distasteful.

Significantly, Khin was absolutely silent on the fact that she herself converted to Catholicism in order to terminate her first marriage when her husband Solomon Feld'shtein refused to grant her a divorce.[8] (Under tsarist law at the time, conversion of one spouse automatically dissolved a marriage between Jews.) When it became evident that she wished to make a Jew her second husband, Osip Borisovich Gol'dovskii converted to Christianity in order to marry Khin. Theirs was an intermarriage of the most bizarre sort, and, though it appears that the couple remained converts, they became increasingly interested in the well-being of those from whom they had ostensibly severed ties.

Needless to say, Khin was far removed from the categories stereotypically assigned to Jewish women of nineteenth-century Eastern Europe. She was neither a *balebuste*, who sought to preserve the customs of her ancient faith, nor a revolutionary, who eschewed her Judaism in order to join a political movement. Rather, Khin regarded herself—despite her conversion—as an "aristocratic Jew," disdaining her "plebeian" coreligionists but gradually coming to sympathize with their tribulations and, in the end, revising both her feelings for and relationship to the Jewish people. As a born Jew, as a member of the upper-income professional class, and as one who hosted intellectual and social gatherings at her home, it is tempting to compare Khin to the so-called salon Jewesses of Berlin of an earlier era.[9] Such an analogy raises the question of whether Jewish women of a certain class experienced a similar process of acculturation, whether they lived in Western or Eastern Europe. To what extent then did Khin's integration into the larger society mirror that experienced by her Jewish sisters in the West a century earlier? What do Khin's imaginary writings reveal about modernizing Jews in the Russian Empire? Khin's position as simultaneous insider to and outsider in both the Jewish and Russian communities will enrich our understanding of identity among Jews of both sexes in early twentieth-century Russia.

* * * * *

Reconstructing a vanished life is never a simple prospect, but in Rashel' Mironovna Khin's case, the task is complicated by the meager resources detailing her childhood and adolescence (from 1861 to 1881) and the period late in her life (after the Revolution of 1917), when she stopped writing original works altogether. Her voluminous diaries date from 1891, when she was already thirty years old, to the outbreak of the Revolution, eleven years prior to her death on December 12, 1928.[10] In the twilight of her life, Khin was hard at work preparing her diaries for publication as memoirs, which never made it to press. She assigned herself the role of chronicler, knowing full well that hers would not, as she stated in the prologue to the memoirs, be a "history, but a subjective reflection of the changing impressions of an imperceptibly-fleeting life."[11] Her aim was to transform the "silhouettes of [her] life" into a record of "life experienced by Russian society of the pre-October reality that was sinking into oblivion." Khin's memoirs are thus an account, albeit incomplete, of both her life and the lives of those of Russian society with whom she associated. The 600-page typed memoirs whittled down from her 4,000-page handwritten, (nearly) daily diary entries (1891–1917) form, along with her fiction and drama, the primary sources of this study. Although Khin's literature is a useful resource, one must, of course, be wary of drawing autobiographical conclusions from it. Nevertheless, it certainly will assist us as we bring Khin and her milieu to life.

The Model of the Modern Jewish Gentlewoman

On March 9, 1861 Rashel' Khin was born to Rebekka Emanuilovna and Miron Markovich, an affluent member of the Jewish merchant class. Her parents lived for the first several years of their daughter's life in Gorki, Mogilev province (present-day Byelorus). The first region with a large Jewish population to be annexed by Russia, Mogilev, together with the province of Vitebsk, later comprised the core of the Pale of Settlement. In 1847, nearly ninety thousand Jews were registered in the communities of Mogilev, and by 1897, that figure had more than doubled. The Khins, however, were not numbered among them by that time, for by the late 1870s, they were ensconced in Russia's interior, living among fellow Jews

Rashel' Mironovna Khin (1900)
From the collection of the Russian State Archive of Literature and Art, Moscow

in Moscow. While Jews had been forbidden to reside in Russia altogether until the late eighteenth century, the nineteenth century saw a series of petitions by Jewish entrepreneurs to the tsarist government requesting permission to reside in the Empire's interior.[12] Their petitions met with success. Privileged groups (really those who could provide privileges to Russia) were allowed to settle in the interior, including Jewish merchants (of the first guild), university graduates, craftsmen, artisans and returned cantonists.

Miron Khin's status as merchant enabled him not only to reside in Moscow with his family, but allowed him to introduce his daughter Rashel' to the sumptuous upper-middle-class way of life. Conforming to the model of the modern Jewish maiden, she attended the girls' third gymnasium (1877–80) in the city. Scattered references to happy days spent studying with other girls are sprinkled throughout Khin's memoirs. After bumping into her old teacher Filadel'f Petrovich Dekapol'skii at a lecture by Vasilii Osipovich Kliuchevskii, the widely admired historian at Moscow University, Khin waxed nostalgic in her diary for her youth "when skies seemed blue and birds always sang . . . how strong [then] was hope [and] young courage."[13] She then, in the same entry, elaborated upon a special friendship with one Masha Ledenova, who despite being the most gifted student in the class, poisoned herself at the age of twenty-two. The pining for better, earlier days surfaces again in 1897 as Khin lamented the bygone 1870s which were a "better time for the gymnasium. Our class seemed so bright—talented, [brimming with] deeply-soulful and elegant women of high capabilities."[14] Though she referred to many of these women by name, it is hers alone that remains for posterity.

The specific contents of Khin's gymnasium instruction can only be inferred, for she remained virtually silent on the details of her childhood education.[15] Undoubtedly, she had been immersed in European languages and literature from youth and evidently graduated with a command of French and German that enabled her to read and converse in both with ease. In her memoirs, written mostly in Russian, she frequently employed French, especially when recording a word-for-word conversation with her intelligentsia cohorts. Moreover, as she mentions only in passing, she lived in Salzburg for a time as a child.[16] Fluency in French and other European languages was, after all, the hallmark of the educated woman, and, like others in similar financial circumstances, she was raised on a steady diet of art, literature, music, and manners intended to raise her up to be a lady.

Upon graduation in 1880, Khin headed to St. Petersburg with a plan to enroll at the "Women's Medical Courses" and prepare for a career in midwifery. In 1872, the St. Petersburg College of Physicians and Surgeons had begun a four-year course of training for women under the auspices of D.A. Miliutin, the Minister of War. The classes offered an attractive professional alternative to Jewish women, who were barred from teaching, and who, by the end of the decade, made up over one-fifth of the total number of alumnae.[17] Khin joined their ranks only briefly, for the courses were shut down by order of the new Minister of War a year after she arrived.[18] Despite her brief tenure, Khin managed to craft a tale drawn from her experiences in the courses. "Iz storony v storonu" (From Side to Side), a novella serialized throughout 1883, was her first published work.[19] It appeared in the journal *Drug zhenshchin* (Friend of Women), which had begun publication only the year before and carried articles on women in journalism, education, literature, medicine and white-collar employment, in addition to fiction.[20] It was one of several magazines focusing on women to spring to life in this decade.[21]

In the aptly-titled "From Side to Side," Khin focused on the internal struggle of the medical student Elena (Lenochka) Belaeva, torn between the competing demands of professional ambition and romantic interests. In fact, Belaeva decides to enroll in the medical courses only at the suggestion of her gymnasium teacher, with whom she is infatuated. On the eve of her graduation with honors, he proposes that since "she is a rose in a pile of thistles," she ought to "go to the medical courses in St. Petersburg, graduate, and go to the people in the provinces."[22] She retorts plaintively, "And you'll remain *here*?" Belaeva follows his suggestion, only after learning that he has become betrothed to her best and only friend. Once in St. Petersburg, she falls in love with a prospective suitor named Uspenskii, but is spurned once again. Uspenskii manages to distract her from her medical studies, which she eventually abandons altogether for a failed attempt at acting, and marries Belaeva's friend and idol, Katerina Semenovna Smirnova. Unable to find satisfaction in a career or love, Belaeva succumbs to death, leaving behind a bastard son. The reader learns in a one-sentence epilogue that the unfortunate and misguided protagonist suffers even in death. It seems that her former lover and father of her child married a wealthy widow and abandoned both the child and memories of Belaeva. "From Side to Side" admonishes the reader that while men may depend on women for emotional or financial support, women who depend on men are doomed. Khin followed her own advice and became self-reliant. But this she did not as a trained midwife, but as a writer.

Within months of arriving in St. Petersburg, Khin radically changed course, relinquishing the scientific toil of the Women's Medical Courses for study of the humanities at the Collège de France and the Sorbonne in Paris. Perhaps she found the Parisian ambiance more to her Western tastes or, equally likely, France's scholastic offerings more appealing to her artistic sensibilities and talents. Khin completed a three-year course in history and literature (1880–82), all the while receiving counsel from another Russian abroad, namely Ivan Sergeevich Turgenev (1818–1883). Turgenev fell in love with the Spanish singer Pauline Garcia-Viardot in 1843, and his attachment to her was largely responsible for his frequent travels and, after 1856, for his prolonged residence abroad. While living in Paris in the 1870s, Turgenev became a fixture in literary circles of the most important French writers of the time, including Flaubert and Zola, who praised him as one of the greatest contemporary realists. Turgenev's works, especially his novels, marked a new stage in the development of Russian realism. His sensitivity to topical issues, his profound interpretation of events and human nature, and the authenticity of his novels' depictions make them a unique chronicle of Russian life from the 1840s to the 1870s. Turgenev returned to Russia in 1879 and 1880, where he took part in the dedication of a monument to Pushkin and readings for the benefit of the Society of Lovers of the Russian Word, a literary and scholarly association established at Moscow University. Khin attended these presentations and admired the author from afar. A year later she would be taken into his confidence when the two met face-to-face in Paris.

A First Encounter with the Russian Cultural Elite

That Turgenev and Khin entered into what is best characterized as a mentor-disciple relationship by the early 1880s is evident from two reminiscences penned by the latter after the former's death, as well as their very brief correspondence.[23] Khin arrived to Paris in the winter of 1880 and, as she put it, "had an opportunity to see Turgenev frequently."[24] In Russia she had met him only "in public places on a platform—in meetings or the theater." But now he was "so close, right next to me and he spoke [to me] so simply, kindly and quietly."[25] Gradually, Khin came to spend hours with him, either seeking his advice, engaging in theoretical conversation, or reading to him aloud. Turgenev advised Khin on practical matters, persuading her to draw up a fixed program of study, rather than flitting willy-nilly to every lecture that struck her fancy.[26] Their central topic of discussion was, of course, literature, and Turgenev gently guided the budding author, reviewing her earliest writing endeavors and sharing his own techniques.[27] He showed Khin, for instance, his "album of heroes," in which he recorded musings on the temperament, tastes, and background of his protagonists, including the famous Bazarov, the central figure in *Fathers and Sons*. While at the theater, Turgenev confessed, his mind would often wander as he pondered: "What would Bazarov think of this?"[28]

As for Khin, she admitted to feeling intimidated by the accomplished master, who was forty-five years her senior. Despite his extraordinary kindness, she always felt "such reverential fear in his presence that during the first moments of meeting, . . . every topic [for discussion] would vanish before [her] eyes, and [she] literally didn't know where to sit and what to say." Noticing her discomfort, the compassionate gentleman would nod his head and exclaim: "You're out of breath again! I asked you not to run up the stairs in such a hurry."[29]

By the 1880s—when the two met—Khin was entering the literary arena along with other female writers of realism who were grappling with themes particular to their own experience: women's nature and identity, the constituents of women's happiness, the competing demands of career and love, and personal relationships with men, children, and other women.[30] Khin, too, was concerned with such issues, as is evident by her use of female protagonists. She resembled her counterparts from a demographic standpoint as well. Most of the women writers who began their careers in the 1880s were urbanites, and most were daughters of professional men, civil servants, or military officers.[31] The realistic short story came of age in the 1880s, and Khin, too, churned out works in that genre for the next two decades. Five stories were collected in a separate volume entitled *Siluety* (Silhouettes) in 1894, and seven more in *Pod goru* (Downhill) in 1900. It was to Turgenev's "unforgettable memory" that she dedicated the second volume.

Turgenev did not live to see Khin's career flourish. Their acquaintance was short-lived, curtailed by his death on August 22, 1883. Weeks before he expired, Turgenev wrote Khin asking if they might meet in Moscow. During their final encounter, the elder comforted the younger, saying: "[Death] is inevitable. The life of a man doesn't count. What continues is his hopes, dreams and ideals."[32] The two writers shared these intangibles even in the span of their fleeting three-year friendship. As their equally transient correspondence reveals, Khin disclosed stunning details of her personal life to him during her years in Paris.[33]

In a pair of letters sent to Turgenev in June and July 1881, she divulged, for example, the fact of her sister's apostasy and the resulting havoc it wreaked on her sister's relationship to her father. Khin explained to Turgenev that she intended to extend her anticipated stay in Paris to act as mediator between the two.[34] Khin's father, who encouraged his daughters to "take [their] education seriously and not squander [their] youth and talents" was disappointed that one had chosen to become a governess, even if it was with the famous Sheremetev family, the wealthiest landowners in Russia for over five centuries. He offered her financial support in return for a promise that she would break her commitment to the family and return home (and presumably to Judaism), an agreement to which she initially consented. Upon reflection, however, she found that "Papa was forcing her to renounce her Christianity, which was as impossible for her as abandoning the Sheremetev family" and thus "denied herself the pleasure of seeing him and her family until a later time." Whether and how the dispute was resolved must remain a mystery; Khin never mentioned the incident again.

The conversion of Khin's sister to Christianity both corroborates and contradicts the nascent research on apostasy in nineteenth-century Russia.[35] That Jews converted in sizable numbers in the Russian Empire during the nineteenth century is undisputed. The most reliable extant statistics—which, like all other numbers referring to Russian Jews in the nineteenth century, must be treated with skepticism—were published by the Russian Holy Synod itself, and establish that 69,400 Russian Jews were baptized in the Russian Orthodox Church during the nineteenth century.[36] The historian Michael Stanislawski has created a tentative typology for apostasy in Russia based on 244 records of Jewish converts reported by the Lithuanian Consistory of the Russian Orthodox Church for

the years 1819–1911. On the one hand, Stanislawski has found a disproportionate representation of female apostates among Jews, growing larger
in each successive generation. By the first decade of the twentieth century, for instance, women made up 65 percent of the converting group.
In addition, most Jewish apostates were young and voluntary converts.
The apostasy of Khin's sister obviously confirms these findings. On the
other hand, Stanislawski's investigation reveals that, like males, most of
the female converts came from the poorest stratum of Russian Jewry.
Khin's sister is, of course, not reflective of this trend. Rather, she can be
classified among what Stanislawski terms either the "true believers in
Christianity" or "those seeking educational or professional advancement." The primary motive of the Khin conversion is not clear from the
evidence at hand; we know only that "forcing her to renounce her Christianity . . . was as impossible for her as abandoning the Sheremetev family." Does this statement imply deeper devotion to Christianity or to the
Sheremetevs? Regardless, it is certain that the Khin conversion was not
motivated by financial need or incentive. After all, her father was prepared to support his daughter if she returned to Judaism.

One final observation by Stanislawski is significant for our purposes.
His typology includes a category known as "haute-bourgeois apostates"—"those who converted after having already achieved significant
economic mobility and success."[37] In the consistory materials there are
only four such converts. Yet as Stanislawski logically assumes, this type
of convert represented a greater proportion in the total number of apostates in the Russian Empire than found in the Lithuanian Consistory, especially if data were available on Jewish converts in St. Petersburg and
Moscow, the major seats of the Jewish upper classes. Khin's Muscovite
circle of acquaintances, as will be shown, confirm that this type of apostate abounded.

Though at this stage in her life Khin did not consider apostasy, she did
experience employment discrimination as a result of her Jewish roots. As
she expressed to Turgenev in the same letter of June 1881: "I hope to secure a teaching position at a gymnasium or at least at a private boarding
school, but lately I think not. Even I, a wealthy Jewish girl, have received
a refusal from everywhere."[38] Khin's hope was that Turgenev would use
his influence to assist her in her search, as she remarked in the same letter: "I haven't noticed any proselytizing tendencies in you, which is a dis-

tinguishing trait of our . . . intelligentsia society." She knew well that liberal intellectuals of Russian birth seldom displayed a "we-they" attitude
in distinguishing between themselves and privileged Jews in the late-
nineteenth century. For them, the dichotomy between educated society
like themselves and the rest of the population was of far more import.[39]

"The Misfit": Fact and Fiction

Khin incorporated her personal experience of ethnic prejudice into a
160-page novella entitled "Ne ko dvoru" (The Misfit), which appeared
five years later in 1886 in *Voskhod*—one of only two of her stories to appear in the Russian-Jewish journal.[40] As the title suggests, the central
character, Sara Pavlovich Berg, failed to find her niche among Jews or
Christians, having been reared in a household where Judaism was regarded, at best, with ambivalence. Her father "tried chiefly to raise his
children so no one could 'recognize' them [as Jews], but at the same time
would not permit either the thought or the possibility of their formal entrance to Christianity."[41]

The story is essentially a recounting of Berg's life as she moves closer
toward her heritage, overcomes her shame of Judaism and revises her humanistic idealism. As a hot-headed adolescent, she challenges her "smart,
smug, clever" father, whom Khin described as the "vivid personification
of the parvenu of Russia thirty years ago" and whose every action "is
meant to prove he is a Russian." "Papa," she asks, "are we Jews?" "Of
course," he replies. She goads him further:

> "But I heard that at Passover Jews drink human blood with
> matzah."
> "Do you drink [blood] at Passover?" Her father angrily retorted.
> "We're not real Jews."
> "How so?"
> "I don't know, though we're not real; all the real ones are dirty."
> "Jews, like Russians, are dirty when they're poor and unedu-
> cated. If you don't want to be dirty, study."
> "But I don't want to be a Jew when I grow up. I want to be
> baptized."[42]

Her words prove prophetic, for four years later while away at boarding school and in the wake of the death of both her parents, Berg turns to Christianity for comfort. Engaging in the most ascetic of practices, she fasts daily, prays on her knees each evening and becomes engrossed in the study of saints. Within weeks, her self-denial bounces her into the school's infirmary, where a sympathetic French teacher visits her. He attempts to coax her back to her people, explaining that "yours is a tribe with a grandiose and tragic history." With his guidance, Berg becomes exposed to Jewish history, reading, for instance, Lessing's drama *Nathan the Wise*.[43] After immersing herself in her people's past, Berg determines to devote herself to the Jews.

Following graduation, she works as a teacher among the very Jews about whom she spoke so derisively during the earlier conversation with her father. As a young woman, she begins to feel compassion and even admiration for the simple Jewish women who go out to work as hawkers, shouldering domestic and financial responsibilities while their husbands engage in study.[44] After a short time, she weds a Jewish philologist and, after the birth of their daughter, searches for work as a tutor to supplement their meager income. In a fictionalized version of Khin's own experience, Berg is denied employment and is told that it is preferable to "take a Russian without a diploma than a Jew."[45] Her dream of Jewish-Russian harmony is disintegrating as Berg laments: "Why can't they develop an understanding of human worth? . . . [Perhaps] it would be better if I raised my [daughter] among my coreligionists. Then I could hate without pangs of remorse . . . I want to love, but they compel me to hate."[46] Berg suffers job discrimination once again when she seeks a position as a governess in the wake of her deadbeat husband's desertion. One potential employee turns her away with the excuse that appearances must be kept up. "Sorry, we can't have [you]," she explains, "We must [maintain] our stature."[47] Denied a livelihood, Khin's heroine is unable to provide for her daughter, whose death by starvation causes her to reassess her dream of Russian-Jewish fraternity.

At long last, Berg is engaged as governess by the wealthy widow Zubkov, who fears being suspected of prejudice more than allowing a Jew to supervise her children.[48] Berg spends a restless first night at the Zubkov home plagued by a nightmare in which alternating scenes of happiness and misfortune rain down. At first, "everything is good, . . .

[all peoples] understand each other, no one is tormented, . . . no one hates and [Berg] herself is happy." But that image disappears as a "miserable, ragged and persecuted *zhid*" [a contemptuous epithet for a Jew] comes into focus while a voice bellows accusingly: "Christ-seller, . . . exploiter . . . good riddance." In vengeful response, the old Jew mutters Heinrich Heine's verses, which Khin quotes in their original German:

Ein Jahrtausend und schon länger
Dulden wir uns brüderlich;
Du—du duldest, dass ich athme
Dass du rasest — dulde ich . . .

A millennium and even longer
We have endured each other in a brotherly way
You—you endure that I breathe
I endure your rage . . . [49]

Khin's clever reference to Heine (1797–1856) resonates on several levels. After all, Heine's life mirrors that of Khin's "misfit," being himself a self-hating Jew who mocked his coreligionists and in the end favorably reassessed his old faith. Despite Heine's traditional Jewish upbringing, his father Samson permitted his wife Betty to remove her son from a private Jewish school and send him to a Catholic lycée. Consequently, Heine's knowledge of Judaism, like Berg's, was fragmentary and confused. Heine's adult apostasy, which he spoke of as an "admission ticket to European culture," brought him no such advantages, and he came to writhe under the stigma of being a convert. Though at times severely critical of Jews and Judaism, he shed much of his hostility as he learned more of Jewish history and culture. The Damascus Affair (1840), which involved a ritual murder libel against the Jews, marked the starting point of Heine's change of heart, even though a year later he married the gentile Eugenie Mirat, an illiterate Paris shop assistant. Khin's protagonist undergoes an odyssey similar to Heine's, but unlike him, though she contemplates conversion and at story's end intermarriage, she partakes of neither.

Berg's refusal to marry a Russian aristocrat with whom she has found true love proves that she no longer abides the notion that Russians will one day fully accept Jews. "I've changed," she tells her suitor, continuing,

My dreams about fraternity among people is a pitiful, childish illusion. Since I was a girl, I thought like a Russian and spoke Russian. My ear was tuned to the sounds of Russian songs . . . [And] everyone mocked this. I have experienced the horror of [such a Jewish] status . . . I knocked on every door looking for work so we wouldn't die of starvation, and all refused me. My child died before my very eyes, and I could do nothing. *Zhidovka* [a contemptuous epithet for a Jewish woman] burns on my lip like a brand . . . I generously offered to sell myself because Orthodox Christians are not squeamish about *zhidovskii* beauty . . . [But] in the end, I was regarded as a wild animal to be exterminated.[50]

At her death of a chronic heart condition months later, Khin's heroine is still piecing together a shattered faith in Judaism and in humanity.

"The Misfit" received a favorable review in *Voskhod* in 1894 after appearing as one of five stories in Khin's collection *Siluety* (Silhouettes). The review was composed by none other than Oskar Osipovich Gruzenberg, a Jewish lawyer whose most prominent case was to be that of the Kievan Jew Mendel Beilis, charged in 1911 with the ritual murder of a Christian boy.[51] As his memoirs indicate, Gruzenberg could easily identify with Khin's misfit. Like the fictional character Berg, Gruzenberg had been raised without benefit of either a Jewish education or adherence to Jewish cultural and religious traditions. As a result, he initially felt no close connection with the Jewish people, though he did, like Berg, feel strong attachments to Russian culture. Nearly echoing her closing monologue, he proudly gushed in his memoirs of 1938: "The first word to reach my consciousness was Russian. Russian songs, fairy tales, nannies, childhood games with playmates—all of these were Russian. I fell in love with this marvelous language."[52] Yet at the same time, since Gruzenberg (and Berg) could not be fully accepted into the mainstream of Russian life without converting to Christianity, they were to some extent outsiders among the Russians. As Gruzenberg completed his law studies at the University of Kiev in 1889, the government issued a decree that non-Christians were to be admitted to the bar only with the personal approval of the Minister of Justice. This meant a virtual ban on Jews. While some would-be Jewish attorneys converted, Gruzenberg elected to persist in the task of pursuing a career as a Jew in the gentile world. He remained a lawyer-in-training for sixteen years until Russia relaxed its stringent policies in 1905, all the while maintaining a sense of responsibility to his people by defending Jews like Beilis.

Besides being somewhat illustrative of the reviewer Gruzenberg's predicament (and Heine's, too), "The Misfit" functions as something of a primer to understanding Khin's own complicated relationship to Judaism and the Jewish people. Though initially published in 1886 when she was merely twenty-five, the story accurately portrays both the point of origin and destination of Khin's own Jewish identity. Like her fictional alter ego, from childhood Khin was immersed in Russian rather than Jewish culture, and, as an adult, took an interest in things Jewish only as mounting restrictions and then all-out violence against Jews goaded her to action. Between these two intervals, at some point during the early 1880s, Khin converted to Catholicism as mentioned above in order to escape from her brief, and apparently unbearable, marriage to Solomon Fel'dshtein, who refused her a divorce.[53] Knowing that Jewish law generally prohibits a woman from initiating a divorce and that Tsarist law regards a marriage between a Jew and Christian as dissolved, her apostasy might be viewed as an end in itself.[54] She converted to seek neither professional advancement nor spiritual sustenance. Catholicism seems to have been irrelevant and incidental to Khin's identity, as evidenced by the fact that she not once referred to it in her memoirs. Moreover, within years of her conversion, she openly engaged in activity on behalf of Jewry.

After 1900, Khin wrote with increasing regularity and concern in her diary about the injustice suffered by her people and even expressed sympathy for their plight. She devoted a dozen entries to recounting horrors perpetuated against Jews, including pogroms, evacuations, military restrictions, and university quotas.[55] She decried especially the indifference of the "Christian '*intelligenty*'" who walked the streets in their holiday apparel and *looked* as the slaughter was carried out [but] did not object" [her emphasis].[56] In the old days, members of the intelligentsia would "make a big fuss . . . about the inequity toward Jews."[57] But even this, she lamented, they did for unworthy reasons. According to Khin, support for Jews or any beleaguered people ought to be grounded in pure humanitarianism. But they made their support contingent on Jews' patriotic acts toward the fatherland. Russian intellectuals' good intentions could not disguise their true opinion that the Jews were "alien scum."[58]

Though Khin never severed her intimate ties to the "Christian *intelligenty*," she began to associate more closely with the organized Jewish community in the Russian Empire. Like other integrated and privileged Jews who had lost direct contact with the Jewish masses, Khin began in the 1890s to raise her voice in their defense.[59] For example, the President of the Society for the Spread of Enlightenment among the Jews, a group established in 1863 for the purpose of Russifying the Jewish masses, invited her to participate in a literary-musical evening in November 1899 to benefit Jewish students enrolled in secondary schools.[60] In addition, she contributed a story and a pair of translations to two different literary anthologies whose proceeds were used, respectively, to support an elementary Jewish school and Jews of Kherson and Bessarabia, beleaguered by the famine of 1899–1900.[61]

In "Mechtatel'" (The Dreamer), which appeared in the first of those volumes, a gentile narrator chronicles the idealism and eventual disillusionment of his Jewish friend, the title character Boris Moiseevich Zon'.[62] Zon' yearns for the day when differences between Jews and Christians will be disregarded and then obliterated, giving way to a time when, as he puts it, the "word 'Jew' will disappear altogether." Khin shared Zon's hope for a basic and pervasive humanism. But like her character, her hopes faded as brotherhood between Jew and Christian became more elusive in the face of mounting prejudice and restrictions against Jews.

As for Zon', despite his Jewish blood and unprepossessing appearance, he is (c.1870s) at the very center of a lively Muscovite circle of conservatory students, musicians, and even a *kursistka* (female student) or two. The group meets at his apartment, "furnished rooms of means" nicknamed the *ermitazh'* (refuge), and is engaged in a routine of lectures, exams, book discussions, and theater attendance, along with occasional teaching stints so that they can "go to the people" and enlighten the ignorant.

As the narration unfolds, the reader learns how Zon's dream of Russian-Jewish unity is chipped away bit by bit. First, he is spurned by his one and only love, a beautiful and coquettish gentile *kursistka*, who, after a two-month betrothal, disappears, leaving behind in writing only that "though I very much respect and esteem you, I cannot marry you." Though never stated explicitly, the reader speculates that she was unable to make a lifelong commitment to a Jew, no matter how cultivated and refined (i.e. Russified) he may appear to be. Several years later Zon's sec-

ond major setback comes to pass when he discovers that his disciple
Liedman has been baptized. It seems that the student has taken his
teacher's humanistic philosophy to its logical conclusion. As Liedman explains it to Zon': "You're a brother to four million [Jews], while I am a
brother to all [people]."

Despite his Russifying bent, for Zon', total abandonment of his ancestral roots is not an option. In one telling conversation, he challenges a
female student of history to take up the study of the Jewish past in "our
fatherland." "The usual impression," he exclaims, "is that Jews sit their
whole life by the Talmud, fascinated with God-knows-what, confused.
. . ." "But," he continues, "Jews have become disentangled from this enigmatic labyrinth of medieval scholasticism." Like his model Isaac Baer
Levinson, the pioneering Russian maskil whom he identifies by name,
Zon' wishes to dispel myths about the Jews and raise their status in the
eyes of Russians.[63] In the end, though, Zon's dreams are not realized, and
Khin's story concludes rather predictably, with Zon's suicide, as a result of
his overpowering despair after being forcibly expelled from Moscow for
no reason but for being a Jew.[64] Yet Zon's suicide note offers still a glim-
mer of hope, melodramatically expressed: "The sun of the twentieth century will shine for you. . . . Be cheerful! Go forward . . . it seems all is not
lost. Suddenly from the black earth . . . a daisy appears and whispers:
'Don't be sad. Spring is coming. Spring is coming.'" The message is obvious. Khin forecasts a brighter future for Jews of the next generation.[65]

The Aristocrat at Odds with the Plebeian

Fictional representations and explicit expressions of sympathy only partially illuminate Khin's Jewish consciousness. To delve more deeply into
Khin's attitudes toward Jews, it is necessary to consult the diaries she
began to keep when she was thirty years old; her last entry was in 1917,
when she was fifty-six. Besides the detailed chronicle of exploits against
Jews as delineated above, Khin's diary abounds with telling remarks revealing her convictions about the stratified nature of the Jewish community and her place in it. In no uncertain terms, she makes clear that two
distinct sorts of Jews exist in her day: aristocrats and plebeians. The former type are educated at the finest gymnasia and universities of Russia or
Europe, schooled in the manners of the West, easily blend with the intel-

lectual and cultural elite of their countries, and reside, so far as Russia is concerned, within its interior. Those of the latter are ignorant of the civilizing ways and ideas of modernity, vulgar in dress and behavior, a conspicuous embarrassment to their refined brothers and sisters, and reside in the Pale of Settlement (or, if not, ought to return there). Needless to say, Khin's education, affluence, and Moscow-based existence guaranteed her "aristocratic" standing. Except presumably for her very early childhood in Mogilev, she associated exclusively with those of her ilk. As an adult, Khin remained virtually ignorant of "common" Jews until the 1890s, when she struck up what would become a lifelong friendship with Nadezhda Evgen'evna Auer—the woman Khin regarded as the apotheosis of elegance and good taste. Ironically, it was through "Nadine," as she preferred to be called, that Khin became reacquainted with the plebeian segment of her people.

Khin described at length how she met Nadine. While traveling by train from Tula (approximately 125 miles south of Moscow) to Moscow in December 1893, Khin spotted her on the seat opposite.[66] The two initially only eyed each other but after an hour were "gabbing as though they were long-lost sisters" on topics ranging from "literature, life, Moscow and St. Petersburg society, scandalous writers and most of all about Paris, about Paris." They spoke in French, which Nadine preferred, but which Khin found to be rather affected. When the two parted, they promised to write—an oath they solemnly kept as evidenced by the 1,066 pages(!) of letters from Auer to Khin housed in the latter's archival holding.[67] We learn from Khin that the "intelligent, delicate, kind and soft-spoken" Nadine, the daughter of a physician and high Russian official, fell in love with and eventually wed Leopold Auer (1845–1930), "a Jew of simple folk."[68] Auer's talent as a violinist propelled him from his native Hungary to Germany and then to Russia, where he became the star of the St. Petersburg Conservatory. Ascending even higher on the Russian cultural horizon, Auer converted to Russian Orthodoxy shortly after 1868, when he was appointed soloist of the Russian Imperial Orchestra. He was ennobled by the Tsar in 1895 and immigrated to America in 1918.[69]

Because of their tight-knit friendship, Khin was privy to a personal view of the Auers' relationship and commented liberally on her observations. In addition to what Nadine confided to her in person and in letters, Khin visited the Auers with regularity and spent weeks at a time at their summer home in Finland.[70] Khin was struck by their unnatural match in light of Auer's Jewish—and plebeian at that—background and Nadine's nonpareil good breeding. As Khin saw it, Auer's recently acquired European elegance could no more wash away the stain of his Jewishness than his immersion in baptismal waters. To her, once a Jew always a Jew. She painted a vivid portrait of her bosom buddy's husband, in whom, she claimed, "one can feel a Jew—in his mannerisms, his jokes, his reasoning, [and] in his bright, enormous, bulging black eyes. . . . He's an outstandingly polished, well-bred, elegant European but a Jew all the same. And not an *aristocrat* Jew, a descendant of the noble Acosta, but a Jew of simple folk—smart, clever, somewhat coarse and kind" [her emphasis].[71]

Khin is referring here to Uriel da Costa, who was born into a crypto-Jewish family in Portugal in 1585 and later returned to Judaism.[72] Da Costa became a popular figure among the cultured classes and was immortalized in stage productions bearing his name. In the Russian Empire, Leonid Nikolaevich Andreev (1871–1919), Khin's acquaintance, penned a drama with da Costa at the center of the plot.[73] As an inveterate attendant of Moscow's cultural events, Khin undoubtedly was familiar with this work. Thus, she compared "Acosta," whose veins flowed with a mix of Jewish and Catholic blood, to the Jewish aristocracy of her own day. Only these Europeanized and educated Jews were capable of blending in with the real Russian aristocracy, and even they, as she would personally attest in her diary while visiting the Auers one summer in Finland, did not always fit in: "Sometimes I feel a little uncomfortable . . . among all this splendor and 'aristocratic' calm . . . essentially the only aristocrat is Nadezhda Evgen'evna *herself*" [her emphasis]. Taking yet another jab at the unfit husband, she continued: "The extraordinary violinist is very 'polished' in the European aesthetic and in all circles of society. . . . But he is a Jew-plebeian . . . and if you took away his violin then he would probably be an excellent broker, lawyer, doctor or whatever you like."[74] At the same time that she mocked his ignoble roots and too Jewishly-familiar appearance and mannerisms, Khin found Auer humorous. She took delight, for example, in his faulty Russian accent, and employed him as the butt of jokes.[75] She was, in other words, attracted to him and his idiosyncrasies, but felt superior to him.

Through Nadine, Khin became connected not only to the common Jew but to the aristocrat as well. She was, in her words, "burning with curiosity to meet [the] 'phenomenon'" known as Ivan Stanislavovich Bliokh, Nadine's acquaintance of forty years.[76] Bliokh (1836–1901) was a financier and Polish Jew who played a leading role in the construction of the Russian railroads. Besides winning international fame for his dedication to pacifism, Bliokh maintained an interest in the Jewish Question and in improving the lot of Russian Jewry, despite his conversion to Calvinism. The testament he left his family upon death begins: "I was my whole life a Jew, and I die as a Jew."[77] After the pogroms of the 1890s, he pressed the government to end discrimination and in a five-volume work, he analyzed the Jews' contribution to the economy. Khin admired the fact that Bliokh "did not conceal his links to the chosen people and that he protected the Jews, pleading in their behalf and speaking out about their fate." She finally made his acquaintance in November 1898 at the Auers'. Bliokh revealed to her over breakfast that he had been yearning to meet the author of "Makarka," a story he had read nearly a decade before in the pages of *Voskhod*.[78]

"Makarka" is Khin's attempt to expose the petty vulgarities of the Jewish parvenu. The title character is an adolescent boy who struggles with his father's unrealistic dream that he will some day become a physician. Khin describes the father as a "cunning, pushy, and ingratiating man who was able to guess the weak spot of people's needs and beat them down."[79] He tormented his children and wife with verbal and physical abuse, resulting in his elder son's running away to join an acrobatic troop. Makarka—a quiet boy and dreamer, who loved poetry and music and remained indifferent to his academic studies at the local gymnasium—is ill-suited to fulfill his father's expectations. As Khin summarized the boy's existence: "From morning until three o'clock, he trembled at the gymnasium; after three o'clock, he trembled at home."[80] The boy finds refuge at the home of his Jewish friend David Blum, whose family he describes (in recognizable Khin terminology) as "real aristocrats." Unlike his home, where "two siblings share a plate and a spoon," the Blums' home is clean and decorated smartly. With their French governess, the Blums are to Makarka "completely and utterly unlike Jews."[81] Speaking perhaps in Khin's behalf, David admonishes Makarka that it is his responsibility and that of all young Jews to serve their people by improving the lot of their coarse and unfortunate brothers and sisters.

The climax of the story develops when Makarka reveals to his father that he has been barred from promotion to the next year of studies at the gymnasium. Their subsequent fighting match escalates into violence whereupon the boy flees the house. Uncertain of a destination, Makarka spends the evening in the damp outdoors, and catches typhus. Throughout his long illness, his remorseful father keeps a bedside vigil and begs for forgiveness. But to no avail. The boy dies. The final scene of the story—Makarka's funeral—once again reinforces the clashing differences between the two families. While Makarka's parents engage in embarrassing wails of grief, the Blums remain refined, laying a single white rose on their friend's grave. Khin's distaste and contempt for the Jewish commoner could hardly be expressed more blatantly.

Her disdain is illustrated further in her reminiscences of Vladimir Sergeevich Solov'ev, a close friend who appears with increasing regularity in her diary from 1895 to 1900. Solov'ev (1853–1900) was a theologian and poet who affected the modern course of Russian literature by influencing Symbolists like Aleksandr' Blok, Andrei Belyi, and Viacheslav Ivanov.[82] Son of a renowned historian and grandson of a Russian Orthodox priest, he lectured at Moscow University but suffered the criticism of reactionaries for the liberal character of his Christianity. An interesting component of Solov'ev's thought is his theological and practical philo-Semitism. In this he was almost alone in Russian mystical Christian circles and differed from his friend Dostoevsky. His positive evaluation of Judaism resulted from his appreciation of the Jews' ability to be an individual nation with a distinct national personality while participating in the universal goal of divine-human interaction known as *bogochelovech-estvo* (godmanhood).[83] Solov'ev was introduced to Judaism through his interest in mysticism. He learned to read Jewish mystical texts and Hebrew Scriptures and also studied Talmud in the traditional Jewish manner, with a partner, Feivel' Gets.[84] Solov'ev opposed Christian missionary activities that targeted Jews and raised his voice in sharp protest against the pogroms of 1881–82. Along with one hundred other distinguished Russian intellectuals, he signed a petition on behalf of Jews, which reached Alexander III but was immediately suppressed.[85] Khin recoiled from such charitable efforts on the part of non-Jews. To her, being the "object of philanthropy" was humiliating.[86] To his dying day, however, Solov'ev continued to defend what he called the "grand race."[87] He was said to have recited psalms on behalf of the Jews on his deathbed.

Khin became personally acquainted with Solov'ev through Nadine Auer and the novelist Boborykin in 1895.[88] Khin and Solov'ev evidently kindled a close association quickly, for by early 1896 Khin divulged to her diary: "He knows almost everything about my life."[89] And the following year, when Khin's father took ill and subsequently died, it was Solov'ev who comforted her.[90] The two spoke openly on topics of both a personal and philosophical nature, ranging from family relations to relations between Jews and Christians. Khin had difficulty understanding Solov'ev's sympathy for the Jews, especially those of plebeian roots. They flocked to him, she said: "They consider him [their] *tzaddik* [Hebrew/Yiddish word meaning "righteous leader"], . . . and they rush at him [like creepy-crawlers] from every crevice of the Pale of Settlement."[91] By way of example, Khin recounted in her diary an anecdote culled from Solov'ev's "inexhaustible source of stories about Jews." One evening Solov'ev decided to bring along Feivel' Gets to a literary gathering at the home of the philosopher and literary critic Nikolai Nikolaevich Strakhov (1828–1896).[92] When the two arrived, an antisemitic conversation was taking place, which with their appearance was not only not silenced, but became even more maliciously animated. Noticing Gets' discomfort, one outspoken fellow began to argue for the necessity of destroying the Jews. Attempting to contain his agitation, Gets responded: "Your god commanded you to love your enemy." As their voices escalated in decibel, others gravitated toward the feuding pair and began to drone: "To destroy. To destroy. To destroy. He is the enemy of the Russian soul!" Grabbing his companion by the arm, Solov'ev ushered Gets out of the hall, apologizing all the while for his error in judgment. "I was mistaken," he admitted later to Khin, "for introducing [Gets] to Russian philosophers, . . . to put him completely out of his element." In contrast to the invader Gets, Khin considered herself, and was presumably considered by others, to be a constituent part of that literary circle, as guaranteed by her education and shared Weltanschauung. In fact, her identification with the intellectual and cultured classes of Russia and her disassociation from Jewish plebeians became so complete that years later she would remark in her diary: "I am not a Judeophile and not a Jew-lover."[93]

An Insider-Outsider among the Russian Elite

Like other Jews of her socioeconomic background, Khin's knowledge of things Jewish was meager. In her Russian-language diary—which is replete with French, German, and even an occasional English phrase or literary allusion—she seldom employed common Jewish vocabulary. While she referred to many Russian-language newspapers and journals, she never once mentioned reading from the Russian-Jewish press. She is even silent on *Voskhod*, to which she contributed two stories and in whose pages her works of Jewish content were reviewed. Moreover, she dated her diary with the Russian calendar exclusively and mentioned not a single Jewish festival or ritual. Her diary provides as well no supporting evidence to suggest that Khin was schooled in Jewish subjects. Her knowledge of Yiddish, and especially Hebrew, appears to be limited in the extreme. Although she did occasionally sprinkle her fiction and diary with references to things Jewish (e.g. an allusion to Lessing's *Nathan the Wise* in "The Misfit," a remark about the maskil Isaac Baer Levinson in "The Dreamer," and the description of Solov'ev as *tzaddik*), these details required little familiarity with Judaism to bespeak. Owing probably more to her social class than her gender, Khin's upbringing resembled that of other well-to-do children: care by a governess, followed by training at a gymnasium, and then study at a university abroad. The final product—a solid secular education—was useful to the men and women who would function in late imperial Russia's intellectual and cultural circles.

And by 1891 Khin was regularly involved in those circles. As the names in her diary reveal, her primary social group consisted of philosophers, literary figures, and, most notably, jurists. Khin gained access to the latter primarily through her husbands, both of whom were attorneys. Little is known of her first spouse, Solomon Fel'dshtein, whom she wed by at least the age of twenty (1881).[94] The two had a child, Mikhail, and, as previously mentioned, within half a decade divorced. Khin then married Osip Borisovich Gol'dovskii, with whom, it appears, she had no children. From clues pieced together from her diary—as well as from his writings and scanty archival holdings, which are appended to those of his wife—

we know that Gol'dovskii was a fairly well-known Muscovite lawyer. As a young man, he was apprenticed to Prince Aleksandr Ivanovich Urusov, a lawyer who came to prominence after defending participants in the Nechaev conspiracy in the 1870s.[95] After working under Urusov for nearly ten years, Gol'dovskii became engaged, like other legalists of his day, in Russia's political machinations.[96] In November 1904, for instance, he attended the private meetings of the *zemstvo* (an organ for self-government established in 1864) in St. Petersburg and then later that same month delivered a speech at a banquet celebrating the fortieth anniversary of the Judiciary Reforms at the Hermitage.[97] Moved by her husband's eloquence, Khin recorded in her diary how his remarks on the attitudes of Jews in general and Jewish lawyers in particular toward their colleagues stirred the crowd of five hundred gathered to hear him.

Like his wife, Gol'dovskii, as previously mentioned, was an apostate who converted for reasons having to do not with religious sensibilities but with practicalities.[98] In order to marry a Catholic woman, he could not maintain his status as Jew. So he converted to Protestanism (perhaps it seemed less extreme than Catholicism) and refused to use his new status to advance his legal career from apprentice to full member of the bar, the latter being a position closed to Jews at the time.[99] Gol'dovskii also resembled his wife in the way that he was drawn to his persecuted coreligionists later in life. Though his beneficence was not extensive, he did become the patron of the then-struggling Jewish playwright and prose writer Semon Solomonovich Iushkevich (1868–1927), who in return modeled a protagonist on his benefactor.[100] In sum, Gol'dovskii mingled with ease among the legal elite of his day but grew increasingly agitated by challenges facing his less privileged brothers and sisters.[101]

That Gol'dovskii should have gravitated to the legal profession comes as no surprise to students of Russian Jewish history.[102] After all, in late imperial Russia, Jews had no access to professorships, civil service posts, employment in the Justice Department, or elective posts in local governing bodies. The far-reaching Judiciary Reforms of 1864, however, had rendered the bar free of whimsical impediments to Jews, at least temporarily and theoretically. These reforms, part of the series of drastic changes created in the wake of the serf emancipation of 1861, introduced into Russia a court system patterned on European models. For the first time, Russian justice was placed in the hands of experts trained in the application of legal norms and theoretically independent of the Tsar's influence. Despite the later emergence of restrictions, Jews succeeded in winning a place in the bar. In the last decade of the nineteenth century, Jews constituted some 14 percent of the Empire's lawyers and 43 percent of all apprentice lawyers—the primary pool from which future members of the bar would be drawn.[103]

Individual lawyers gained fame among the literate Russian populace as important criminal trials, including the speeches of attorneys for the defense, were widely publicized in the press owing to the Censorship Reform of 1865.[104] One such lawyer was Anatolii Fedorovich Koni (1843–1927), who shared a thirty-year intimacy with Khin, as is evident by his regular appearance in her diary and their voluminous correspondence, found in both of their archival holdings.[105] Koni was rarely far from Khin's thoughts after their first meeting, which was arranged by their mutual acquaintance Urusov in the late 1880s. Their long-standing friendship led eventually to Khin's son Mikhail becoming apprenticed to Koni.[106] A jurist and man of letters, Koni gained renown in connection with the famed trial of Vera Zasulich, who was accused of attempting to assassinate Governor Trepov of St. Petersburg in 1878. A jury acquitted Zasulich, but not before her case became a triumph of public opinion. Russians regarded this trial by jury and its verdict of not guilty as an open protest of public conscience against the oppression of autocracy.[107] Koni, the presiding judge, rode the trial's coattails to popularity. And decades later he would regale charmed listeners assembled at Khin's home with his reminiscences.[108]

Gol'dovskii and Koni made up only two of the legal swarm buzzing about Khin. A.I. Urusov, Gol'dovskii's above-mentioned mentor, frequently came round, as did Vladimir Ivanovich Taneev (1840–1921), the lawyer and materialist philosopher whom Khin scornfully labeled a "throwback to serfdom" and a dying breed preoccupied by his "own eternal cares."[109] Despite her unfavorable opinions, Khin welcomed Taneev's visits and juicy bits of gossip about important people like Mikhail Evgrafovich Saltykov-Shchedrin (1826–89), the journalist who co-edited *Otechestvennye zapisky* (Notes of the Fatherland), and Alexei Mikhailovich Unkovskii (1828–93), the court-appointed defense for Alexander II's assassins.[110] Other jurists of late nineteenth-century Russia flitted in and out of Khin's life as well, including Boris Nikolaevich Chicherin (1828–1904), a law professor at Moscow University and former tutor to Alexander II's oldest son, and Maksim Maksimovich Kovalevskii (1851–1916), a law professor at St. Petersburg University and later the founder of the Constitutional Monarchist Party.[111] As his later political affiliations suggest, Kovalevskii, like Chicherin and most other lawyers influencing Khin, espoused ideas of moderation and gradualism in solving Russia's political problems. Opposed to Marxism, they supported the doctrine of a constitutional government that would lead to ethnic and religious pluralism in a newly-configured Russia. Their political ideals led some of these liberal jurists to condemn antisemitism, an act which ingratiated them to Khin and other Jews embittered by growing intolerance in their homeland.

After 1897, Khin played host to her assorted guests at Katino, the country estate in the outskirts of Moscow purchased in June of that year. "I bought Katino," she boasted, "[It is] a beautiful large house, [with] two wings, a magnificent staff of servants, a fruit garden and park, a kitchen-garden, a small pond; an excellent, ideal setting."[112] While this short but descriptive notice neglects to inform us of the financial source for such an expensive acquisition, it does stress that the owner is the thirty-six year old Khin alone. Perhaps she used earnings from her published writings to purchase the estate, though more likely she dipped into the inheritance presumably bequeathed to her a year earlier upon her father's death.[113] Khin used Katino as a refuge from the urban pace of Moscow, where she shared an apartment with her husband and son, and from her frequent and tiring journeys abroad. Around her she gathered illustrious friends and acquaintances, who, growing accustomed to Katino's bucolic setting and calm ambiance, returned time and again. A typical day at Katino might unfold as such: a morning in writing solitude, an afternoon devoted to walking the glorious grounds, and an evening given over to a lavish dinner prepared by Nadine Auer, readings by Koni, and a piano recital by Gol'dovskii.[114] As exemplified at Katino, as Russia's autocracy began its slow descent, members of its privileged classes indulged for the last time in cultural sport of trifling import. Prior to the dark days that opened the twentieth century, evenings at Katino were occasions for spirited discussion disconnected from the reality that would bring this era and these carefree gatherings to an end. But as Russia convulsed with upheaval after upheaval—from student riots in 1902 to war with Japan in 1904, from the Revolutions of

1905 and 1917 to World War I—guests at Katino increasingly concerned themselves with affairs of the state and their future within it.

From the Personal to the Political

Khin was no exception. Beginning in 1901, there is a marked shift in emphasis in her diary from the personal to the political. With the eye of a journalist and the convictions of a commentator, she began to record the dizzying changes affecting her native land. Often she gleaned data from local newspapers, citing her sources and then following up with personal remarks, as in February 1902 when she discussed the disturbances crossing the Empire that would culminate in Revolution three years hence:

> There are student riots in Moscow and Petersburg. They say 850 people have been arrested. It's all so extraordinary. . . . [The riots have spread] to Kiev and to Kharkov as well. The university in St. Petersburg has been closed since February. In general, Russia is a mess! . . . Such an absurd country—our Russia. Everything happens at the wrong time, whether too early or too late . . . [the newspaper] . . . reports that students were arrested and exiled to Siberia for five or ten years. I don't want to believe this, though in Russia anything is possible. . . .[115]

Khin's sympathy for the students and indignation toward the government were further inflamed the following month when the political unrest affected her own family. The government deported her aunt's son Maks for a period of four years for his alleged involvement in revolutionary activities. Her angry uncle deplored his son's "nihilism" and instructed his wife never to utter his name in their household again. Though "in his heart, of course," Khin reasoned, "he adores Maks and is utterly shocked by this 'unheard of scandal.'"[116]

Political clouds began to gather on Russia's horizon as early as 1881 in the wake of Alexander II's assassination. Partly as a rejoinder to what he considered to be the failed progressive course of his predecessor, Alexander III (1881–1894) reversed the Empire's policy direction. His subjects responded initially with mere consternation, which quickly escalated into violence that rocked the Empire and eventually caused its demise.

Seen by some historians as reactionary, the new Tsar attempted to bring Russia into line with an illusory pre-Petrine ideal by implementing counterreforms that struck blows at liberties secured during Alexander II's reign. The new ruler severely curtailed freedom of the press, judicial independence, and self-government. And on account of his anti-intellectual and anti-intelligentsia stance, professors and students at universities became suspect while quotas for admission to institutions of higher learning proliferated.

As is well known, these counterreforms had a great impact on the Jewish community, which was restricted in 1887 by a 10 percent quota for secondary schools and schools of higher learning within the Pale, 5 percent outside the Pale and 3 percent in Moscow and St. Petersburg. These numbers were further reduced when Nicholas II (1894–1917) took over the reins of power.[117] Khin herself acted to reverse the numerus clausus. She reported in her diary on September 26, 1904 her efforts to petition the government about "university acceptance, above the famous norm" in behalf of "sons very close to my heart." Angrily, she expressed her displeasure at the charade of "lot casting" for those endeavoring to "rush into the temple of science [where there were] eighty spots for eight hundred people."[118]

Khin's actions were typical of the efforts of many Jews in the broad stream of Russian politics. Responding to growing antisemitism and incensed by (and fearful of) pogroms, Jews in increasing numbers became convinced that their ultimate future lay in activism aimed at wresting full equality of rights from the government. Many joined political movements of a primarily Jewish (e.g. the Bundists) or Russian (e.g. the Social Revolutionaries) orientation that offered opportunities to transform Russia through revolution.[119] Others, like Khin, opted for a less radical approach. They allied themselves with liberal political parties like the Constitutional Democrats (Kadets), who were organized with an emphasis on civil liberties and a constitutional government. The Kadets were especially attractive to Jews, for they were willing to raise the Jewish Question and the pogroms, using them as a means of attacking the government and unmasking its reactionary policy.[120]

It is likely that Khin's interest in the Kadets stemmed from her husband's involvement with the party, including its very formation. In 1904, Gol'dovskii journeyed to St. Petersburg to discuss Russia's future with one hundred-eighteen prominent men. The participants included Ivan Ilych Petrunkevich, who, with Paul Nikolaevich Miliukov and Maksim Vinaver, was responsible for the foundation of the Kadet party a year later.[121] Throughout 1905 the couple regularly attended the party's meetings, though Khin herself remained ambivalent toward its aims.[122] In all likelihood, her views were not unlike those of other liberal Russians who were concerned primarily with the protection of persons and property from arbitrary authority. Their liberalism was tempered by the belief that there could be no limiting of supreme power at times of turbulence and by their distrust of popular assemblies and popular sovereignty.[123] The banality of Khin's political judgment is revealed in such comments as, "Someone needs to combine a constitution with autocracy."[124] To her, a constitution should be introduced only when the monarch deems it necessary. So when in October 1905, under the pressure of strikes and public demonstrations, Nicholas II finally issued a manifesto promising basic freedoms to the entire population, Khin hailed the event as "blessed."[125] But, as for Russia's parliamentary experiment known as the Duma, Khin cast a vote of thumbs-down. Alluding to a line from Pushkin's well-known fairy tale in verse "Skazka o tsare Saltane" (A Tale about Tsar Saltan) she maintained, "[The Duma] will turn out to be neither a little mouse nor a little frog but an unknown beast."[126] She continued with specific criticism: "The Duma *is concerned with discussion and the preparation of bills.* The workers will be deprived of a voice. The peasants will predominate in numbers, but the *kulak* [rich peasants] and nobility will prevail in action. The [influence of the] intelligentsia will be reduced. . . . Smart people say that this is a step forward . . . making it difficult to return to how it was. Therefore, smart people are happy. But I'm not smart. In my soul, I have no happiness [her emphasis]."[127]

Whatever her political leanings, Khin recognized that Russia had in "these terrible and grand days [of October 1905] made *history*" [her emphasis].[128] She was, however, to flee the epic-making environs of Russia for France shortly after the Revolution of 1905. Fearing violence against Muscovite Jews, she and her husband moved temporarily to Paris. There Khin renewed her acquaintance with old friends like Anatole France and Oktave Mirbeau, and even dined with Georgii Gapon (1870–1906), the priest who had led the Petersburg workers to the Winter Palace in January 1905 with a petition of protest for the Tsar.[129]

Dramatizing the "Woman Question"

While the revolutionary turbulence swirled about her, Khin's career took a new direction. Since her literary debut in 1883, Khin busied herself exclusively with the writing of fictional prose in the realist tradition, composing thirteen short stories or novellas in as many years. All were published in journals and/or as parts of anthologies. But then suddenly drama began to flow from her pen; a total of five plays appeared in roughly a decade starting in 1897. Significantly, two of the five were accepted into the repertory of the Malyi Theater. The oldest of Moscow's theaters, the Malyi opened in 1824 and exercised a great influence on the development of Russian culture, furthering the establishment of realism and romanticism on the Russian stage. Theater historians have, in fact, linked the Malyi's activity with the evolution of progressive social thought and the growth of the liberation movement.[130] Its productions reflected and stirred up feelings of protest against the yoke of autocracy and reaction.

By the 1890s, when Khin was regularly attending performances at the Malyi, its importance was diminishing.[131] As a result of pressure from conservative circles, mediocre plays and second-rate farces dominated the Russian stage. Khin bemoaned this change in Russia's cultural fate. As was her lifetime wont, she compared Russia to the "massively-talented" France, where drama was "profound, but also cheerful and always humorous."[132] In her homeland, in contrast, "a ban lies over everything interesting, making it impossible to mention anything political." Thus, she concluded, "[Russians] unwillingly make do with stupid and vulgar [racial] jokes or indecent songs. . . . Educated Europeans must look at us like barbarians. . . . In [Paris] alone, it is possible *to live* [her emphasis].[133]

Perhaps to bolster her country's flagging reputation, Khin joined the ranks of Russian playwrights, composing drama in her native tongue. Her first work, *Okhota smertnaia* (Desire to Die), premiered on the page and not on stage. The one-act play of a mere eleven pages appeared in 1897 in *Prizyv'* (Appeal), a literary collection designed to benefit elderly and ailing artists and their families.[134] *Desire to Die* explores the psyche of a novice painter who feels trapped by marriage, motherhood, and archaic notions of female capabilities. "Every evening when I lie down," the despairing protagonist reveals, "I think, another day has passed. So what? What nonsense." After her husband accuses her of being a dilettante and her mother instructs her to be concerned exclusively with her children, she resigns herself to her disagreeable fate. The full articulation and realization of women's liberation had to await Khin's next play *Porosl'* (Budding Sprouts), a creation that came to light eight years later as the campaign for women's rights in Russia was gaining in complexity and fortune.

For nineteenth-century Russians, the "Woman Question" was the term designating the whole matrix of issues regarding women's education, work, and position in the family.[135] From its beginnings in the 1850s, the movement toward female emancipation was propagated almost exclusively by male intellectuals.[136] Yet by the 1880s, women's works began to be published in growing numbers, and female writers, too, alluded to the "Question" and created more nuanced portrayals of their own sex.

Though she made no direct reference to the "Woman Question" in her diary, Khin did describe her frustration and ire when excluded on account of her sex from a literary circle being formed by her friend Boborykin. Although Khin was one of a cluster of educated females growing aware of their restricted status, she failed to obtain the support of these other women and eventually abandoned her idea to start a similar group for those of her own sex.[137] Additionally, Khin wrote in her diary of becoming provoked by the lecturer Kliuchevskii's seeming endorsement of a well-known sixteenth-century manual, the *Domostroi*, which instructs that the man is the master of the house, while the woman is merely an ornament shining in her husband's crown.[138] Significantly as well, Khin's first published work was an anthropological study of sorts on women's fate in courtship and marriage through an investigation of lyrics of ancient folk songs.[139] Khin's sympathy for the cause of women can be further detected by the fact that she contributed a translation of George Sand's "Hamlet" to *Sbornik na pomoshch' uchashchimsiia zhenshchinam* (Collection to Assist Women Students), which appeared along with the works of other esteemed literary women of her day like Zinaida Gippius, Ol'ga Shapir, and Tatiana Shchepkina-Kupernik.[140]

As enumerated above, Khin featured women as protagonists with regularity in several of her short stories. But her tour de force for the female sex occurs in *Porosl'* (Budding Sprouts). Here she depicts in five acts a Turgenev-like generational struggle between those with contradictory ideas and aspirations. But unlike the masterful novelist of the 1860s who influenced her so profoundly, Khin's fictionalized conflict arises exclu-

sively among women. Not fathers and sons, but mothers and daughters
are at the center of this drama. To be precise, two pairs of gentile mothers and daughters are among the play's twenty characters: Sofiia
Vasil'evna Gribin, the thirty-six year old wife of a lawyer along with her
fifteen-year old daughter Iulia; and Sofiia's older sister Katerina Vail'evna
Linevich along with her twenty-five-year-old daughter Ol'ga. The action
of *Budding Sprouts* takes place over the course of two months in late 1905
on the Gribins' Chekhov-like country estate on the outskirts of Moscow.

The play is concerned with the future direction of the lives of the
daughters—the "budding sprouts" of the play's title—who are on the
cusp of maturity and, for Ol'ga at least, of independence.[141] The mothers, on the one hand, plot that their daughters will do as they have done:
marry wealthy gentlemen and settle down to a life of running estates and
raising children. Katerina dreams, for instance, of a wedding between
Ol'ga and Boris Anton'ich Shatilin, a philology student with a promising
future. The daughters, on the other hand, see their prospects differently.
With Iulia's free-spirited tutor Margarita as their model, they yearn to
take advantage of the array of opportunities that had opened up for Russian women in the past four decades. With the impetus of nihilism of the
1860s (popularized in Turgenev's famous generational novel and crystallized in Chernyshevskii's *What is to be Done?*)—with its emphasis on personal and sexual freedom, intellectual fulfillment, and experimental
lifestyles—a women's liberation movement of sorts was born. While at
first the movement was mostly theoretical in nature, influencing only a
small proportion of the population, by the end of the century, a host of
additional factors had brought about greater possibilities for greater
numbers of women: emancipation of the serfs and the attendant break-
down of the gentry family structure; the advent of modernization and ur-
banization in the 1880s; more educational options available to women,
including studies at the college-level, especially after 1894; and the revolutionary spirit and modes of behavior that captivated and became appropriate for both sexes.[142] So, by 1905, both Iulia and especially Ol'ga
anticipate for themselves a life far different from that of their mothers.

The "budded sprout" Ol'ga makes this goal perfectly clear in the play's
climactic scene (act 5, scene 3). After disappearing for two days, she returns home to inform her mother of her intention to break with the role

history and her own mother have assigned to her. The inflamed conversation between the two erupts into the following diatribe:

Mother: Where have you been for two days?
Daughter: In Moscow. I saw Boris at the station. He's gone abroad.
M: Do you love him?
D: No. Let me live how I wish. I'm not fifteen. I don't want to marry. I don't want the "family life." I don't want to have a master, caring for his children, [his] career . . . [his] needs. I don't want to care for children . . . to lie to myself that this is the "highest happiness." I don't want, at the end of twenty-five years, to be in the scene we're in now . . . I don't want to vent anger against my own daughter for leading a stupid life . . . she'll want to be her own person and not my portrait. Tell me please why [all the independent] women are found only in Turgenev's novels? Why do all the Natalias [of *Rudin*] [and] Elenas [of *On the Eve*] . . . leave the framework of generally-accepted morals. We could have living models. . . . Do you regard me as a black sheep who's a special exception? Not so! I am only more bold than the others. I know my own goal, and I don't want to pretend. Don't you say yourself that we are women of a new era, who also have a raison d'être?

. . . .

M: You're an egoist. You gratify only yourself. You're an ingrate. You love nothing. . . . You're interested in nothing — not your country, not your people. . . . You savages dress in modern costumes and adopt cultured behavior. . . .[You have] one goal: to make an effect! This is no ambition, but only a small, unfortunate trifle.

. . . .

D: Allow me to give you some advice, Mama. We'll be far more comfortable if you let me have the same freedom that I give to you. You are a fanatic, a *politikantka* [a woman involved in all the fashionable political causes], a *femme superieure* . . . I have nothing against your kind. But you must become reconciled with the idea that I look at things differently. . . . I envy those who live boldly. I have a skeptical mind.
M: This is empty skepticism, of an ignoramus who rejects everything that he doesn't understand.

. . . .

D: Simply, Mama . . . I don't know you. . . . This is the influence of
Russian air. . . . I have also lost equilibrium. But this will no longer
be the case. I promise! I'd sooner be in Paris.

Khin's characters are acting out a paradigm shift that was taking place in
fin-de-siècle Russia. The daughter is devoted to pure art and regards the
actions of her mother as trifling and meaningless; while the mother considers her daughter to be a selfish aesthete removed from life and dis-
tanced from the pragmatic needs of her homeland. Generational conflict
in literature had, of course, first manifested itself two score years earlier
in Turgenev's *Fathers and Sons*. But in 1905, Russia's changed historical
circumstances gave daughters the opportunity to break free of the molds
sons endeavored to escape from forty years before. In *Budding Sprouts*, the
playwright accomplishes for women what her mentor had done for men.
Like Turgenev, Khin expressed fictionally a new reality; but unlike the
novelist, her forum for expression was the stage. Indeed, once the drama
passed the censors' scrutiny, it appeared at the Malyi Theater in the early
part of 1905.[143]

In her next play, *Pod' sen'iu Penatov'* (Under the Protection of Penates),
Khin also focused on discord between parents and children.[144] But this
play was to have an altogether different fate than *Budding Sprouts*, as it had
an altogether different venue. Its action takes place in Moscow at the time
of the Decembrist Uprising, an unsuccessful conspiracy staged in 1825 to
overthrow Nicholas I. The play focuses on the headmaster of a gymnasium who has cut himself off completely from any contact with the political insurgents and expects the same of his son and niece. Defying their fa-
ther-uncle, the young pair leaves home in order to take up the cause of
the Decembrists. The censors, citing the probable insurrection that this
play would incite among its audience, banned it from the stage.[145] They
did, however, permit the four-act comedy *Nasledniki* (Generations), Khin's
fourth play, to be performed at the Malyi Theater in October, 1911.[146] Her
fifth and final play *Ledokhod'* (Drifting Ice) was also Khin's last published
work.[147] Appearing in print in 1917, *Drifting Ice* concerns the founding of
the leadership of the 1905 movement and Khin's own growing preoccupation with Russia's worsening political climate.

Faith in the Intelligentsia Nonetheless

When she returned in 1914 to her native land after her self-imposed exile to France in 1905, Khin was caught up in a daily struggle for survival along with all Russians. With neither leisure nor peace of mind, her writing became generally circumscribed to miscellaneous correspondence and the daily diary kept faithfully until 1917. "A troubled sea boils endlessly," remarked Khin, as "the Moscow of old, . . . constructed as it was out of white stone, . . . is transformed into a red metropolis of Socialism."[148] At the same time that the Tsarist Empire was disintegrating, bringing down with it the surety of prosperity and stature of its privileged classes, World War I was wreaking havoc on the unprepared and ill-equipped Russians. The second half of Khin's memoirs (1913–1917) are peppered with doleful accounts of the effects of war. "Yesterday I was in the city, and Moscow was deserted," she wrote in mid-1914, "Everyone spoke to us about the war with the unconcealed indignation of simple people who feel they are on the edge of an abyss."[149] Khin feared that Russians were growing accustomed to war and its depravities, and looked forward to the day when Russia would rout Germany. She likened victory to a "mission . . . a triumph of the *soul* over *materialism*"[her emphasis].[150] Yet Russia's soulfulness did not, to Khin's chagrin and way of thinking, extend to the Jews. She grew angry with Russian indifference to the plight of her people—some 600,000 of whom had been expelled from the Western borderlands on account of accusations of treason.[151] According to Khin, even the Kadets were "sluggish" toward the Jews; "vacillators" was how she came to characterize her old party.[152]

With each passing year, Khin's faith in Russia dimmed. She marked the tenth anniversary of the 1905 Revolution with these words: "Civilization is moving toward barbarity! . . . Other peoples move toward their own heyday. But we still do not . . . pray to God that we will move toward yesterday."[153] Within two months, she asked, "When did the bloody hurricane come that exploded all the roots of the old world? What will survive for us?"[154] But Khin responded to the chaos by committing herself to taking part in the political experiment washing over Russia. As she scribbled in her final diary entry on March 17, 1917: "We . . . Russian intelligentsia do not understand that Russia must undergo such pangs in order to give birth to its freedom. All must participate."[155] In the eleven-year gap from this entry's writing to her death on December 28, 1928, we never hear from Khin again and know no details surrounding her death and burial. But her parting words reinforce her fundamental connection to the Russian intellectual and cultural elite to whom she played host and with whom she mixed on a regular basis throughout her life.

* * * * *

Given her social role, Rashel' Mironovna Khin might be cast as Russia's salon Jewess. As a shorthand summary, the term serves well enough. Like Rahel Varnhagen, Dorothea von Courland, and others of eighteenth-century Berlin, Khin presided over a coterie of women and men, Jew and gentile, gathered simultaneously for a social and intellectual event. In both cases, wealthy, educated and cultivated Jewish women created an ambiance in their homes that lent itself to social mingling of an unprecedented type. The salons of Berlin that operated between 1780 and 1806 were part of a wider European phenomenon. Besides Berlin, important clusters of salons existed in Paris and London, as well as in the capital cities and provinces of the Russian Empire.[156]

On closer examination, however, the term "salon Jewess" does not adequately describe Khin. First, it is important to note that the Berlin salonières acted as mere hosts to their distinguished guests and did not themselves engage in writing the literature and philosophy that were topics of discussion at their gatherings. In contrast, Khin was a published author of two collections of short stories (one of which was reissued twice over) and a pair of plays seen on Moscow's prominent Malyi Theater stage. Even more significant differences are found in the behavior patterns of the Berlin salonières and Khin vis-à-vis Jewry. On account of high rates of intermarriage and conversion among salon Jewesses, Jewish historians have typically censured them and cast them as deserters of their faith.[157] Those who chose apostasy often did so in order to marry gentile suitors. Not Khin. In a strange twist of fate, she converted to dissolve her Jewish marriage, and then, to make matters more curious, married a Jew who converted to Christianity in order to marry her. For the couple, faith mattered little and had little to do with national ties. In the multinational Russian Empire, being Jewish did not necessarily mean observing Jewish ritual or subscribing to Jewish belief. Rather, it was an ethnic distinction conferred at birth—and though, according to Khin, it could never be obliterated altogether, even by apostasy (as in the case of her sister's conversion), good education and fine breeding could attenuate it to the point where integration into the highest echelons of Russian society was possible. As members of this elite corps, the couple grew increasingly concerned about beleagurered Jews in the last decade of the nineteenth century and began to rally on their behalf, even as Judeophilism permeated the ranks of the Russian intelligentsia in general.

Yet we might do well to question the stability of Khin's position among Russia's privileged class. If her fiction is reflective of reality, then the messages of both "The Misfit" and "The Dreamer" indicate that the social integration of Jews into intellectual and artistic circles was far from complete. The records of Khin's life indicate that she had a truly impressive network of friends and acquaintances. But readers of her memoirs cannot ignore the uneasy sensation that Khin's frequent naming of important Russian figures involved in her life was somehow an attempt to bolster her own significance in the Russian setting. Moreover, while her antipathy toward what she called "plebeian" Jews was characteristic of Westernized Jews—regarding them as invaders (like Gets in Solov'ev's story) or as aliens (like Auer)—their presence perhaps reminded Khin of her tenuous foothold in the Russian cultural and intellectual landscape.

Khin's life and literature provide an alternative model of accommodation to modernity on the part of a Jew in the Russian context. She definitely did not stoke the home fire with Jewish tradition, as is generally assumed of Eastern European Jewish women. But she also did not favor auto-emancipation, revolution, or defection from Russia itself—the better-known paths chosen by Russia's Jews. Instead, she persevered in her commitment to tolerance as espoused by the educated Russian society, which embraced her and which she embraced. Rashel' Mironovna Khin, a salon Jewess of sorts, struggled mightily between a love for Russia and a latent, but real and growing, identification with Jewry.

4

A Jewish Life Behind the Scenes

Feiga Izrailevna Kogan (1891–1974)

Russian Symbolism

Any critical attention that Feiga Kogan has received until recently is owing to her contributions to Russian rather than Jewish culture. The author of books of Symbolist verse and several textbooks on basic principles of meter and rhyme, her reputation is modest. She is known mostly among aficionados of her teacher Viacheslav Ivanovich Ivanov (1866–1949), a favorite theorist among second-generation Russian Symbolists who gathered at his famous salon known as the "Tower."

Symbolism is a rather approximate label to describe the movement that spread from France to Russia and from poetry to the other arts in the final decade of the nineteenth century. The name itself was not always used in the movement; the terms "Decadence" and the "new arts" also had currency. A school that originated in opposition to Naturalism and Realism, Symbolism sought to convey impressions by suggestion rather than by direct statement. Symbols, of course, have been used for millenia to unite the external sign with the thing it signifies. As generally interpreted by the practitioners of this movement, a symbol connoted a sign that needed to be deciphered and thus invited the participation of the reader or viewer to penetrate the mystery. At times, however, the Symbolists' views of the correspondence between what was below and what was on the surface were not terribly conducive to interpretation. This, coupled with a general defiance of traditional syntax, made Symbolist literature, occasionally, exceedingly obscure. At the same time, however, Symbolism's characteristic unconventionality made for brilliant phrasing, rhythm, and expressiveness of lyrics.

Russian Symbolism began to assert itself in 1892, a year after Kogan's birth.[1] Whereas the French were somewhat limited in their view of Symbolism, regarding it mostly as an approach to writing, some Russian Symbolists sought to make their art form into a whole philosophic system, a worldview that could encompass all thought and even become a way of life, equating the objective world with a façade that had to be overcome in order to obtain a higher reality. To them, Symbolism was somehow more real than the world perceived merely by the senses.

One of the chief exponents of such a view was Ivanov Ivanovich Viacheslav, who, along with Aleksandr Blok and Andrei Belyi, represented the leadership troika of the second wave of Russian Symbolism.[2] In contrast to members of the older generation, who wrote generally before the turn of the century and who are regarded as more decadent and more influenced by French Symbolism, members of the younger generation wrote in the first two decades of the twentieth century and are usually depicted as more idealistic and religious. Ivanov is representative of this trend. According to him, "Everywhere—I repeat this again and again—there is a Bethel and a Jacob's ladder," and he sought through his art to make such a ladder manifest in everyday existence.[3]

In his lecture, "The Precepts of Symbolism," delivered in March 1910, Ivanov articulated his fundamental beliefs.[4] He began by remarking on the impossibility of expressing oneself in an honest way and thus resorting to symbols as the only means for self-expression. Yet ironically, Ivanov proceeded to explain that *self*-expression must be limited to an elite corps of poets who were entrusted with this sacred act. He regarded Symbolism as a reminiscence of ancient religious practice, when the priests would interpret the secret world for the masses. For Ivanov, in twentieth-century Russia, Symbolism was a restoration of that religious language, and its practitioners were replacements for the priests of yore. Indeed, in early twentieth-century Russia, the poet was theurgist—in Ivanov's words—"a religious organizer of life, an interpreter and consolidator of the divine connection of that which exists." It followed, therefore, that the means by which a poet created art, namely Symbolism, could not be considered merely art. It was a way of life as well. This lesson Ivanov imparted to his students, among them the young Feiga Kogan, who came of age during the height of the Symbolist movement in Russia.

Unlike her teacher, Kogan was a Jew but a devout Symbolist all the same. She buried outward signs of her Jewish lineage beneath layers of christological allusions employed regularly by student and teacher alike; direct reference to her background and themes relating to Jewish life and tradition do not appear in her published writings. Consequently, biographers and critics have paid scant attention to her Jewish background and how things Jewish may have influenced her, despite the fact that her unmistakably Jewish name is affixed to all her writings.[5] While Feiga is a common Yiddish name, Kogan—the English equivalent of which is Cohen—is like a clarion call announcing Jewish ancestry. Nevertheless, Kogan has staked out no place as yet in the cultural history of Jewry in late Imperial Russia.[6] This chapter, chronicling her life and literary contributions, comes to amend the record.

The rich contents of Kogan's archives—consisting of autobiographies, an autobibliography, manuscripts of her published and unpublished verse and prose, a volume of unpublished and reinterpreted Bible stories, reminiscences of acquaintances, translations of Hebrew texts into Russian, and miscellaneous correspondence, including several letters even to Joseph Stalin—reveal that Kogan was involved simultaneously in both the cultural life of Russian Jewry at the beginning of the twentieth century and the second wave of Symbolist literary activity in the Russian language.[7] Specifically and dramatically, she transformed her childhood interest in the Hebrew language into a vocation as she toiled, literally, behind the scenes to bring Jewish theater to life in the Russian Empire. Kogan was a founding member of Habimah, the first Hebrew theater in the world and the forerunner to the National Theater of Israel. She played an off-stage role assisting actors in correct pronunciation of their Hebrew lines. At the same time, she labored to bring Hebrew writings, including the folklore of the Rabbis of the Talmud and the biblical book of Psalms to Russian readers through her imaginative interpretations and fastidious translations. Her abiding love of Hebrew led her to lasting relationships with figures active in the language's revival movement including Uri Nissim Gnessin, the author responsible for introducing a psychologically-oriented prose style into Hebrew literature, and Elisheva (Elizaveta Zhirkova Bikhovskii), the non-Jewish Hebrew poet referred to as "Ruth from the banks of the Volga."

The historical context surrounding Kogan's life raises the larger question of how Jews who wrote in Russian were classified, and classified themselves, in the earliest decades of twentieth-century Russia. Should we, for instance, consider Kogan a "Russian writer" or a "Jewish writer"? To what extent did her ethnic background inform her writings? Feiga Kogan's life and literary output will be resurrected and explored not only to show how she concealed her Jewish identity behind a Russian front but to consider why she felt it necessary to do so.

* * * * *

Regrettably, historians must resort to scattered, selective, and faded memories to trace the trajectory of Feiga Izrailevna Kogan's life. At seventy-eight, she undertook the task of writing what she called an autobiography.[8] The hand-written account is at times alive with vivid descriptions of her experiences but at others woefully weak in detail. Given the genre, of course, the text is hampered by its retroactive perspective; Kogan penned it over a half-century after the related events. To fill out the historical record, then, one must study as well her published and unpublished writings. Yet they offer little by way of biography, for Kogan's major literary interest was Russian Symbolism, a trend that eschewed realism and revealed little about its authors. Nevertheless, where possible, personal details have been squeezed out of her literary oeuvre. The analytical overview that follows is thus culled from a variety of sources, including the aforementioned, along with Kogan's correspondence and secondary references to her.

A Poet is Born

On August 7, 1891 Khasi Eselevna and Izrail Simonovich Kogan welcomed their daughter Feiga into a Jewish community in shock. Months before, the Tsar had issued an expulsion order for Jews residing illegally in the capital city. Of the fifteen thousand Jews forced to leave, many had lived in Moscow for several decades or were even born there. They were granted a period of three months to a year to dispose of their property and many were compelled to sell out to their neighbors at derisory prices. For some unknown reason, the Kogan family remained among Moscow's 8,000 Jews in a general population of one million.

As the Jewish population of her hometown shrank, young Kogan thought herself destined to participate in Moscow's outburst of literary

Feiga Izrailevna Kogan (left) and her sister Ita (1909)
From the collection of the Russian State Archive of Literature and Art, Moscow

productivity. "I began to read by the age of five," she maintained, "but poetry composed itself within me even earlier." She continued: "[The verses] somehow came to me by themselves, and it was as though I heard them within me."[9] These opening lines from Kogan's autobiography signify more than precociousness on the part of their author. As an adult looking back at herself as a young girl, Kogan is indicating here her early self-awareness as a poet, a consciousness that developed, she claimed, even as a toddler. It was as if a poetic soul took hold of the youngster's body, making itself felt before the child acquired the linguistic skills to articulate the innate but inchoate sensations.

It is important to note that, to some, Kogan's notion of child-poet is incontrovertible. Take, for instance, Kornei Chukovskii, the author whose name is virtually synonymous in Russia with children's literature. He set out to discover and formulate the whimsical and elusive laws of how children think, and in his popular *Ot dvukh do piati* (From Two to Five), he argued that all children are natural poets. In his words:

> It seems to me that beginning with the age of two, every child becomes for a short period of time a living genius. Later, beginning with the age of five to six, this talent begins to fade. There is no trace left in the eight-year-old of this creativity with words, since the need for it has passed; by this age the child has already fully mastered the basic principles of his native language. If his former talent for word invention and construction had not abandoned him, he would, even by the age of ten, eclipse any of us with his suppleness and brilliance at speech.[10]

Unlike most, Kogan's poetic consciousness did not dissipate by age ten. Rather, her childhood—which she characterized as "an enormous black hole in the heavens" (she was a sickly child frequently under the supervision of a nanny)—was considerably enhanced by words and their magical power that enabled her to transcend her reality.

As might be expected, Kogan was a good student and thrived at a local municipal grammar school in Moscow. "I can still recall now," she reminisced in her late seventies, "the pleasant faces of our teachers and the sounds of the words of the splendid Russian language."[11] Though numbers were not her strong suit, with the help of her only sister Ita, who was four years her senior, Kogan passed the requisite mathematics exam and was admitted to one of the thirty-five Marinskii girls' gymnasia in existence at the beginning of the twentieth century.[12] Established by Empress Maria, the school catered mostly to the children of the gentry and bourgeoisie who paid yearly tuition so that their daughters could participate in a seven-year course of instruction that included religious teaching and preparation for housework, along with classes in Russian language and history, math, geography, natural science, calligraphy, singing, and needlework.[13]

Of modest means, Kogan's parents presumably struggled financially in order to send their offspring to such an institution.[14] From her autobiography, we know that her father was a furrier who owned a shop where he peddled fabric and fur remnants. Kogan's mother helped her husband with his business and managed their humble dwelling, a three-room apartment that housed two female boarders in addition to the family of four. In 1902, tragedy struck when a thief stole ninety rubles from the store. The shock and trauma of the robbery riled Kogan's father so that he took sick and died a year later. In a desperate move, Kogan's mother instructed her daughters to abandon their gymnasium training and become seamstresses. Stunned, they flatly refused, and Kogan managed to remain at gymnasium by virtue of the generosity of a German teacher. Her sister Ita picked up odd tutoring jobs that enabled her to fund her own education.

As two of approximately twenty Jews at the First Marinskii Girls' Gymnasium in Moscow, Kogan and her sister were exempt from the usual course on "God's law" (*zakona bozh'ego*) but forced to attend common prayers, an experience Kogan found altogether humiliating. Additionally, the school administration required its Jewish students to prepare for an examination on Jewish history using Simon Dubnov's text and administered by Yakov Isaevich Maze, the government-appointed community rabbi of Moscow from 1893.[15] Among other achievements, Maze participated in the famed Beilis trial and contributed to the important Hebrew publication *Ha-melitz* (The Advocate).[16]

In addition to the Jewish past, Kogan was well aware of the pogroms being staged against her people in the present, as well as the general political chaos blighting the Russian landscape. She recalled with fright the bellowing of the custodian in her apartment building one late autumn evening, crying: "Tonight you Jews will be killed."[17] Transported that night to a safe refuge, she heard in the morning that there had been a riot of workers and students. The year was 1905, and Kogan also participated in so-called "gymnasium riots," a none too politicized activity that amounted essentially to distributing subversive pamphlets and singing revolutionary anthems with verve. In Kogan's words, the chief peril facing her in those revolutionary days was the constant threat of expulsion from school, a fate she managed to dodge, graduating on May 3, 1908.[18] It was not until seven years later that she landed in a St. Petersburg police station on account, undoubtedly, of revolutionary activities.[19]

Upon graduation from gymnasium, Kogan felt ashamed of her ignorance and devised a program of independent study. Each day the seventeen-year-old would turn up at the *Rumiantsevskii* Hall (the forerunner to the Lenin Library) to devour books and articles on a range of subjects including physics and literature, philosophy and astronomy. Eternally attracted to the written word, Kogan built up a large storehouse of knowledge from her self-described "free lessons," while simultaneously turning out poems that would be published in 1912 in an anthology entitled *Moia dusha* (My Soul).[20]

While a student at gymnasium, Kogan had tried her hand at poetry but, judging them saccharine, apparently destroyed the early attempts. No poems from that era remain for contemporary readers to evaluate for themselves. Yet written memories do reveal the extensive influences upon the inexperienced poet: "I howled from happiness on account of Pushkin" and later "died over the new sounds . . ." of the Symbolists.[21] Maintaining an "affinity for Dostoevsky," Kogan claimed to have come "formally under the influence of Blok and internally under the influence of Tiutchev" (1803–1873), attempting to combine the lyricism of the former with the mysticism of the latter.[22]

This fusion of lyricism and mysticism is apparent to the reader of the fifty-eight poems contained in *My Soul*. Written between 1908 and 1912, Kogan's poetry sings with, what one critic called, "reverential pantheism."[23] Inspired by the exquisite landscape of Tula, to where she retired many a summer, Kogan claimed during that time to have written poetry "on every scrap of [available] paper."[24] "Molitva" (Prayer), for instance, is an ironic hymn of praise to the season autumn, which is responsible for bringing on inevitable death, but which closes the circle of life. Kogan's youthfulness and inexperience are much in evidence in this collection. As the poet herself said in retrospect of the book: "[It] was feeble and juvenile, but the text gave a vague promise of potential . . .."[25] Kogan was, after all, only twenty-one when the book appeared and as young as seventeen when she penned the earliest compositions in the volume. Yet, the awkwardness is coupled with a heartfelt sincerity fueled in part by her innocence.

While dozens of the poems contained in *My Soul* may attract the attention of literary critics, two deserve the full attention of the Jewish historian. The knowledgeable reader will be struck by the poet's allusions to Jewish tradition and her ambivalence toward the same. Kogan composed the first, titled "Prorok" (Prophet), in 1910.[26] While its five stanzas are arranged in an uncomplicated ABAB rhyme scheme, its underlying message is anything but simple.

Break the holy tablets,
Go away, where God is eternal!
They will not understand your sadness
and your anguish, Prophet! . . [the ellipsis appears in the original]

What are you searching for in a foreign land?
The time has not come.
The mournful voice of the Prophet
did not yet sound here.

A crowd of years—thousands of them—passed
before the sound of feasts and battles—
and they are like the old, the slaves and the children,
the ecstasy of prayer is alien to them.

Leave them alone with their illusionary happiness,
with their illusionary peace:
You will be unable to disturb the earthly passions
with your immortal sadness.

Break the holy tablets,
Go away, where God is eternal!
They will not understand your sadness
and your anguish, Prophet! . . [the ellipsis appears in the original]

Kogan's poem is unremarkable in its overarching message: human beings are given to their earthly, mundane matters and so fail to heed the call of the visionary. The speaker of the poem instructs the prophet to look elsewhere for an audience receptive to his message. She chastises him for coming, in vain, before the appointed time. Presently, the poet suggests, the inhabitants' complacency prevents them from hearing the prophet's mournful cry. Of course, in the Russian Empire of 1910, this poem could easily have been read as a political wake-up call to Russians failing to unite with revolutionaries. Perhaps Kogan was joining other Symbolists like Aleksandr Blok, who over time turned away from a dreamy, backward-looking romanticism toward the bitter and painful reality of modern life.[27] Accept the new order, the poet seems to cry.

In the second and third stanzas, Kogan introduces a unique subtheme, which is particularly resonant for Jewish readers. Though they are directed at the prophet alone, her words suggest alienation from Russian society: "What are you searching for in a foreign land?" she asks. Already by 1910, a sizable proportion of the Jewish population of Russia had immigrated to the United States to lay down roots in the proverbial *goldene medine* (golden land) and begin the climb toward upward mobility. Pogroms rocking Russia in 1903–05 only hastened their departure. At the same time, a much smaller percentage of Jewry was heading to the Promised Land of their Bible to create a political state of Jews. While Kogan joined neither group, she surely knew of these developments and, as well, of the nearly age-old notion that the Jews' lot is one of perpetual wandering and exile. Especially given the blatant nod to the Hebrew Bible suggested by the poem's title and central character, Kogan may have been directing her words to a Jewish audience. If so, the message must be interpreted anew as a warning to her coreligionists to abandon their smug optimism for the realism represented by the bloodshed against Russian Jewry over the past several years. Perhaps Kogan, too, was beginning to doubt that a Jew could find salvation in Russia. While only implied in "The Prophet," a poem buried in her archives and never published suggests an unmistakable estrangement from Russian society.

In "Adonai" (Hebrew for "my lord"), which she wrote in Russian, Kogan reveals her hidden desire to flee the land of her birth for the more comfortable land of her ancestors.[28] The poem, composed in a rhythmical prose that attempts to replicate that of the Bible, is among Kogan's most stirring. The poet first introduces the central character, who, paralyzed by her feeble condition, is incapable of extricating her ailing body from the very place causing her degeneration:

> If my days were like a deep light
> that is pouring over the fields of the South
> and my hands were like strong flowers growing under the sun
> and my legs were strong and powerful
> in order to bear my body throughout the day and night,
> I would walk one thousand days to the shore of the sea
> And I would divide its waves with my hands
> to touch the dust of my land.
>
> Instead my hands are like greenhouse flowers
> and my legs are weak and shackled
> to the pavement of the city.

It is as if the protagonist herself is the "greenhouse flower," artificially growing in an unnatural environment. Denying her roots, planted as she is in an infertile soil, she is an outcast and an alien who has come to speak a foreign language.

> The pale sky of the North is over my head
> And the tongue of the North has long become the tongue of my
>   songs.

The poem closes with two dialogues: one between the protagonist and the strangers about her, the other between the protagonist and her God.

> And the people of the North are walking about
> and look at me with their cold eyes [saying]:
>
> What can you do, sick child,
> having no fatherland, but having only the great books of your
>   people?

O, I can make my life simple and beautiful
and my days serene and kind, and my song pleasing to God.

And I also can *secretly* love the wind [emphasis added]
that I hear blowing from the mountains of Lebanon.
and the fire which is pouring through my eyelids
straight into my heart.

How many days, *Adonai*, will pass
like slow waves through the sands and mists
before I meet You?

And how many of Your children will pass
under the slow sun of the North
before the green waves of the forests on
the mountains of Lebanon will be covered in mist?

"Adonai" gives voice to Kogan's private sense of exile and longing to return to her God. The hope remained hidden from Kogan's reading audience, however, for in no published work was the poet as explicit as in this one that did not see the light of day. Her book *My Soul*, with its misleading title, did not reveal the inner religious musings of its young author. If Kogan's poetry was a vehicle for working out her identity issues, she kept the products of her labor to herself.[29]

"Adonai" also shows signs of Kogan's high level of Jewish literacy, which is confirmed by excavating the contents of her archives. Her papers testify that Kogan's knowledge of things Jewish was rich; her attachment to the Jewish people was deep. Born of two Jewish parents, she was raised in an observant home. Kogan's mother, Khasi Eselevna, was from an old Hasidic family, and she maintained the customs and practices of Jewish tradition in her own household. Kogan recalled how she, her parents, and her sister would observe all the Jewish holidays. Her mother, she claimed, would each year "swoon from exhaustion" after cleaning and preparing for Passover.[30] From early on, Kogan was involved in communal Jewish life as well, for her father was as she described it "head of the Moscow Synagogue."[31] Proud of his position, Kogan would often, as a child, accompany him to worship services, and he would lead her by the hand into the men's section where, she boasted, "everyone enjoyed me."[32]

The central aspect of Kogan's Jewish identity was, however, her interest in the Hebrew language. A series of rabbis' wives tutored her and her elder sister in her people's ancient tongue, albeit in an unsystematic way. Learning by rote as she did, Kogan envied Jewish boys who, from her perspective, "studied as they ought to have. Soon they could not only read, but also understand and speak [Hebrew]. They regard us 'maidens' [her quote] with scorn."[33] Despite her inadequate education, Kogan grew attached to the "gentle and immutable" sounds of the language. She would prance about her apartment as a young girl, yodeling little ditties in Hebrew to her heart's content. The words were, for her, "a large part of childhood," and ignited within her a love for language in general. As she told it, her adoration of Hebrew motivated her to "worship the richness of Russian."[34]

To a limited degree, Kogan incorporated the two languages of her youth into a single work that appears in *My Soul*.[35] "Na Kreste" (On the Cross) is a two-stanza poem composed in Russian with the exception of the opening verse of each stanza, which is in Aramaic, the language of the Talmud and the vernacular among Jews living in the time of Jesus. As the title suggests, "On the Cross" is laden with christological imagery, and, in fact, even the Aramaic components of the poem are excerpted from the New Testament. The Christian Bible contains Aramaic words and phrases, which the disciples heard from Jesus and took care to remember and record. One such example, found both in Matthew 27:46 and Mark 15:34, is "Eli, eli, lamah sabaḥtani?" (My lord, my lord, why do you forsake me?).[36] Kogan selected this as the centerpiece and theme of her poem "On the Cross." As in the New Testament, she, too, retained the original language; a Russian translation appears only in a footnote. "On the Cross" expresses the dying words of a disinherited man, pleading with his god for salvation.

> *Eli, eli, lamah sabaḥtani!*
> I die on the Lord's day . . . [ellipsis in the original]
> The radiant shadow has fallen over me
> in the distant fog.
>
> *Eli, eli, lamah sabaḥtani!*
> O hear miserable Me!
> How I die unanswered
> on the deserted, sorrowful ocean.

The poem represents a strange fusion of Christian and Jewish voices. It is as if the former is perceived through the latter: the Jewish poet gives voice to personal despair through the voice of Jesus, himself a Jew. To use the Russian expression, Kogan here "sits between two chairs," on the very edges of Christianity and Judaism. Like the good Symbolist that she is, Kogan searches Christian texts for symbols that convey more than their literal meaning, choosing an Aramaic passage from the New Testament to do her bidding.

Kogan's Growing Attachment to Hebrew

By 1916, Kogan enrolled in a two-year course of Hebrew study offered by the Society for Lovers of the Hebrew Language (*hovevei sefat ever*), an organization established in 1907 by, among others, her former gymnasium teacher Yakov Maze.[37] Devoted to developing and disseminating literature, as well as teaching the rudiments of the language, the Society supervised forty chapters throughout the Russian Empire by 1911. The class offered in Moscow furnished Kogan with the ideal opportunity for improving her Hebraic skills. She joined other students in resurrecting the ancient tongue, a trend that had gained momentum since the 1880s among those wishing to create a Jewish national spirit and movement.

The classes provided Kogan with more than an education. Through them she became acquainted with individuals who would, in direct and indirect ways, shape the course of her life. She struck up a friendship with a classmate, Elizabeta Ivanova Zhirkova (1888–1949), a non-Jew with a strong yearning to learn Hebrew, whose extraordinary linguistic skills, according to Kogan, made her a quick study.[38] Upon her mother's death when she was three years old, Zhirkova was sent to Moscow to be educated under the supervision of an aunt from England. A girlhood friend, the daughter of a pious philanthropist named Raskin, introduced Zhirkova to Judaism and its languages. At a young age, she learned Yiddish and acquired a spiritual connection to Jews. Like Kogan a devotee of the Symbolist movement, Zhirkova began to publish verse in Russian at the age of twenty-one and published an article years later on Aleksandr Blok.[39] Her efforts in Jewish languages started with Russian translations of works by S.Y. Imber as well as Hayim Nahman Bialik's rendering of Yehudah Halevi's "Tzion halo tishali," a popular expression of longing for a return to the Land of Israel read on the ninth of Av, a day of mourning on the Jewish calendar. In 1925, Zhirkova actualized a personal longing when she moved to Palestine with her husband Simon Bikhovskii, whom she married in 1920. A year after her marriage, her original poetry in Hebrew first appeared, along with critical articles, in publications such as *Ha-tekufah* and *Ha-po'el ha-tza'ir*.[40]

Elisheva, as Zhirkova came to call herself, regarded the world of Hebrew as her own. Though she claimed to have two souls within her— "one Russian, the other Hebrew," by 1919 the latter came to dominate and demand, as she put it, that she compose solely in that language.[41] Only months later, she admitted that her love of Hebrew had grown to encompass the whole of Judaism: "I am a Jew in my heart and soul," she wrote in October 1919.[42] Kogan noted the obvious parallels between the lives of Zhirkova and the biblical Ruth—a Midianite woman who married an Israelite and then cast her lot with her husband's people—in a review of her friend's work published in *Khronika evreiskoi zhizni* (Chronicle of Jewish Life).[43] She praised Zhirkova's short book, a song about distant Zion, for "its indubitable candor" expressing "a dream of blending with strangers who are familiar in spirit."

Zhirkova and Kogan were obviously kindred spirits. As expressed in "Adonai," Kogan, too, was suffering from alienation, though of a different sort. While Zhirkova felt estranged from her roots, Kogan was being drawn to hers and thus alienated from the Russian society around her. Their love of Hebrew brought them and bound them together for years, despite even geographic separation. Following Zhirkova's move to Palestine, the two corresponded in Hebrew. Although their letters are not extant, Kogan maintained that they wrote regularly, exchanging poetry and thoughts on their mutual interest in the ancient tongue.[44] Among Kogan's papers, for instance, lies Zhirkova's translation of Halevi's "Tzion halo tishali."[45] The friendship kindled during their school days at the Society for the Lovers of the Hebrew Language proved mutually beneficial.

The same course was responsible as well for bringing Kogan into contact with a man who would have a decisive influence not only on her but on Jewish culture in general during the second two decades of the twentieth century. Kogan's teacher was none other than Menahem Gnessin (1882–1952), who was identified in those days simply as the younger brother of the Hebrew author Uri Nissim Gnessin (1881–1913). Within a decade, however, Menahem would gain prominence in his own right as an actor and pioneer of the Hebrew theater. Originally from Starodub, Ukraine, in 1903 he followed his brother to Palestine, where he remained for approximately a decade. Returning to Moscow in 1912, he began to teach for the Society for the Lovers of the Hebrew Language.

In 1916, when she began the Society's course of study, Kogan immediately gravitated toward Gnessin, whom she admired for his "noble Sephardic pronunciation of the [Hebrew] words."[46] Like most involved in the revival of the ancient tongue, teacher and student preferred the latter to the Ashkenazic pronunciation, which sounded similar to the Yiddish they were seeking to render obsolete. Kogan fondly remembered Gnessin's inspiring lessons, after which students would take to the streets of Moscow practicing their conversational skills. When quizzical onlookers asked in amazement what language they were speaking, the students, according to Kogan, responded: "Why in noble and beautiful Hebrew."[47]

A Jewish Life Behind the Scenes

Both teacher and student were among a group who maintained that the theater was the most effective vehicle for drawing attention to Hebrew. Created when all the Western nations had long-established theatrical traditions, the Hebrew stage was intended first of all to be the chief instrument of the Jewish cultural renaissance. For obvious reasons, theater could, like none of the other arts, revive the ancient tongue in a way that simultaneously validated it as a living language. It thus became a powerful weapon in the fight to establish Hebrew as the Jewish community's vernacular. The hope was that the theater's significance would reach far beyond the purely artistic.[48] To do so, of course, it was necessary to win over large audiences of Jews. Needless to say, only a tiny minority of Jews in Russia—and worldwide for that matter—understood spoken Hebrew at the time. It is indeed remarkable, then, that despite the lack of a ready-made audience, the Hebrew theater emerged and flowered in the Russian Empire. In this instance, the stage was not necessarily reflecting life, but creating it.

The Hebrew theater of Russia was partially an import from Palestine. The secondary schools of Palestine, where children were being exposed daily to the sounds of their people's ancient tongue, became the first testing ground for Hebrew drama. During the last decades of the nineteenth century, plays by literary greats of the Hebrew renaissance were making their way onto the schools' stages. The first such performance in Hebrew was ironically a translation from the Yiddish of Moses Leib Lilienblum's *Zerubavel*.[49] Creators of the Hebrew theater—like their counterparts in other Hebrew genres—regarded Yiddish as an embodiment of the spirit of the ghetto and thus felt little urge to draw upon its theater, which had been established in 1876.[50] The Hebrew plays met with success; audiences came not so much to see the productions staged by the children as to hear the sounds of the ancient tongue. In 1905, adults literally took the lead in Jaffa when Menahem Gnessin launched the Amateur Dramatic Arts Company, an organization devoted to the production of plays in Hebrew.[51] He played the title role in *Uriel Acosta*, the company's first production and a recent favorite among Yiddish theater-goers across Europe.[52] In 1912, Gnessin went abroad for theatrical training, and the company disbanded when the Turkish High Command took over Jaffa and banished Jews from the town.

Once in the Russian Empire, Gnessin met his match in Nahum Zemah (1887–1939), who since his late teens had recognized the importance of theater in reviving Hebrew. As a Hebrew tutor to youth, he spent his leisure time organizing and directing the local children in plays in the language. His zeal only intensified as an adult, and in 1912, at the age of twenty-five, he organized a Hebrew-speaking group of actor-amateurs in Bialystok. Newly-arrived to this center of Jewish cultural life in Byelorus, Gnessin joined Zemah and the other actors in 1913 when the troupe performed a drama by Osip Dymov (pseudonym of Joseph Perelman, 1878–1959) at the logical venue of the eleventh Zionist Congress in Vienna. Although well received, the show generated no income. World War I then halted the troupe's efforts altogether, though many of the actors reassembled in Moscow in 1917—Gnessin among them—to form a company they called *Habimah* (the stage) under the leadership of Zemah.

Zemah was not only the founder and theatrical director of Habimah but its chief visionary and primary recruiter. He persuaded Hannah Rovinah to abandon her kindergarten-teaching job in Saratov for the Hebrew theater of Moscow and Shoshanah Avivit to strive for a more professional stage than the one she was appearing on in Odessa. The latter recalled how Zemah appeared unannounced at her home, paraphrasing Ezekiel 37 as he expressed his desire to "draw the future nearer, . . . to return to life the dry bones of [my] people on the boards of the stage." For her part, Avivit could only wonder, "Is he serious or is he trying to amuse me?" Zemah continued, as if in a trance: "[Habimah] will appear in all countries, before all nations. We will sail the seven seas."[53] Indeed, Zemah's vision was not far from reality. Founded in the midst of the Russian Revolution, it brought revolutionary changes to Jewish culture. As the first professional Hebrew theater in the world, it came to project the Hebrew stage as a vital, continuous entity for the Jewish people and formed the nucleus of the National Hebrew Theater, a title it earned in 1958, after settling in Palestine in 1933.

As previously mentioned, Kogan played an off-stage role in Habimah's development, coaching actors in the correct pronunciation of their lines.[54] Those unfamiliar with Hebrew received scripts transliterated into the Cyrillic alphabet. It then fell to Kogan to familiarize them with the fine nuances of articulating Hebrew so as to sound authentic. Among her students were Shoshanah Avivit and Miriam Elias. Presumably she owed a debt of gratitude to her former teacher Gnessin not only for enabling her to guide her pupils in reciting their lines using correct Sephardic pronunciation but for introducing her to Hebrew theater in the first place.

When Kogan met Gnessin in 1916, she had already been nurturing a love of theater for eight years, since her graduation from gymnasium.[55] Told by others that she had a "very beautiful voice," she enrolled in courses offered at the State Institute of Declamation (later known as the State Institute of the Word) in 1911–12, where she engaged in exercises in rhetoric and elocution.[56] Drawn both to the theater and to the Hebrew language, it was only natural that Kogan should become involved in Habimah. Combining the two interests, she used her training in both to train others. While Kogan never appeared in front of the curtain, she did participate with the rest of the company in acting lessons provided by Evgeniia Vakhtangov, the student of the celebrated theater director Konstantin Stanislavskii (1863–1938).

Stanislavskii, who was responsible for single-handedly laying the foundation of modern theater in Russia, exerted a profound and personal influence on Habimah. His interest in the fledgling company derived from the pan-European fascination with exotic and enigmatic cultures.[57] An interest in the Orient had arisen in Europe in the late 1870s and had influenced different cultural trends at the turn of the century, including the composer Gustav Mahler (1860–1911) and the artists Henri Matisse

(1869–1954) and Paul Gaugin (1848–1954). According to Stanislavskii, Russia's Habimah could provide a springboard for new theatrical experiments. Meanwhile, Zemah adopted Stanislavskii's famous method, in which the actor was urged to merge with the role. In 1898, when Stanislavskii founded the Moscow Art Academic Theater to put his method into play, two studios were affiliated with it: the Chekhov Studio and the Armenian Group. Habimah was later added as a third. Despite his ignorance of Hebrew, Stanislavskii was regularly involved with Habimah, instructing its actors and giving them his (gentile) disciples to serve as directors of their productions.

On October 8, 1918 the great director attended Habimah's first public performance, four one-act plays by Jewish writers. Faces on and off stage that evening formed a panoply of important figures in Kogan's life. Rabbi Yakov Maze of Moscow, her former history instructor, delivered a short blessing before the curtain was raised. Menahem Gnessin, her former Hebrew teacher, starred in the leading male role. And the understudy Shoshanah Avivit, her current pupil, sat in the wings ready to rush on stage should the leading lady, Hannah Rovinah, fall ill. Kogan was enthralled with the production, claiming years later to have never seen a finer ensemble of actors.[58]

Kogan's enthusiasm for the troupe and its goals would never wane. Her glowing review of *The Dybbuk,* the play that established Habimah's reputation, appeared in *Evreiskii vestnik* (Jewish Herald).[59] Additionally, as her papers reveal, she spent years clipping articles from newspapers and journals relating to the company's activities.[60]

From historical documents we might even conclude that she was instrumental in insuring the theater's financial solvency by encouraging her teacher Viacheslav Ivanov to fight in Habimah's behalf with the *Evsektsiia,* the Jewish section of the Communist party. Faced with the fact that millions of Jews speaking their own language and maintaining their own social institutions existed in Russia, the Communists created the *Evsektsiia* as a temporary agency to deal with them until such time as they assimilated among their neighbors. The *Evsektsiia* was modeled on the national sections that were then being established to direct party work among other non-Russian peoples. Voicing his resistance to Habimah, the Commissar of the *Evsektsiia* Simon Dimanstein (1886–1937) described it as "an enterprise needed by no one except a handful of nationalistic bourgeoisie who want forcibly to bring a dead language back to life, bring the Jewish people back to religious superstitions, separate them from the masses, and prevent their class progress."[61]

Following Dimanstein's lead, the government threatened in 1922 to withhold a subsidy from Habimah. So Viacheslav Ivanov stepped into the fold to defend the theater, engaging in a battle of words with the *Evsekt-siia's* head.[62] Ivanonv himself had long been involved in Russian theater by this time. In keeping with his theory of art, he promoted a theater of mystery in which the spectator would be transformed into a participant in a religious rite, achieving the mystical communion in which Ivanov saw the highest goal of art.[63] For him, all barriers between actor and spectator ought to be abolished. That Ivanov became a vocal proponent of Habimah may indeed have had something to do with his association with Feiga Kogan. As her hand-written notes indicate, Ivanov instructed Kogan in poetry classes from late February to early August of 1920 under the auspices of the Moscow State Institute of Declamation.[64] Additionally, at Kogan's initiative, the Institute organized a poetry circle under the leadership of Ivanov.[65] It appears likely that Kogan played a role in her instructor's intervention in behalf of her beloved Habimah.[66]

While Kogan maintained strong ties to Ivanov over the next decade, her direct involvement with Habimah terminated within years of its origination. As she described it, a "serious nervous disorder" forced her to leave the troupe.[67] This single, laconic reference to illness is explained nowhere among Kogan's papers. Like other ambitious Jewish literary women of her generation, perhaps she, too, succumbed to mental stress brought on by the unconventional course of her life, in traditional Jewish terms. Nearly thirty, she was unmarried and childless, and would remain so throughout her lifetime. Moreover, the fruits of her literary talents did not fit neatly into any of the cultural molds gelling among Russian Jewry in the second decade of the twentieth century. Those involved in the Jewish cultural renaissance may have taken notice of her writings if they had but known of their existence. They were, of course, unlikely to search the books of a Symbolist poet—Jewish or not—for inspiring national sentiment. And Kogan kept concealed from the public eye her poems directly relating to Jewish themes, as well as a collection of stories based on Jewish sources that she worked on assiduously during this period.[68]

Beneath the Surface is a Jew

On the ninety pages of a small notebook, scribbled in Kogan's longhand are fifteen stories that are short retellings of lengthy narratives contained in the first two books of the Hebrew Bible. Extending from Adam and Eve to Moses, Kogan's interpretations are based on *Sefer ha-aggadah* (The Book of Legends), a massive compendium of Rabbinic legend and lore that had appeared in Odessa only five years earlier.[69] The latter was more than just a collection of charming Jewish stories and sayings; it was a monumental and successful attempt on the part of creators of modern Jewish culture to assimilate and appropriate their classical heritage.[70] Two leading representatives of the Hebrew renaissance in Russia were responsible for its compilation: Hayim Nahman Bialik (1873–1934), already recognized as the national poet of the Jewish people, and Yehoshua Hana Ravnitsky (1859–1944), editor, journalist and co-founder with Bialik of the prestigious Hebrew publishing house Dvir. The two had chosen this project and this material to spearhead the revival of a Hebrew national ethos for their contemporaries. Kogan relied on a Russian translation of *Sefer ha-aggadah* by the poet Shimon Shmuel Frug (1860–1916), who is known as the first to incorporate Jewish themes into Russian verse.

Kogan geared her Bible stories toward youth. After teaching Hebrew extensively for many years, she wanted to "make certain that these stories would excite and move children." The volume was intended for publication in 1917, but it never saw the light of day. If it had, though it might have been useful in familiarizing children with the Bible, it would have done nothing to improve their Hebraic skills. For it was written in Russian. Either Kogan did not at the time have the requisite experience in Hebrew to compose in the language or she felt her intended audience did not have the requisite experience to read in Hebrew. Whatever the case, the collection was useful in its own way. Seeking to join what she called, "unconnected entities"—"the stern style" of the Bible with the "vitality" of the *aggadah*—she successfully blended the two into readable, rhymed prose that read well aloud. In fact, Kogan demonstrated as much when she recited selections of her tales, informally, before a short story circle and, formally, at the department of short stories at the State Institute of the Word.

Throughout her twenties and early thirties, Kogan supplemented her education by taking courses, as well as by joining literary circles and theater groups where she honed her skills and plied the wares of her labors. As described, she was a student at the State Institute of Declamation and by 1920 was enrolled at the State Institute of the Word. All the while, she busied herself with her verse. Of the hundreds of poems stored in her archive, only a minority appeared in print. Characteristically, those she shared with the public in her volume of poetry published in 1923 were ethnically neutral, nary a trace of Jewish content among them. Kogan's *Plamennik* (The Torch), a sixty-page volume of twenty-seven poems, is a case in point.[71] The renowned Russian Symbolist Valerii Briusov credited the poet with possessing a certain level of technical proficiency and found her poetic stylizations of Russian folk sayings and children's songs rather appealing.[72] Kogan, in contrast, described the book as carelessly published and consequently unsuccessful.[73]

The contents of two poems in *The Torch* bear directly on the question of Kogan's concealed identity and beliefs. As its title suggests, "Bogu" (To God) is one such poem. The earliest sample of the collection, "To God" was penned in 1914 when Kogan was twenty-three years of age. In it, she connects the idea of God with love in a way reminiscent of the Song of Songs. Like the ancient biblical book, she characterizes the divine as her beloved, speaking intimately to God in language ordinarily reserved for lovers.

You laugh magically with me,
You flow in the depths of my being,
You rise like a momentary wave in me, without ebbing.

I am not able to express even in a wondrous song
how, in Your deepest night,
I am drawn in by Your unknowable darkness,
I mark my days [by You].

But behind the darkness, protected by love,
everything is treasured and cherished,
You listen with a smile, Beloved, to
how I'm speechless here.

Though evocative of an attachment to her God, the poem offers no hint of the specifics of Kogan's theology. Perhaps what is manifest is Ivanov's influence over the young poet. "To God" may well be an imitation of the elder's "Eros," a poetic synthesis of religion and sensuality that appeared in 1907 and was undoubtedly known to the composer of these verses.[74]

Kogan sounded a unique voice in the pages of the The *Torch* as well. The penultimate poem in the collection—untitled and without date—is notable for both its form and content.[75] When read aloud in its original, the simple AABB rhyme scheme of its six stanzas becomes a melody that accompanies a popular Russian folk dance known as the *chastushka*, which emerged in the nineteenth century.[76] The poem's sprightly presentation stands in contrast to its solemn message. It begins:

> I am God's orphan
> I open the gates
> with a small key—a small lock
> with a silken handkerchief.

Here the poet plays with the reader, offering a riddle of sorts. The handkerchief is, of course, a symbol for the tears of this orphan, whose inferiority is depicted in the stanzas that follow.

> People drive me away,
> and I hide myself
> near the fence.
> I will become inconspicuous
> like a small, gray beetle
> or like a dirty mouse.

> The heavens will glance in the morning
> with its quiet beam,
> it will reach into the depths [of a small mouse hole]
> and I will stand on this blue beam
> and take out the key of tears.

The reader is left to wonder which lock the key will open. And the poem's end provides an answer: the gates of heaven.

And I will ask Christ
to stay with me at least for a day
in the white chill,
in the pigeon's cold.

And Christ will say kindly:
"You have poured many tears.
We love the likes of you.
Come in, wanderer, miserable one."

The opening stanza then returns, like a refrain:

I am God's orphan
I open the gates
with a small key—a small lock
with a silken handkerchief.

The message of the poem seems self-evident: luckless people who have strayed from their God inevitably appeal to that very God, who will ultimately take pity upon them and save them. For the informed reader—the reader conversant with Kogan's extensive Jewish background—the poem is puzzling as much for what it states as for what it withholds. It is important to note that Kogan did not invent the ingenious phrase "God's orphan." It is a common expression found in Russian folklore. Nonetheless, Kogan's use of the phrase in a poem published in 1923 demands explanation in light of the Jewish attachments she had been forging up to this period. As made abundantly clear in the fifth stanza, the internal logic of the poem indicates that the God referred to is the Christian one. This poem then begs us to ask why Kogan would publicly portray Christ as the savior when that notion conflicted with her private beliefs. After all, not a scrap of evidence exists to suggest that she wanted to or did, in fact, become an apostate at any point in her long life. On the contrary, her unpublished records demonstrate that she privately turned toward her roots, cultivating an interest in her people's ancient tongue and composing poetry in private that show her true Jewish stripes.

An unpublished poem from 1920 entitled "Bog" (God) presents an important contrast to the two poems discussed above that appeared in *The Torch*. In "God"—as in her 1914 "To God"—Kogan borrows from Ivanov once again, but sparingly. Like her mentor, she employs Old Slavonic words and a solemn, religious idiom, but that idiom, for Kogan, is wholly Jewish. She soars here on Jewish wings, ascending to heights accessible only to knowledgeable Jews. She introduces themes and imagery culled from her background; at one and the same time she is classical and innovative, a Jew and a Symbolist. Although there is nothing amateur about this poem, it was never published. But according to Ruth Rischin, Kogan did present it to the Poetry Circle, where it received Ivanov's enthusiastic praise.

Kogan supplied a fitting epigraph to the poem, which appeared as a scribbled note in the corner of the typewritten copy of "God" found in her archive.[77] Borrowing from the French scientist and religious thinker Blaise Pascal (1623–1662) Kogan offered, in effect, a defense for holding fast to theology in post-Revolutionary Russia: *Dieu d'Abraham, Dieu d'Isaac, Dieu d'Jacob, non des philosphes et des savants.* (God of Abraham, God of Isaac, God of Jacob, not of philosophers but of scholars.)[78] Like Ivanov, Kogan was an intellectual who was also a person of faith, but the faith she cherished remained concealed in unpublished works.

While the simple title "Bog" (God) masks the intricate message of Kogan's poem, its subtitle "Pustynia" (Desert) provides a foreshadowing of the parallels she will draw between the situation of her people in their religious wilderness of the past and that wilderness in the present. Kogan begins by drawing the reader back to the time of the ancient Israelites. She evokes imagery from the Book of Exodus that specifically focuses on the attributes of the God of Israel:

When you lead Your people
through the Sinai desert,
You concealed the future destiny
beyond the tent, under the heavenly sanctuary,
the emanations of the inaudible worlds
kept us from perilous storm,
and You were a cloud in the azure
and You were a flame in the night.

The divine protected the people Israel on their journey, and the poet observes that the same is occurring in her day as contemporary Jews "walk through the desert."

> And now [*dnes'*—Old Slavonic] when more stiff-necked,
> loving Your commandments,
> as in days of old [*drevle*—Old Slavonic],
> we are walking through the desert
> awaiting You,
>
> You are guiding us, invisible Fire
> or inaudible Darkness,
> And the quiet wings of the *shekhinah* flutter,
>   [Hebrew for divine presence]
> guarded by clouds.

In a footnote, Kogan accurately defined *shekhinah* as the "female emanation of God," which "traveled with the Israelites into exile." The use of a footnote indicates that rather than simply putting her thoughts down for her own benefit, Kogan was indeed writing "God" for an audience. After all, informational footnotes are aimed at an audience. But none viewed this footnote or poem. Perhaps, as Kogan had suggested after the publication of *The Torch*, censors had removed much poetry from her 1923 volume, including "God."[79]

Whether or not "God" was expunged from her volume, the fact remains that in the early 1920s censors were keeping a close watch to insure that no hints of religious faith—Jewish or otherwise—were being introduced into literature. As mentioned above, already by 1918, the Communists had created the *Evsektsiia* within its own structure to carry out party policy among the Jews. Regarding the values and institutions of the Jewish community as alien to Marxist ideology and to the new society that was to be based on it, the *Evsektsiia* took over local Jewish organizations and institutions and set out to eliminate not only the Zionist movement and Jewish religion but also the "bourgeois language" of Hebrew. Yiddish, meanwhile, was allowed to flourish, for it was deemed the language of the proletariat.[80] Surely, Kogan's poems with Jewish content would have been suspect, even if they had been written in Russian. Still, readers are left to ponder whether it was external censorship or Kogan's self-censorship that accounts for the poem's not having been published.

By referring to God as *shekhinah*, the name associated with exile, Kogan here intimates to the reader the turn her poem will next take.

> I dream with pain in the foreign land
> of the flowering camps of Israel;
> copper horizons of the desert,
> and golden waters of the Jordan;
> Carmel sun-filled vine,
> and sapphire of the Dead Sea,
> and sacred roses of Sharon,
> And banquets of fragrant lilies.

Revisiting the theme introduced in "Adonai," Kogan expresses alienation from the "foreign land" of her birth. Situated in Russia, she longs for the natural beauty of the Land of Israel, continuing:

> I remember the moment
> when the Great one
> split the Red Sea for us,
>
> [from here the poem is hand-written, rather than typed:]
> And all the people tread on the precious shore
> and Miriam sang,
> and in the distance
> the beauty of the songs sounded,
> and the air responded with reverberations
> the prophetic lips quivered:

Here, the poet lilts from past to present, giving voice to the hidden recesses of her soul through Miriam, the prophetic sister of Moses, who after the miraculous splitting of the Sea of Reeds, expressed her praise to God in a spirited dance with timbrel in hand.[81] Kogan, like her foremother, sang a psalm of thanksgiving to God, with which the poem concludes.

You allowed me to take part in these songs
in this prophetic exile
and gave me uncertain knowledge
and the ardor of the righteous heart.
So now with earthly sounds and my mortal music
let me glorify Your regal Name
beyond the seas of the sun.

The speaker suggests here that life in exile is bearable as long as the refugee has access to the "songs," the language of one's people. The sounds of Hebrew reached Kogan, even in the Russian Empire, and sustained her in her exile. For that she was grateful to God.

Like every writer, Kogan was presumambly concerned about her audience. In her desire to appeal to the largest Russian-reading public possible, she could no more draw on Jewish symbolism than she could compose in the language of her ancestors. Surely, Kogan knew as well that the early-1920s ban on expressions of religiosity had turned by the mid-1920s to the Communist party encouraging national cultures. The party invested in schools, theaters, newspapers, and magazines in non-Russian languages, including Yiddish, in order to promote its new policy of "socialist in content, nationalist in form." Kogan watched from the sidelines as the state financed the rapid expansion of publishing in Yiddish. Her interests lay elsewhere.

The Poet becomes a Theoretician

Kogan persevered in her study of Russian literature and theater at the State Institute of the Word. Upon graduation in 1925, she became an instructor at the Institute, a position she relinquished when Valeri Briusov invited her to become his assistant.[82] After this point, the details regarding her professional life are sketchy. Generally, it is known that through the years, she held a number of positions, ranging from lecturer on Russian language and literature at the State Institute of Dramatic Art[83] to producer of literary evenings and concerts in Moscow.[84] All the while, as she put it, she happily tutored the children of Jewish families in Hebrew and participated in amateur productions through the auspices of the Central Amateur Teaching Theater.[85]

It was poetry, however, that remained Kogan's "eternal calling to the end," as she put it.[86] The hundreds of poems collected in her archive attest to her words, as well as her productivity. Nearly every decade throughout her prodigious life, she would assemble her most recent compositions into a typed volume, the last dating from 1964 when she was seventy-three years old, and a decade before her death. Never published, they are monuments to the perseverance of a woman, who, even in the absence of an audience, responded steadily to her poetic impulses.

In contrast, based on her publication history, it would appear as though Kogan had abandoned poetry altogether by the early 1920s. After all, *The Torch*, which appeared in 1923, was the last collection of her verse to be published. And by the latter half of that same decade, Kogan began to churn out books on the theory of poetry. It would seem that, within a space of ten years, she had turned wholeheartedly to theorizing about poetry rather than composing it, what with the publication of three books on the subject within the same decade.[87] In 1935, for example, her *Tekhnika ispolneniia stikha* (The Art of Performing Verse) appeared, an instruction manual aimed at potential young readers of poetry that enumerates the basic principles on which verse is constructed. By the 1940s, Kogan was to describe herself as a "teacher and theoretician in the art of reading [poetry]."[88]

Not coincidentally, Kogan's transformation into a theoretician coincided with the wane of Symbolism in Russia. Acmeism, with its stress on craftsmanship and clarity, emerged around 1910 as a direct response to Symbolism's abstraction. As the former ascended, Kogan's books of theory understandably met with far greater success than those of Symbolist verse. Moreover, so far as the censor was concerned, it appears that Kogan had, by turning to theory, chosen the path of least resistance. But her battle with the censor was far from over.

In the 1930s, Kogan completed a monograph on the poet Vladimir Maiakovskii. After meeting with the approval of several officials, the book was scheduled to be published in the fall of 1941. The manuscript lay dormant, however, and after various aborted attempts, Kogan appealed to Stalin to intervene in her behalf. In a letter to the Soviet leader, she asked for a re-evaluation of the book, which she regarded "not as a private work, but as a powerful investment in the general upbuilding of our Soviet culture."[89] Although Stalin ruled in her favor, the work was never published. While interesting in and of itself, the incident is especially intriguing for it shows that Kogan, like the majority of her coreligionists had, at least outwardly, Sovietized by that time.

Inwardly, though, as her private papers reveal, Kogan was maintaining ties to her Jewish roots. The first piece of evidence to suggest as much is a 243-page handwritten Russian translation of the Book of Psalms, begun in the 1920s and completed by 1960.[90] Following once again in the footsteps of her teacher Ivanov, who prepared new editions of various scriptural texts for the Vatican, Kogan assiduously translated the Book of Psalms from a Hebrew edition.[91] Translating the lengthy biblical book over the course of several years served the dual purpose of reinforcing her Hebraic skills while strengthening her interest in lyrical poetry.[92]

The second piece of evidence suggesting Kogan's sustained Jewish attachment is a letter penned to Ilya Ehrenburg (1891–1967), the most renowned Soviet journalist of his generation. The two had much in common. Born in the same year to middle-class Jewish families, both spent their childhoods in Moscow and attended the city's prestigious high schools. As adults, they appeared to be thoroughly integrated into Russian and, later, Soviet culture. Yet, each took a unique interest in the Jews: Kogan attached herself to the Hebrew language all her life, and Ehrenburg expressed his outrage against antisemitism throughout his career.[93] Such activity gained Kogan's admiration, and in 1962 she told Ehrenburg the same in a letter she signed "one of the old Russian intelligentsia."[94] Ehrenburg replied in a short note, cordially thanking her for her support and for the volume of her poetry that had accompanied the letter.[95]

In 1964, two years after corresponding with Ehrenburg, Kogan donated the bulk of her papers to the Russian State Archive for Literature and Art in Moscow.[96] Besides demonstrating a sense of historical consciousness, the action shows Kogan's assumption that her life's work was worthy of preservation, if not investigation. By handing over her unpublished, self-revelatory papers, she was signaling a willingness to put her life—public and private—under the microscope for anyone to examine. When she died eight years later, in 1974, at the age of eighty-three, she may have realized that the way in which she (privately) blended aspects of Russian and Jewish cultures to form her identity deserves attention and explanation.

* * * * *

Kogan's life and works complicate our understanding of Jewish identity in pre-Revolutionary and Soviet Russia. On the one hand, she sought to become a bearer of Russian culture, and, in albeit modest terms, she succeeded. Though not a household name in Russian literature, she published three volumes each of Symbolist verse and poetic theory, and many more articles on those subjects. Moreover, she was personally involved with two of the most important Symbolists of her day: Briusov and Ivanov. The quality of her writings is admirable. They indicate an original poet and thinker who is deserving of critical attention, which she received in her day. On the other hand, Kogan early on connected in an esoteric way not to her native tongue but to the ancient language of the Jewish people. As a child, even without comprehending the words, she was enchanted by its sounds. Her love for the language only deepened as she engaged in formal Hebrew instruction. Hebrew became Kogan's Jewish touchstone. Participating in Hebrew theater and translating Hebrew texts became her Jewish rituals. Not religion, not nationality, but culture—as manifest through language—defined her as a Jew.

Defining oneself as a Jew through the Hebrew language was a monumental task in the early part of this century, especially for a woman living in pre-Revolutionary and then Soviet Russia. As has been explained elsewhere, Hebrew was just then being invented as a secular, literary language.[97] While Moscow became, after Odessa, a center of Hebraic creativity, Kogan had almost nothing to do with the progenitors of that renaissance in her hometown. Except for her course at the Society for Lovers of the Hebrew Language and her brief stint with Habimah—which covered a period of a maximum of three years—her papers indicate no connection to men or women involved in the Hebrew revival. Though she persevered with her translations, Kogan did so with neither assistance nor recognition. Moreover, as the Communists amassed power, Jewish religion and the Hebrew language were rendered theoretically obsolete. In practical terms, too, they were to peter out.

Notably, those involved in the Hebrew revival generally regarded themselves as Jewish nationalists. Unlike her friend Elisheva, who found ultimate fulfillment in the land of Israel, Kogan lived her entire life in Russia. She never mentioned a desire to emigrate, and only once did she come close to baring her Jewish soul publicly. In "The Prophet," she wrote in an ambiguous, if not disguised, way about her people's unpreparedness for salvation. Whether her intended audience was Jewish or Russian remains uncertain. Two other poems, necessarily buried in her archive, speak directly about a Jewish allegiance. "God" portrays the land of Israel in glowing terms, while "Adonai" explains how living in an alien environment has so debilitated the Jews that they cannot return to their land.

Kogan once explained that Hebrew was the catalyst for her lifelong "fascination with the sounds and rhythms" of words in general.[98] But born into Muscovite society and educated in a secular gymnasium, she expressed herself in the language accessible to her. As she poetically rendered it: "[T]he tongue of the North has long become the tongue of my songs." As an adult, however, she expressed sorrow over the fact that Hebrew had not been the language of her girlhood.[99] If it had, she surely would have composed in it. Instead, she gave herself over—professionally and personally—to Russian language and culture. Her attraction to Symbolism in general and Ivanov's style in particular resulted in her composing not a few poems with a Christian idiom. As has been demonstrated, like a good pupil, she imitated her teacher, hoping perhaps for approval, even acclaim. At the same time, though, she was grateful that the "songs" of Miriam—that is, Hebrew—reached her. The ancient tongue was her secret inspiration.

The eminent historian Salo Baron might have regarded Kogan as an "inverted Marrano"—his uncharitable term for a Jew in Russia who tried to hide his or her Jewish background behind a veil of Russianness.[100] But the contents of her archival holdings reveal that, in fact, she nursed a complex Jewish identity behind the scenes. Categories such as "Russian writer" or "Jewish writer" fail to capture the full extent of Kogan's professional and personal identity.

5

Blending Bread and Matzah

Sofiia Dubnova-Erlikh (1885–1986)

A Russian-Jew

> I was approximately seven years old when . . . an unfamiliar woman
> asked me: "Who are you?" and . . . I responded without thinking
> about it: "I am a Russian Jew." This response remained with me my
> whole life long.[1]

The Jewish academic community typically casts Sofiia Dubnova-Erlikh
as either the daughter of Simon Dubnov, the pioneering historian of the
systematic study of the Jewish past in Eastern Europe, or the wife of Genrikh Erlikh, a principal leader in the Jewish socialist party known as the
Bund. She herself was wont to describe women in relation to men: " . . .
I frequently think that we [girls and women] take years to learn how to
be daughters, sisters, friends of our lovers, wives, and mothers. We try to
learn but we never finish our studies."[2] In fact, Dubnova-Erlikh's familial
relationships to men played an exceedingly large role in her life. Her father anointed her his "spiritual heir" and set about training her for a life
devoted to enlightened thinking and cultural engagement.[3] Her husband
exerted a strong political influence upon her, and her two sons absorbed
her attention and became the subject of her finest verse.

Yet, at the same time, Sofiia Dubnova-Erlikh was a poet, political activist, critic, translator, and memoirist in her own right. Her literary corpus tells the remarkable story of one woman's tireless involvement and
significant achievements in two disparate cultural spheres. Over a lifetime spanning one hundred one years, Dubnova-Erlikh engaged in Jewish socialist party politics and literary activity focused on Jewish interests, on the one hand, and Russian Silver Age poetry (1890–1922), on

the other.[4] Russian was her mother tongue and she published over fifty works in that language, ranging from verse (original and translations) and criticism to biography and history.[5]

Born on March 9, 1885 in Mstislavl (Byelorus), Dubnova-Erlikh was the eldest child of Simon and Ida (Friedlin) Dubnov. At the age of five, she and her parents, along with siblings Ol'ga and Yakov, moved to Odessa, where her father began to instruct her according to John Stuart Mill's educational system until the age of fourteen, when she entered a gymnasium. Upon graduation in 1902, Dubnova-Erlikh studied at the Bestuzhev Higher Courses in St. Petersburg, a four-year degree program equivalent to that of the university, offered to women with parental permission and the fifty-ruble annual tuition.

Simultaneously, Dubnova-Erlikh was initiated into both the literary and political worlds when in 1904 her first poem, "Gaman" (Haman) was to appear in the Russian-Jewish weekly *Voskhod*.[6] In her satiric verse, she covertly identified the Tsar's Minister of Interior V.K. Plehve with Haman, the villain of the biblical Scroll of Esther who in seeking the Jews' demise ultimately causes his own end. While her relatives praised her as a prophet who predicted Plehve's fall (he was assassinated shortly after the poem was written), her subtlety did not elude the Russian censors, who confiscated the poem and axed it from the journal's galley proofs. Meanwhile, Dubnova-Erlikh's proud father gushed over her verses, exclaiming to the essayist Ahad Ha'am: "Our daughter is the hero of the day."[7] That same year, university officials expelled Dubnova-Erlikh from her courses for participating in a student protest. Undeterred, she entered the history-philology department of St. Petersburg University in 1905 and later, in 1910–11, studied comparative religion and the history of world literature at the Sorbonne.

Meanwhile, her family had moved to Vilna, the hotbed of Jewish politics in the Russian Empire, where Dubnova-Erlikh became eventually an active member of the Social Democratic Labor Party and the Jewish Labor Party, and an anti-militarist propagandist. As she explained in her memoirs: "The anxiety of our generation was destined to become intertwined with the anxiety of our era."[8] She sealed that fate in 1911 by marrying Genrikh Erlikh (1883–1941), a Warsaw-born law graduate of Petersburg University who was prominent in the Bund.

In deed and in printed word, the couple worked to promote the ideals of Jewish cultural autonomy and Socialist internationalism. Dubnova-Erlikh, for instance, contributed to various political journals, including *Nashe slovo* (Our Word), an organ of the Bund edited by the political leader Vladimir Medem, and even ghostwrote her husband's speeches.[9] By 1918, the Dubnov-Erlikhs relocated to Warsaw, where they remained for over twenty years with their sons, Aleksander and Viktor. When the city fell to the Nazis in 1939, Erlikh was arrested by Soviet authorities and Dubnova-Erlikh moved her family to Vilna, where they lived until 1941. When she reached the United States in 1942, she learned of her husband's death and her father's murder by the Nazis. Dubnova-Erlikh remained politically active in her new land as well, advocating civil rights and protesting the Vietnam War.[10]

Despite her literary false start in 1904, Dubnova-Erlikh's writing career flourished well into her nineties. Her poems, essays, and translations—all reflecting her dual interests in high arts and politics—appeared in journals and newspapers in Russian, Yiddish, Polish, and English.[11] Moreover, she produced three volumes of poetry, several histories on topics relating to the Bund, and a biography of her father entitled *Zhizn' i tvorchestvo S.M. Dubnova* (The Life and Work of S.M. Dubnov).[12] Because of her father's renown, the latter, which was originally written in Russian and subsequently translated into Yiddish and English, became the most conspicuous of Dubnova-Erlikh's writings. In fact, scholars of Jewish history and literature have paid little or no attention to her other works, which are thus virtually unknown, except among a narrow audience of well-educated students of Silver Age poetry. In the seventh decade of her life, Dubnova-Erlikh turned to writing her own memoirs and produced, over the course of ten years, 792 pages of Russian longhand chronicling her life against the backdrop of Russian-Jewish history.[13] The memoirs—which have been titled *Bread and Matzah* and are brimming with names and dates, anecdotes and analysis—seem to be based on a daily journal or notes of some sort, but make no reference to the same. The present study draws copiously from the memoirs, as well as from the entirety of her literary oeuvre.

As the pupil and daughter of a master historian, Dubnova-Erlikh developed a strong historical consciousness, which informs her memoirs to a large extent and her literature to a far lesser one. Comprehending the

historical significance of her own age—she repeatedly drew parallels between it and eighteenth-century France[14]—Dubnova-Erlikh presented
her life as one specific example of a woman's contact with important literary and political movements of the day. She knew she could offer an
extraordinary perspective: she was aware of her involvement in circles
peopled with men who would make history. She not only took pride in
her insider status, but understood that it made the telling of her life story
all the more essential and worthy of being told. Dubnova-Erlikh's familial
ties, and position in society as a result, make her unique among the
women in this study.

She is unique in other ways. In contrast to Markel-Mosessohn,
Shapiro, Khin, and Kogan, as will be shown, Dubnova-Erlikh not only
cherished the memories of her childhood home but strived to create a
similar environment for her own two children. Although her education
ostensibly put her on equal footing with enlightened Jewish men, and although she regularly interacted with women and men involved in revolutionary movements who typically rejected bourgeois notions of male-
female roles, Dubnova-Erlikh patterned her life after generations of
Jewish women whose primary responsibility was to their husband and
children. The domestic and child-rearing responsibilities that consumed
a significant proportion of her time did not, however, prevent her from
producing an impressive bibliography of her own. Nevertheless, as will
be argued, she returned again and again in her writings to the unique
ways in which being a woman informed her life experience. Motherhood, for instance, was crucial to how she understood herself and her
place in society.

It is tempting to divide Sofiia Dubnova-Erlikh's life and work neatly
and facilely into two distinct compartments: the Russian and the Jewish
segments. But, as our discussion will show, this is exactly what Dubnova-
Erlikh resisted throughout her lifetime. Like her father, she envisaged a
future era when barriers isolating the Jews from the outside world would
be broken down and Jews would recognize that the fate of their nation
was inextricably linked to that of humanity as a whole. She admonished
Zionists for their Palestino-centrism and traditionalists for their voluntary isolation, calling upon Jews to forge living links with their native
lands. She taught this credo by example, mastering the elements of her
people's modern culture along with that of her motherland and conse-

quently identifying herself from a young age as a "Russian Jew." The fitting title of her memoirs *Bread and Matzah* demonstrates her desire to blend, self-consciously, Russianness and Jewishness into an organic whole. How—both under her father's tutelage and despite it—she did so will form the focus of our investigation.

Patrilineal and Matrilineal Descent

As the daughter of a famous man whose life has been documented by generations of scholars, the sources for tracing Dubnova-Erlikh's ancestry are plentiful.[15] One need only peruse, for instance, the initial chapter of *The Life and Work of S.M. Dubnov*, which Dubnova-Erlikh herself penned in 1950 by drawing on Dubnov's autobiography and her reminiscences, to determine her roots.[16] With an historian's brush, she painted a colorful panorama of life in a small town in Byelorus called Mstislavl. There, since the end of the eighteenth century when Yosef Dubno had moved his family from Volhynia, generations of men had borne the family name with a distinction earned by learning rather than wealth. Simon Dubnov's father Meyer-Yakov (1833–1887) was the son of an esteemed rabbi but worked as a steward for his well-to-do father-in-law, who bought up timber from Byelorussian landowners and floated it southward. When Simon's father died at the age of fifty-four, his mother Sheyne assumed financial responsibility for her eight children by peddling crockery at the local marketplace. Her life was exceedingly different from that of Dubnova-Erlikh's maternal grandmother Mera (Miriam) Freidlin, whose life is highlighted in the opening pages of *Bread and Matzah*.[17]

Dubnova-Erlikh's attention to her grandmother is noteworthy on two counts. First, although her father was by all counts the greatest single influence upon her, women, too, inspired her. Secondly, her description of Mera Freidlin provides a rare view of the obstacles a Jewish woman had to overcome when she was educated for a secular world but forced into an arranged marriage with a traditional Jew. This scenario is the mirror image of the well-documented phenomenon of enlightened Jewish men who authored autobiographies revealing their dissatisfaction with arranged marriages to traditional Jewish women.[18]

As a young girl in Mstislavl, Dubnova-Erlikh's grandmother Mera used her knowledge of Russian, Polish, and German by serving as translator

(*Left to right*) Sofiia Dubnova-Erlikh, her husband Genrikh Erlikh,
and their friends Sara Grosser and Bronislav Grosser (c. 1910)
(B. Grosser was a leading spokesman of the Bund)
Photo courtesy of Victor Erlich

for her father, a wealthy merchant who engaged in trade with foreign buyers. Among them was a Polish landowner who grew fond of his associate's golden-haired daughter Mera. The pair corresponded by stealthily placing letters in the hollow of an old tree trunk. When this arrangement was discovered, the suitor promptly removed himself from Mstislavl, and the sixteen-year old girl was married off to a middle-aged Hasid with sons. To her great relief, Mera became widowed at a young age and as such was free to choose her own mate: the respectable merchant Hayim Freidlin. Their marriage was based on love, and Mera became an exemplary wife and mother and managed their prosperous household in consonance with Jewish custom.

Mera's daughters appeared to be following in their mother's footsteps. During the late 1870s, while attending the local private school in Mstislavl, Ida and Fanny helped to organize a small circle for self-education. It met regularly at their parents' home, which housed a small library. When Simon Dubnov returned to his hometown in response to a summons for military service—which he subsequently avoided—he gravitated toward the library circle and the Freidlin sisters. After three years, Ida and Simon's friendship, nourished mostly by the latter's lengthy discourses on the contents of his favorite literature and his commentary on the same, blossomed into romance. Despite the amorous episode of her youth, Mera Friedlin opposed this union and called upon matchmakers to present eligible bridegrooms who possessed either Torah learning or capital. Upon hearing this plan, the Freidlin sisters fled Mstislavl with the dream of attending university. Penniless, they returned home within months to see their dying father.[19]

Reunited in Mstislavl, Ida and Simon planned a joint future, which consisted of "working together, . . . moving to St. Petersburg and then Paris, and transforming [their] path of thorns into a smooth and joyful one."[20] At this stage in their lives, this meant behaving according to the principles of positivism, materialism, and utilitarianism, a triad of interrelated philosophical systems that gained currency among Russian youth in the 1850s and 60s. Reacting against an older generation of idealistic Romantics, whom Turgenev described as "the fathers," the youthful adherents of these philosophies—the "sons"—were pragmatists who sought to cure society of its moral and physical ills by leading exemplary lives devoted to useful work. Flouting any traditional aspect of culture and society that did not conform to the dictates of empirical science, they jetti-soned all forms of religion, maintained a casual attitude toward dress and appearance, and talked of liberating women as a show of rejecting bour-geois convention. The last-named goal, together with their disdain for the traditional Jewish marriage ceremony and an awareness that civil marriage was not a legal option in the Russian Empire, resulted in Ida's and Simon's decision to live together—unmarried—in the capital.

Once in St. Petersburg, Simon became increasingly absorbed in jour-nalism as Ida prepared to enroll in the local Medical Institute.[21] Her pro-fessional plans, however, would come to naught as she, like her mother before her, surrendered to a life in the shadow of her man. Within a year or two, as the couple prepared to return to Mstislavl so that Simon could study without the distractions of St. Petersburg, they legalized their rela-tionship in a Jewish ceremony of the lowest common denominator. In the words of the groom: "In the presence of several casual witnesses, a dejected young man in a threadbare jacket placed a ring on the finger of an embarrassed young woman and quickly muttered the marriage vows."[22] Ida's plan for escaping the petty bourgeois existence of her par-ents had indeed boomeranged. For, when they took up residence in their hometown once again, the couple had, insofar as their private life was concerned, assumed, and would maintain through the years, the very gender roles assigned to them by middle-class domesticity and Jewish tradition: Ida managed the household and finances, while Simon studied. However, the subject of his study remained altogether untraditional with its focus on European philosophy, and their home remained altogether irreligious as a result of Dubnov's rejection of the "blind patriotism"—the unquestioning loyalty to the Jewish people—of his youth.[23]

Educating for Life

Sofiia (Sonia) Semenovna Dubnova was born into this unconventionally conventional household on March 9, 1885. In preparation for his first child's arrival, Dubnov had reviewed the literature on child psychology and development, as well as the sections of John Stuart Mill's autobiogra-phy describing his boyhood, in order to create the requisite conditions for enlightened child rearing.[24] Until mid-adolescence, Dubnova's sole teacher—unlike her younger sister and brother who attended local schools at an early age—was her father. Dubnov fully expected his daughter to be his spiritual heir, a plan that Dubnova-Erlikh claimed "hastened [her] intellectual growth but imposed a heavy burden upon [her] childhood shoulders."[25] Rising to the challenge, she mastered not only the fundamentals of natural science, but history, math, and the languages and literature of both the Russian and Jewish (i.e. Hebrew and Yiddish) cultures as well. Dubnova-Erlikh was as conversant with the poetry of Pushkin and Lermontov and the history by Kliuchevskii as with the poetry of the Bible and Bialik and the history by Graetz. "In my upbringing," she explained, "national Jewish lines were interlaced with the humanities in general."[26] The course of study was unsystematic, meandering from one topic to another, dictated only by Dubnov's enthusiasm for the subject matter.[27] Yet by the time she "graduated" from her father's program, Dubnova-Erlikh easily passed the entrance examination for the local gymnasium in Odessa, where the family had been living since 1890.

Dubnova acquired her father's love of poetry around the family table, where one evening a week they would engage in readings whose ritualized nature bespoke a religious experience. By the light of the kerosene lamp, Dubnov would read aloud to his daughter as if intoning the prayers of his youth. As Dubnova-Erlikh recalled: "Opening the book to the correct place, Papa would slowly read in a voice hoarse from physical trembling."[28] Living among these "sweet and prayerful sounds," it was not long before she herself took up the poet's pen. By the age of nine, she began to draft compositions in Russian, which she would turn over to her father for his review.[29] Although occasionally his criticism would dissolve her to tears, the poems generally found favor in his eyes. Initially, she wrote in the guise of a man, using masculine gender forms when speaking in the first person, but broke the habit upon realizing that "female poets [could] exist right alongside male poets."[30]

Dubnova-Erlikh's earliest known poetry sounded a note of Jewish nationalism, couched in imagery drawn from nature. She shared with her father a personal theology bordering on pantheism, a doctrine identifying the divine through natural phenomena.[31] The "cult of nature" had seized father and daughter alike.[32] In her mid-teens, Dubnova-Erlikh declared that her "lyre was lit up by the silver moon, and [she] sang loudly" about the "lot of [her] ancient people." At fifteen, she penned

"Videniia" (Visions), and though the text is lost, in a partially-extant prologue, the poet asserted: "Northern [i.e. Russian] fairly tales and legends pale in comparison to the images of the country [i.e. Palestine] where Kinneret is ringed with floral gardens and Sharon is dressed in green garments in the glistening sun."[33] Lest the reader accuse her of chauvinism, however, Dubnova-Erlikh explained that her extolling of the beauty of her people's ancient land was a mere literary device. "Unlike [the Jewish national poets Shimon Shmuel] Frug and Bialik, who regarded Palestine as a land of the future," the young poet considered it "a distant land of the biblical past."

It would seem that Dubnova-Erlikh was echoing the sentiments of her father, whose strong belief in positivism had given way, over the first decade of his daughter's life, to skepticism and doubt. In the late Tolstoi and in Ernest Renan, Dubnov had recognized his own need to reclaim his lost faith. From the late 1880s, he began his way back to Judaism, seeking to build a bridge between the old and the new, the particular and the universal. By 1897, when his daughter was twelve years old, Dubnov had reached the point where he could present publicly his own complete world-view: a secular Jewish nationalism, which came to be known as Autonomism. In contrast to the Palestino-centrism of Zionism, Dubnov's ideology envisaged the gradual transformation of traditional Jewish culture and self-government within pluralistic modern nations throughout the Diaspora.[34]

After twelve years of imbibing her father's lessons, Dubnova-Erlikh had assimilated her father's ideology into her very being. As an adolescent, she championed Autonomism and even defended it against the attacks launched by her friends, the sons and daughters of her father's associates. As a result of "grow[ing] up in the peculiar atmosphere of a religious ghetto," she explained, they clung to "an anemic Palestinophilism."[35] So she set about setting them straight by employing her father's arguments and rhetoric. Yet her unwavering belief in Autonomism at this stage in her life is belied by an episode described in her memoirs. When Abraham Menahem Mendel Ussishkin (1863–1941), a Zionist leader involved early on in immigration attempts, informed Dubnova-Erlikh that Palestine needed young women like her, she planned to emigrate, but was restrained by her father.[36]

As a teenager, Dubnova-Erlikh also began to question her father's strict avoidance of Jewish observance. She had grown accustomed to Dubnov's attempts to transform religious symbols into nationalist ones as, for example, the family's custom of reciting Frug's epic poem "Ha-kos" (The [Kiddush] Cup) each year at the Passover seder around a table laden with matzah *and* bread.[37] While the prohibition against eating leavened products during the holiday meant nothing to Dubnov, his daughter's ignorance of Judaism drove her to the synagogue. Sitting among the women in the balcony, Dubnova-Erlikh quickly became the focus of attention as the others noticed her unusual proficiency in Hebrew. Although she attended regularly for a some time, her religious training was short-lived. The words of the prayers, which she "conscientiously translated into [her native] Russian" did not "speak to [her] heart."[38]

Dubnova-Erlikh would continue to maintain, at best, an ambivalent attitude toward religion. She came closest to defining her religious sensibilities when she spoke in retrospect of her attachment to Symbolism, the literary movement of late nineteenth and early twentieth-century Russia that was bound up with religious and philosophic problems:[39]

> Symbolism held out the promise of broadening the boundaries of our perceptions. It needs to be said that, despite my attraction to Marxism, at times my desire was to believe Vladimir Solov'ev [the high priest of Symbolism] who said: "All that is evident to us is only shadows, only a reflection of what is invisible to the eye." . . . The religious experience of my adolescence had left an [inadequate] impression on me: I felt as though I was at the threshold of [acquiring] a mystical sensibility, but I did not dare cross over that threshold. [Thus] I rejected, finally and for all time, the primitive formula of the Marxists that religion was an opium of the masses.[40]

Dubnova-Erlikh was acknowledging here a spiritual yearning that might have been fulfilled by religion. She did not reject it outright, but rather regarded it as an option for creating meaning beyond humanity's empirical existence, into a mystical dimension. She would have nothing to do, however, with its outer trappings, and explained her teenage participation in Jewish worship as a need for social intercourse with humanity and not with God.[41]

Dubnova-Erlikh herself was not lacking for human contact throughout her adolescence. The Dubnov home in Odessa, where they lived from 1890 to 1903, became the gathering place for figures made famous by their monumental roles in the Jewish cultural renaissance. Considering it an important aspect of her education, Dubnov included his eldest daughter in discussions with his visitors, even permitting her to eavesdrop on his private conversations with intimates like the essayist Ahad Ha'am and the fiction writer Mendele Mokher-Seforim (pseudonym of Shalom Yakov Abramowitsch). While she was acquainted with the daughters of each gentleman—the former had one named Rachel, whom they called Rosa; the latter had three, two of whom eventually studied medicine abroad and the third became a musician—she preferred the company of the older set, whose intellectual interests attracted her. While impressed with the content of the debates of the members of the so-called Odessa Circle, Dubnova-Erlikh was critical of their pronunciation. "Generally speaking," she recalled, "the people in *our* [emphasis added] circle used the limited Russian of the maskilim, accenting words incorrectly, and only Papa had no trouble articulating his thoughts in clear, literary language."[42]

During her adolescence, Dubnova-Erlikh's personal contacts were not limited to the middle-aged men who populated her father's study.[43] Her two younger siblings offered companionship of a different sort. Ol'ga (1886–1944), born a year after Dubnova-Erlikh, was the black sheep of the family. She criticized her older sister's conformism and longed to leave the confines of her childhood home. Graduating from gymnasium with honors, she became estranged from her parents as a result of her relationship with Mikhail Ivanov, a non-Jewish peasant's son. Learning of his interest in things Jewish, including possibly joining the Bund, Dubnova-Erlikh tried to reconcile her parents to the young man. At the same time, though, she admitted to her sister that she disapproved of intermarriage, even if it were to be sanctioned by Russian law. Hopelessly in love, Ol'ga eventually married Ivanov abroad and became the mother of twins. The sisters seldom saw each other, and there was little intimacy between them until Ol'ga returned to her family's home during the Second World War. She died on a train departing from Leningrad during the blockade.[44] In contrast to the sisters' relationship, Dubnova-Erlikh remained exceptionally close to her brother Yakov (1887–1957). Although they were only two years apart in age, she mothered him and introduced him to her favorite pastime—writing poetry. Yakov became a mathematician of some repute and remained in Russia until his death.[45]

As for girlhood friends, Dubnova-Erlikh had few. She preferred the company of books to children, and surely the long delay in starting at the local school made contact with others less accessible. When she entered an Odessa gymnasium for the first time, she wandered about like a lost soul until she wrote her first essay and zoomed to the head of the class.[46] At the beginning of the twentieth century, Odessa could boast of an impressive array of educational options for Jewish boys and girls. The social and economic position of the *maskilim* in the port city drew them near to the local authorities and enabled them to gain considerable influence within the community and the shaping of its institutions. So while nearly five thousand students attended two hundred *ḥadarim* (traditional Jewish schools), 6,500 children attended forty Jewish elementary schools categorized as public, governmental, or semi-public. The language of instruction was Russian, while Jewish subjects held an insignificant place.[47] Dubnova-Erlikh noted that though the majority of students at her all-girl gymnasium were the daughters of Jews of the merchant and professional classes, a small number of Russian girls matriculated each year as well.

Unimpressed with her teachers—whom she tagged "men in a case," using Chekhov's phrase—Dubnova-Erlikh organized a supplemental learning circle with the help of Berta Bernshtein, whose older sister Esfir' agreed to conduct lectures on Russian cultural history for the younger girls and, at their request, administer examinations as well. Esfir' Bernshtein was then a student at the Bestuzhev Higher Courses for Women. In an attempt to curb the flow of Russian women to foreign universities, Alexander II had authorized, as early as April 1876, the creation of women's higher courses.[48] Classified as private courses, they had no degree-granting powers nor any claim to state subsidies but did, over time, in certain cities become akin to university programs, four years in length. The high annual tuition of fifty rubles, which was equal to the cost for the regular university, severely curtailed admission from the lower social orders; Jews of the merchant class could afford to send their daughters and did so. In 1885–86, for instance, Jews represented almost 17 percent of the student population of the St. Petersburg Higher Courses.[49] The only Higher Courses to survive the reign of Alexander III, those in St. Petersburg became a center of revolutionary activity in the last decades of the nineteenth century. Possessing at first only the vaguest notion of revolutionary activity and objectives, Dubnova-Erlikh and her cohorts listened with rapt attention to Esfir' Bernshtein's descriptions of student demonstrations. They retorted by reporting their own version of protest: at school assemblies where the patriotic cries of "God, Tsar and Church" were required, they stood with their lips closed.[50]

In addition to enhancing her knowledge of things Russian with the Bernshtein sisters, Dubnova-Erlikh maintained an interest in things Jewish by joining a group of what she called "nationally-spirited Jewish youth" who performed plays in Hebrew. They chose to perform a drama by Bialik and even managed to cast him in a small role. Rather than following the script as written, though, he would improvise from rehearsal to rehearsal, sending the other actors into a tailspin. The show, however, never went on; the entire project fizzled as news of the Kishinev pogroms (April 6–7, 1903) reached Odessa, and Bialik departed for that region.[51]

Upon graduating from gymnasium with honors, Dubnova-Erlikh followed in the footsteps of her erstwhile teacher Esfir', heading North to St. Petersburg for an education oriented toward both the literary and the political. Before leaving Odessa, she read Marx's *Das Kapital* in an attempt to gird her emotional attraction toward socialism with an intellectual basis.[52] From 1903, she attended the history-philology (i.e. liberal arts) department of the Bestuzhev Higher Courses for Women (Vasil'evskii Island, 10th Line No. 31–35) and began to read journals devoted to Symbolist poetry. On February 3, 1904 she was formally inducted into the fraternity of political activists when she attended a student assembly protesting professors' actions in support of the government. Experiencing for the first time the exultation of "linking with the people," she claimed that it was at that moment that political activism became an "inalienable part of [her] life."[53] The school administrators expelled all participants in the protest, which meant for Dubnova-Erlikh, as a Jew, the loss of the right to remain in the capital. Vowing to return to Petersburg at a later date, she departed in the spring of 1904 for the home of her parents, who had moved from Odessa to Vilna.

Joining the Political Unrest on Her Own Terms

Vilna of the early-twentieth century, with its varied and intense political activity among its large Jewish population, was the perfect testing ground for Dubnova-Erlikh's emerging political consciousness. Not yet ready to join a specific party, she experimented by attending an assortment of meetings. She was joined in this pursuit by Mendele Mokher-Seforim's two elder daughters, with whom she became reacquainted in Vilna and who claimed to be Socialist-Democrats. The threesome attended a meeting of the Bund, the Jewish Labor Party founded in 1897 with the goal of transforming countries into socialist societies in which the national cultural rights of all minorities would be guaranteed by law. The Bund's cultural orientation was pro-Yiddish; it was, after all, the language of the Jewish masses it claimed to represent, and the polyglot Dubnova-Erlikh felt at home in this linguistic milieu. After the meeting, the three young women contemplated joining the Bund. Mania Abramowitsch voiced her concern that isolating Jewish workers into their own party seemed like surrendering to nationalism, a tenet at odds with the cosmopolitanism of socialism. But Dubnova-Erlikh disagreed. To her, the existence of a party of the Jewish working-class seemed as natural as the existence of any other national party.[54]

It is hardly surprising that Dubnov disapproved of his daughter's deepening interest in socialism in general and the Jewish Labor Party in particular. Their heated arguments on the subject typically concluded with the father storming to his study, the daughter bursting into tears of anger.[55] Dubnov was an evolutionist, and Marxism spoke of social change in revolutionary terms; whereas he believed the basic social unit in which human beings came to organize their lives was the nation, Marxism spoke of the preeminence of class division and class war. Dubnov failed to see that his daughter's attraction to the Jewish Labor Party may indeed have been an outgrowth of her continued allegiance to Autonomism—albeit in a wholly different context. After all, the Bundist position that the Jews were able to thrive in the Diaspora and that there was no need for them to be transferred elsewhere was a guiding principle of Dubnov's Autonomism as well. But the Bund's socialist aspirations and exclusively Yiddish bent clashed with Dubnov's Autonomism, which advocated the upbuilding of Jewish national minority rights within democratic societies with a multiplicity of cultural and linguistic traditions. At bottom, Dubnova-Erlikh, a daughter of Autonomism's passionate spokesman, was as well a daughter of a passionate generation entangled in the revolutionary fervor of early twentieth-century Russia. As such, she would fling herself headlong into activities in behalf of the Bund while enduring her father's ire for the same.

Meanwhile, Dubnov made clear to his daughter his dissatisfaction with her behavior on another count. In the summer of 1904, a visitor arrived to Vilna from Odessa whose name was known to Dubnova-Erlikh from her gymnasium days. He was, she contended, her favorite Odessa youth, and his biography was no less fascinating to her than his writing.[56] Born into a middle-class Jewish family in 1880, he was educated in Russian schools and, except for training for his bar-mitzvah ceremony, had no exposure to Jewish culture. In 1898, he departed for Berne and Rome, where he studied law and served as foreign correspondent for two Odessa dailies. He returned to his hometown in 1901, joining the editorial staff of *Odesskiia novosti* (Odessa News) to compose brilliant daily feuilletons that became widely popular. In the spring of 1903, when the danger of a pogrom in Odessa seemed imminent, he joined the initiators of a Jewish self-defense group. And after the pogrom in Kishinev in the same year, he immersed himself in Zionist activities. By the time Vladimir Jabotinsky met Dubnova-Erlikh, he was a rising force in the Zionist movement. He had a dazzling oratorial style that would turn him into one of Jewry's most celebrated interwar leaders. He surely made a lasting impression on Dubnov's daughter, who described him as "at first glance . . . very ugly. He had large, fleshy lips and a sharp, jutting chin that pressed his face like a monkey. But this . . . dissipated when his dark, sparkling eyes glanced at me. It was difficult to grasp the expression of his eyes—they were obstinate, . . . and also at the same time vague . . . and his voice was richly modulated, making simple words extraordinary." Dubnova-Erlikh and Jabotinsky spent the better part of the summer together reciting poetry, acting and singing, and debating their contrasting, developing political stances. Five years his junior, Dubnova-Erlikh came to trust and seek his judgment, even turning over her private notebook to him. However, she remained unpersuaded by his ideology. On politics, the two agreed to disagree.

Although there is no evidence that their friendship blossomed into ro-

mance, Dubnov remained suspicious of Jabotinsky's intentions toward
his daughter. Distrusting the young activist's politics, he feared that his
daughter might be corrupted by the charismatic man. For the first time,
Dubnov forbade his daughter from seeing her new acquaintance, a prohibition that met with insurgency as the two met in secret. For her part,
Dubnova-Erlikh had clearly fallen under Jabotinsky's spell and described
in quixotic terms her unmistakable feelings for him: "The bonds of
friendship can be blurred, and for a long time after [that summer], I became anxious thinking of our meetings, surrounded by the magic of poetry and the aroma of the short Lithuanian summer."[57] Like most women
her age, the nineteen-year old longed to fall in love but feared that her
plain appearance would hamper that process. "I looked into the mirror,
and my heart sunk . . . my cheeks seemed too flushed, my nostrils too
wide and my gray-green eyes too ordinary."[58] Poetically, she described
herself as a "nun of a distant cloister" who yearned to break free from
her father's grip so as to participate fully in the experiences of life.[59]
Ironically, Dubnov's careful instruction in history and linguistics would
lead his daughter away from him and into the very activities he found
unacceptable.

Dubnova-Erlikh would gain independence from her father by deepening her involvement in her brand of politics as stormy Russia headed for
her own revolution. As early as 1905, she was working on behalf of the
Bund, lecturing circles of gymnasium students on the history of the
French Revolution as a paradigm for activism. A year later, because of her
exceptional Russian skills, she was sent to Grodno (in present-day
Byelorus) to agitate among Russian soldiers.[60] When, at the Bund leaders' directive, she returned to Vilna, Dubnova-Ehrlikh heard a speech delivered by the Bund activist Vladimir Medem (1879–1923) and felt an
immediate kinship with him. Though born into a Jewish family in
Liepaja (Latvia), Medem was baptized as a youth and regarded himself as
a Russian. Politicized in Kiev while studying the law, he made his way
back to the Jewish community by immersing himself in activities on behalf of the Jewish masses. Dubnova-Erlikh was drawn to Medem's cultural sensibilities. She was delighted with the way he wove together politics and culture. As she described it, his speech combined "romantic
élan and the sobriety of politics." In him, Dubnova-Erlikh undoubtedly
saw herself reflected: "His childhood was suffused with . . . literature,

music, and passionate family affection. During adolescence Pushkin and Chopin directed him. From these roots he developed a desire for harmony which . . . collided with [our] clamorous epoch."[61] As editor of the Bundist organ *Nashe slovo* (Our Word), Medem invited Dubnova-Erlikh to write literary criticism for the Russian-language journal. She accepted, and her writing career was launched.

Literary Debut

On July 29, 1906, the first of a two-part article appeared in *Nashe slovo* under the simple byline Sofiia D.[62] This work about the Russian playwright Semon Solomonovich Iushkevich (1868–1927) was Dubnova-Erlikh's literary debut.[63] This was two years after censors confiscated her satiric poem depicting the Minister of Interior V.K. Plehve as the archvillain Haman before it could be published in *Voskhod*, as related above. Dubnova-Erlikh's interest in Iushkevich stemmed from the fact that he occasionally wrote on Jewish themes. Encouraged by Maksim Gorki, among the most famous of Russian Judeophiles of the day, Iushkevich composed plays and narrative works that sought to introduce Jews to the gentile community in a realistic light.

A full four years after calling Jews' attention to Iushkevich's short stories, Dubnova-Erlikh alighted upon the Polish works of Eliza Orzheshko (Orzeszkowa in Polish, 1842–1910) and returned to writing on the theme of gentile authors with an interest in Jews.[64] A Polish-born landowner's daughter with sixteen volumes of belles lettres, prose, and brochures, Orzheshko had studied Jewish history and Hebrew, read the Bible, and was familiar with the Talmud. She published three novels on Jews, and at least two were translated into Russian. Her short stories also appeared in various organs of the Russian-Jewish press.[65] Following her death in 1910, Dubnova-Erlikh published a lengthy tribute to Orzheshko in the literary journal *Evreiskii mir* (Jewish World), and months later turned it into an entry for *Evreiskaia entsiklopediia*.[66] Not coincidentally, Simon Dubnov sat on the editorial boards of both publications.

The eulogy for Orzheshko was one of eleven pieces on Jewish literature Dubnova-Erlikh contributed to *Evreiskii mir* over a period of seventeen months beginning in October 1909. Most of the articles featured the works of emerging Jewish masters of the pen like Sholom Aleichem and Hayim Nahman Bialik, both of whom she had met as a child in her father's study in Odessa.[67] In the eulogy, Dubnova-Erlikh extolled Orzheshko for depicting Jews with more than the "superficiality" they typically received in the pages of Polish history and literature. According to the author, Orzheshko combined a "courageous inquisitiveness" and "penetrating patience," which enabled her to "illuminate the dark corners of Jewish life." Moreover, Dubnova-Erlikh thanked Orzheshko for being a "publicist" who "preached the slogan of her era—the blending of Jews with the surrounding population." In an article entitled "The Jews and the Jewish Problem" published in 1882, Orzheshko defined the "Jewish problem" as the "abnormal circumstances in which the Jews found themselves" and advocated a solution in assimilation.[68] For this, she won the support not only of "Polish-Jewish assimilators" but of Dubnova-Erlikh herself. Like her father, Dubnova-Erlikh maintained in 1910 that the spiritual peaks of Jewish history had been reached when barriers isolating the Jews from the outside world had been broken down and when the Jews had come to see the fate of their nation as inextricably linked to that of humanity as a whole. As acknowledgment perhaps of her father's influence, she signed the article *Mstislavskaia*, the feminine equivalent of his occasionally employed pseudonym *Mstislavskii*, itself a derivative of his hometown.

While the common byline points out an ideological consistency between father and daughter, Dubnova-Erlikh's literary achievements were without equal in her family. Whereas her father's important historical works in Russian remained within the Jewish purview, Dubnova-Erlikh sought to create original poetry in Russian that conformed to the principal style of the day. Within a span of ten years, she produced nearly one hundred poems, some of which appeared in print in 1911 in a single volume. Dubnova-Erlikh was, in other words, a published author not only in the Jewish but also the Russian press. In 1910—the very year in which her works appeared in *Evreiskii mir*—her poem "Proshchanie" (Farewell) was published in the Russian-language journal *Apollon*, an important organ for modernist verse founded by Nikolai Gumilev, the husband of Anna Akhmatova.[69] As its title implies, "Farewell" is an ode to death, employing stock Symbolist imagery drawn from nature.

A Blend of Cultures, a Bifurcated Literary Corpus

By the time she was published, Dubnova-Erlikh had made good on her promise to return to the capital. In 1906, the entire Dubnov family had moved from Vilna to St. Petersburg, where her stream of life flowed from university courses in philosophy and literature to political demonstrations to Bund meetings to literary circle gatherings to Jewish cultural events. Amid these activities, she felt herself "caught in a web of contradictions, straining to listen attentively to the many voices of the epoch and trying not to give [herself] over too hastily to one conclusion."[70] Ultimately, she did not choose one path, but balanced her commitments to the Jewish community in political and cultural terms with immersion in the vibrant Russian cultural life of the city. As for her political involvement, government records reveal that by 1906 she was being monitored by the police. As one report indicates, "At a meeting of Jewish Bundists at the university [in St. Petersburg] . . . the crowd was so large that there was standing-room only. The participants were students . . . [among them] was the Jew Dubnova, the daughter of the historian, who spoke."[71] Meanwhile, her literary interests brought her into contact with some of the most important innovators of Russian culture of her era. She met celebrated poets associated with Symbolism like Valeri Briusov, Aleksandr Blok, Andrei Belyi, Zinaida Gippius, Maximilian Voloshin, and Nikolai Gumilev. She regularly attended performances at the Stray Dog, the cabaret that became a central meeting point for the movement. In addition, she was instrumental in forming *Kruzhok molodoi* (Young Circle), a political-literary group where she befriended the author Kornei Chukovskii, who took her to the Tower, the famous salon hosted by the mystical Symbolist Viacheslav Ivanov.[72]

Establishing a connection between the realms of revolutionary politics and Silver Age culture was no easy task. Dubnova-Erlikh explained, "It was difficult because among the literary 'elite,' grouped around the journals *Vesy* and *Apollon*, it was common to view Marxism as something quite primitive. . . . On the other hand, in the revolutionary circles there was a prejudice inherited from a number of generations against innovation in literature and art and there was a habit of labeling every deviation from realism as Decadence."[73] Whether she studiously ignored the mutual antagonism, learned to compartmentalize her disparate interests or simply refused to acknowledge the differences between the two, Dubnova-Erlikh managed to maintain intimacy with both. This ability allowed her to participate equally intensively in radical politics and Silver Age culture.

For Dubnova-Erlikh, interest in Russian culture went hand in hand with interest in Jewish culture and led to her involvement in the Jewish Historical-Ethnographic Society (which had before 1908 been a modest, narrowly specialized commission) founded by, among others, Dubnov and Maksim Vinaver (1862–1926), the lawyer and communal activist who later helped to found the Kadet party.[74] The Society was designed to spark curiosity in the Jewish past among Jews of the St. Petersburg intelligentsia brought up on Russian literature alone. The hope was that these newly-interested Jews would develop a closer connection to their people. Engaged in collecting and publishing materials as well as presenting lectures, the Society functioned until the late 1920s. Dubnova-Erlikh became an active member, even delivering a paper in 1910 based on documents in Polish on Berek Iuselevich (1763–1809), an officer in the Polish army who became an heroic symbol for Jewish nationalists after leading a Jewish regiment of light cavalry. The presentation apparently met with success. As Dubnova-Erlikh recalled,

> Representatives of Petersburg Jewish society sat at the meeting. Several of them were interested to hear what the daughter of the historian had to say. Some frowned on my being carried away by the revolutionary pitch; not all had sympathy for the Jewish legion. In response to my speech, there was no little fervor: it was gratifying to debate on equal footing with men who had previously looked down on me. Papa was a tinge embarrassed, but the president of the organization Maksim Vinaver embraced me with tears in his eyes.[75]

To Dubnova-Erlikh, simultaneous involvement with the cultural elite of Russian society and of Jewish society of St. Petersburg was neither forced nor far-fetched. She described herself as a "Russian Jew" (*russkaia evreika*), explaining laconically that her "combination of Russianness (*russkogo*) and Jewishness (*evreiskogo*) did not begin mechanically but rather organically."[76] Indeed, her literary activities and writings prove how naturally she moved from culture to culture; yet she found no way, if even she had tried, to combine them in a single work. Her literary corpus of the pre-Revolutionary period is divided into two parts along a Russian-Jewish fault line. For a Russian audience she wrote poetry in Russian. For a Jewish audience she wrote literary criticism in Russian.

The bifurcated nature of Dubnova-Erlikh's pre-Revolutionary writings is no more obviously demonstrated than during the year 1911, when her favorable review of a newly-translated volume of Bialik's poems appeared in *Evreiskii mir* and a collection of her own poems was published in collaboration with the journal *Apollon*.[77] Except for the fact that both periodicals appeared in Russian, they had little in common. *Evreiskii mir* was a short-lived and little-known organ generated by members of the Jewish intelligentsia featuring items of literary interest by Jewish authors writing in Yiddish or Hebrew, translated for an audience of Russian-reading Jews. *Apollon* was a popular journal of modern poetry intended for an audience of Russians interested in the latest works of those like Anna Akhmatova. The contrast between the two is most striking when one imagines Dubnova-Erlikh's personal encounters with the men involved in each publication, as described in her memoirs. On the one hand, she was becoming reacquainted with the writers who peopled the pages of *Evreiskii mir*, specters of a mostly-failed Hebrew and Yiddish literary revival whom she had met first in her father's study as a girl. At the same time, she was becoming involved with figures like Nikolai Gumilev, the suave editor of *Apollon*, whose seductive advances Dubnova-Erlikh spurned.[78] To the former group, she was merely the talented daughter of a colleague; to the latter, a writer with great potential in her own right. Significantly, it appears that each group was unaware of Dubnova-Erlikh's writings for the other: The largely older audience that read the organs of the Russian-Jewish press would hardly be interested in the new Russian literature they disparaged. Dubnova-Erlikh herself had noted her father's negative evaluation of the new literature:

Sucked into the whirlpool of the capital, [his daughter] was rarely at home. As the [father] wandered through his silent, empty dwelling he sometimes went to her desk. Beside the small Bible,

which he had given her and which they both considered a "talis-
man," lay the latest philosophical and literary anthologies and the
verse of modern poets. These books were alien to him. The poetry
was especially bewildering; it seemed mannered and convoluted.
He shut the book, muttering in annoyance, "Decadence." And in
his memory rose the enjoyable, cozy evenings beneath the hanging
kerosene lamp, devoted to Lermontov, Nekrasov, Fet.[79]

Despite (or perhaps because of) her father's distaste for the modern
poets, Dubnova-Erlikh's first volume of verse to appear in print is Symbolist in flavor. In a collection of nearly eighty poems entitled *Osenniaia
svirel'* (Autumnal Reed Pipe), the poet creates impressions—mere snap-
shots—that strive to affect the human senses. The first poem, which explains the collection's title and sets a mood for the whole, illustrates Dubnova-Erlikh's unpolished Symbolist efforts:[80]

> The intoxication of autumnal quiet sings in my soul,
> It swings slow sounds,
> And my song is simple like a rural reed pipe,
> A reed pipe of sunset and separation.
>
> In [the song] the dream is surrounded by white North
> And the purple sunset is silent.
> The heather reddens, and the light sound of leaves
> bashfully falls in the mist.
>
> You threw the gentle one into the sleeping rustling grass
> And a remote path broke into bloom,
> And sadness went away to wander in the evening sadness of the
>   groves.
> Loving, conjuring, fading.
>
> And a pine needle pierced [my] breast.
> And torment grows red in the fire of the rowan trees.
> And my song is a reed pipe,
> And my song is an arrow strained by your bow.

The wind rustling, flickering the bowstring,
The arrow flies into the transparent sunset,
And the arrow welcomes autumn and drowns in her blueness,
In mute and grateful anguish.

That the poem is marred by obscurity and imitation is evident from
Dubnova-Erlikh's own retrospective evaluation of *Autumnal Reed Pipe*.
Years later, while reviewing the "yellowed pages of [the book] published in 1911," she expressed a desire to strike large chunks of the
verse from the book that "seemed confused and obscure, in the cast of
Symbolism."[81] She acknowledged, nonetheless, that they evoked a certain mood and era in her life. She persevered in her poetic pursuits,
bolstered by the support of those she called "her teachers," including
Ivanov, Briusov, and Blok, who praised her collection after receiving
copies from the poet.[82] Surely, the magnificent poem "Mat'" (Mother),
in which Dubnova-Erlikh found her own voice, was partially responsible for their accolades.

"Mother" is one of many poems in the collection that focuses on the
experiences of women. In fact, Dubnova-Erlikh devoted an entire section
of *Autumnal Reed Pipe* to "representations of women" and included
therein poetry on, among others, Mona Lisa and Ariadne.[83] "Mother" is a
dialogue between the title character and her daughter over the course of
the latter's adolescence. Composed with a lyrical simplicity that echoes
folk poetry, the poet spins a tale of growing generational tension, master-
fully evoking the Fates. The omniscient narrator opens the poem:[84]

Mother is at the window early
Bent, quietly weaving . . . [ellipsis in the original]
    Daughter, are you alone like before?
A year passed.

The folds of her morning garments are tender—
Her shoulders are inflamed with sweet bliss.

Mother continues to weave. Dawn is gone.
Noon is at the threshold.
    Daughter, are you white like before?

Time passed.
Behind the innocent whiteness of the garment,
An agitated breast heaves.

> *Daughter, my eyes are becoming dim—*
> *Where are you, Daughter, on which paths?*
> *Make sure you don't intertwine the red thread*
> *   into my white pattern . . .* [ellipsis in original]

Mother has no command over Destiny—
The thread of passion is already intertwined.

> *I am blind. My circle* [of life] *is closed.*
> *Where are you, Daughter? The paths are intertwined.*
> *But my hands still weave by habit . . .* [ellipsis in original]
> *Daughter, you sadden me. Where are you?*

A distant voice quietly flows:

> *I'm asking for the last time*
> *You weave the thread of passion.*
> *I know how to live by the sun.*
> *Now weave and hurry up.*
> *Only don't mix up the threads.*
> *In order to make it by evening, Mother,*
> *Weave me a white shroud.*

Here, timeworn metaphors (e.g. red for passion, white for purity and death) gain new life in a meditation on the intricacies of a changing mother-daughter relationship. A rebellious daughter longs for life experience; her mother longs for the pure daughter of old. Whether or not the poem is autobiographical in nature remains an open question.

The Conventions of Marriage and Motherhood

Surely, by 1911 when "Mother" appeared in the published collection, Dubnova-Erlikh was on her way to independence from her parents. She had recently returned from a year of study at the Sorbonne in Paris, to which she had been drawn "like a magnet," kindling the amusing fantasy that she would "run into Gavroche."[85] While the French Revolution was, of course, long over, Dubnova-Erlikh mingled with contemporary revolutionaries like Trotsky's sister Olga Davidovna Kameneva (a pseudonym for Bronshtein) and even came face to face with Lenin.[86] Her relationship with one revolutionary in particular would result in the weakening of ties to her mother and father, inasmuch as marriage results in distancing between child and parent.

When Genrikh Erlikh arrived in Paris in 1911, Dubnova-Erlikh had already made his acquaintance in Petersburg. Born and raised by Jewish parents of means in Lublin, he joined the Bund in 1903 while a student at the University of Warsaw and was arrested several times for revolutionary activities and expelled from the university. Later he graduated in law from St. Petersburg University and became a member of the central committee of the Bund. The details surrounding the couple's reacquaintance and budding romance are few. Dubnova-Erlikh is uncharacteristically terse throughout her memoirs in describing all aspects of their relationship and subsequent marriage. What is clear is that Erlikh "opened up for [her] a whole new social world in Paris;" the "nun of a distant cloister" had apparently come out of her convent.[87] At the end of the academic year (1910–11), Sofiia left for Finland to vacation with her parents at a relative's summer home, and within weeks Genrikh followed her there, where "in the earthly resinous quiet, it was maturely decided to join [their] lives."[88]

Sofiia's parents were generally happy with the decision. Remembering his own youth, Dubnov agreed to assist the couple in arranging a wedding ceremony involving the most minimal of requirements. He dashed a letter off to the rabbi of the Choral Synagogue in St. Petersburg explaining that he and his wife would not be present at the ceremony because his wife had recently undergone surgery. On September 9, 1911 the young couple stood, as Dubnova-Erlikh described it, "under an old [wedding] canopy. [Sofiia was wearing] . . . a gray woolen dress with a handbag on [her] shoulder. The witnesses were three elderly congregants. G[enrikh] mixed up the words of the ritual, and [Sofiia] corrected him in a whisper."[89] When the marital document was turned over to Sofiia, she noted the new surname assigned to her and, at that moment, vowed never to part with her maiden name. Thus Sofiia Dubnova-Erlikh was born. The hyphenated name would appear as a byline on future publications.

Dubnova-Erlikh's mother expressed the hope that marriage would tame her daughter, whom she feared was capable of taking reckless steps.[90] While marriage to a revolutionary was hardly the tranquil existence her mother dreamed of for her daughter, Dubnova-Erlikh did enthusiastically assume the roles of wife and, later, mother orchestrated by convention. In a way remarkably similar to her own mother and grandmother, she willingly subordinated her own aspirations to those of her husband. While he was involved in intensive political activity that kept him from his family for weeks or even months at a time, she engaged in management of their household and children and squeezed writing opportunities out of the limited available moments. Yet unlike her female relatives, Dubnova-Erlikh had a career of her own and a marriage based on equality.

After the couple returned to St. Petersburg following a year-long visit to Munich, pregnancy and then motherhood became all-consuming. Two sons were born within a span of two years: Aleksander (1912–1985) and Viktor (1914–). Concerned about how her mother would react to the nocturnal visits of various radical socialists, Dubnova-Erlikh refrained from asking for her assistance with the children.[91] This, coupled with her husband's frequent absences, meant responsibility for childrearing lay solely with her. Occasionally, Dubnova-Erlikh managed to assist Erlikh with his writing. To take but one instance, when he was slated to deliver a speech before the Duma on the pogroms against Jews, Dubnova-Erlikh wrote the text in its entirety as Aleksander played at her feet on the study floor.[92] Indeed, as Dubnova-Erlikh put it, "The rhythm of life [had been] interrupted . . . and the wheel of her life had completely turned." She was unperturbed by the drastic change, though; motherhood had "illuminat[ed] life with unexpected light" and drawn her back to the writer's tablet.[93]

Since the publication of Autumnal Reed Pipe five years earlier, Dubnova-Erlikh had sworn never to write poetry again unless the "words t[ook] shape in [her] soul."[94] Those words began to form, ironically, out of the very experiences that had prevented her from writing in the first place: Motherhood begat "Mat'" (Mother), a cycle of six poems evoking the anguish of a mother living through war and revolution. Writing in the wake of newly-emerging literary styles that valued clarity as well as craftsmanship, Dubnova-Erlikh sought "to respond to life, to encounter it" in language far more accessible to the reader.[95] To that end, she attempted to write simply, which proved no easy task for a poet whom, she claimed, had "grown accustomed to the convoluted nature of Symbolism."[96]

In "Mother" (a cycle of poems with the same name as her poem found in *Autumnal Reed Pipe*), Dubnova-Erlikh succeeded in her self-appointed task of exposing the seemingly contradictory emotions of tranquillity and unease that stir mothers, especially those forced to live in the shadow of warfare. In the first of the six sections of the exquisite cycle, the poet invites her reader to share a glimpse of languorous maternal routine, made blissful by its very repetition, dampened only by the absence of the father:[97]

> I feed the baby on the porch,
> as the sunset reddens the ploughed fields.
> The present day, like yesterday,
> is still in the same tender cycle.
>
> The breast is heavy from milk,
> The persistent mouth of the baby hurts my nipples.
> Like the distance, which is sleeping in the fog,
> the soul is quiet and broad.
>
> The soul is calm. The journey is finished.
> The seed is nurtured and ripened.
> The body is twisted from aches,
> But God's law shines forth.
>
> Over the son, I think of [his] father.
> My true friend, my eternal friend,
> Will you come? The ploughed fields are darkening
> and our son sleeps on the porch.

As in *Autumnal Reed Pipe*, Dubnova-Erlikh summoned imagery from nature, but here employed it as foreshadowing for the darkness she will evoke in the second section. The darkening ploughed fields augur the passing of years that bring the birth of a son who like his brother will go out into the world, leaving a bereft but self-aware mother in his wake:

> My younger son sleeps in the white heat,
> The elder plucks violets at the roadside.
> I know—the intoxication of anxiety will age in the cup,
> which is full of spring.
>
> You will take my blood and strength
> And you will leave—each to the one you are destined for.
> My singed soul
> squandered the vernal wealth.
>
> I'm indifferent to everything—[my] heart is not sad.
> For love there is neither borders nor goals.
> My older son kisses the dust of flowers.
> The younger sleeps in a tottering cradle.

Only in the third section does the mother reveal the underlying cause of her anxiety. Ordinary maternal fears are exacerbated by the unrest steadily growing around her family. As expressed below with poetic flair, she fears for her children's lives.

> There is awesome strength in the sad complaint
> of my children's helpless hands.
> In [my] heart the fright of gentle eyes
> will sting with its stinger.
>
> It is possible to leave your most dear thing
> to murder your own joy,
> only do not reject these little hands
> only do not forget them.
>
> It is incomprehensible to me
> whether blood or soul forges the links.
> It seems to my heart—they cannot be forgotten
> even in the grave.

Embedded in section four is the mother's gratitude to her children. Because of them, she will survive. The tasks and anxieties associated with childrearing, though burdensome, provide her with a raison d'être. Here, Dubnova-Erlikh returns once more to the now familiar imagery drawn from nature, which will be embellished further in the section that follows.

> Next to me you are growing up slenderly
> like two young trees.
> I'll spend my quiet days until the end
> in tireless care.

> Perhaps, I am unable [to endure] more,
> I do not shake the dust of the earth,
> I will only fan our violent spring
> with the autumnal quiet.

> You will not protect me from grief,
> my path is pensive and ascetic.
> You granted light burdens of anxiety
> to [my] dusky heart.

The climax of the cycle is reached in section five as the intimacy between mother and sons is broken as the mother abruptly turns from her tender brood outward to address herself to young women. Lest they interpret the litany of woes articulated in the earlier sections as a sign that they ought not enter maternity, she admonishes them to bear children. They, like Mother Earth, must bring forth life, aspects of which become loving metaphors for children's sweet hands, active feet, eager mouths with the strokes of Dubnova-Erlikh's masterful pen.

> Young woman, give birth to a child
> And you will become the mother of the world.

> And you will fall in love, brightly saddened,
> with everything small, timid and lonely:

Delicate twigs of spring
which are covered with fuzz,
Playful drops of rain
like the patter of small feet,
And young greedy grass
[suckled] by the swollen nipples of the earth,
And sad, red heather
on the roadside dust,
And the wind that sings lullabies,
rustling the swaying fields . . .

Young woman, do not be afraid of pain,
Tender one, give birth to a child.

The cycle ends with a coda that jolts the reader back to the cruel reality
at hand. In the sixth and final section, the mother turns back to her sons
and grants them permission to take the life she just exhorted others to
give. In the ravages of war, even murder is permissible, so long as it is
done with an awareness of what is being taken.

Only the cruel one has no wrath now
There are too many sorrows in the world.
Son, ascetically serving sacred objects—
If you must, you should murder.
The compelling call of revenge is bright,
But do not murder in vain.
Remember how you suckled innocently
at the maternal, warm breast.

The sophisticated balance of tenderness and cruelty struck in
"Mother" attracted the attention and admiration of Dubnov's colleague S.
An-ski (pseudonym of Solomon Zainwill Rapaport, 1863–1920), the author and folklorist who was responsible for composing the Bundist anthem "Di shvue" (The Oath). Dubnova-Erlikh had befriended An-ski six
years earlier after meeting him in her father's study. Though twenty-two
years her senior, An-ski had taken an immediate liking to Dubnova-Erlikh and invited her to accompany him to Finland for a meeting of So-

cialist Revolutionaries. She accepted, and the two remained close friends thereafter.[98] Upon completing the cycle, Dubnova-Erlikh entrusted it to An-ski. He recognized the artistry of the verse and, with the poet's permission, sent it to Maksim Gorki, who had recently become the literary editor of the antiwar journal *Letopis'* (The Chronicle).

Not only did Gorki promise to publish the poems, but his enthusiasm for her work led him to invite her to consider employment at *Letopis'*.[99] Within weeks, excerpts of "Mother" appeared in the journal, though in a slightly varied form; censors had expunged the lines sanctioning murder. Three years later the cycle was published as a separate volume.[100] Meanwhile, to her delight, Dubnova-Erlikh had joined the ranks of employed journalists. Gorki hired her with the intent of enlisting her help with editing and with providing his readers with a systematic introduction to Jewish literature, including Sholom Aleichem's stories and Bialik's poetry. Commenting on the new position at *Letopis'*, Dubnova-Erlikh asserted that she had dreamed for many years of becoming involved in the literary fellowship she had merely observed as a child.[101] As an adult, she formed her own connections to literary and political figures, becoming a frequent fixture at the editorial offices of *Letopis'*, where she interacted with others on an equal footing and reveled in the camaraderie.[102] The new position might have furnished her, finally, with an opportunity to draw upon and blend the two cultures she so cherished. But no sooner had she started at the magazine when the events of 1917 unleashed a tornado that caused, among other things, a cessation of its printing press.

Living in St. Petersburg and active in politics, the Dubnov-Erlikh family was in the eye of the storm. Erlikh became a member of the executive committee of the Soviet and was away from his wife and children day and night, updating them by telephone on the progress of the Revolution. For her part, Dubnova-Erlikh remained focused on her children but engaged politically as well. She was saddened by the bitter infighting among political parties and hoped the mass demonstrations being staged with upwards of a million people would act as a means for unifying the factions. Her own family was a case in point of the political divisiveness of the age. As members of the Bund, Dubnova-Erlikh and her husband aligned themselves with the Mensheviks, while Dubnov, after some wavering, began to support the Kadets.[103]

Immersion in New Cultures

Before long it became clear that Dubnova-Erlikh's beloved St. Petersburg was no longer a viable place in which to raise children. In 1918, hunger drove the family over the border to Poland, where they remained for the greater part of two decades. Leaving one set of parents for another, Dubnova-Erlikh and her sons initially stayed in Lublin at the Erlikhs', while her husband shuttled back and forth to Warsaw, a center of Bundist activity. The family of four reunited and settled in Warsaw by the winter of 1919. Though Dubnova-Erlikh was fluent in Polish, she continued to speak to her sons in her native tongue until her dying day.[104] Nevertheless, she became immersed in the cultural life of her adopted country as a theater critic.

Dubnova-Erlikh regularly contributed a column on theater to *Di folks-tsaytung,* a Bundist newspaper in Yiddish edited by her husband. While the work took her away from her sons in the evenings, she found the pace exhilarating until her elder son Aleksander registered a complaint about her absence. He longed for evenings past spent reading poetry or prose together, or recounting the day's events with his mother at hand. Torn by her dual allegiances, yet concerned lest her children not gain independence, Dubnova-Erlikh turned to composing poetry as an outlet for her anxieties. In her notebook, she scribbled the following:

> When you depart for school,
> in a brown beggar's cap,
> nibbling bread,
> I know your path
> and every crossroad along the way,
> and in the muffled din of the street
> I go to you inaudibly.
> But when you become an adult
> and are treading confidently and strongly
> you will return in the morning mist
> (how strange—so tall!),
> my heart will become sad,
> I will not see your steps upon the earth,
> my near one, my distant one.[105]

The close relationship between father and daughter had repeated itself in the next generation. In fact, following a path remarkably similar to her own, her younger son Viktor studied literature and history at home with his mother and math with a tutor. He enrolled at a local school at a relatively late age, by which time he had developed a strong affinity for poetry.[106]

Despite her son's protest, Dubnova-Erlikh carried on in her role as theater critic. Her employment brought her one evening in 1920 to a performance of her old friend An-ski's play "The Dybbuk," staged by Habimah, the troupe devoted to creating theater in Hebrew.[107] Perhaps a combination of nostalgia for her girlhood involvement in Hebrew drama and of sentiment aroused by the recent death of the playwright resulted in a gushing review. Dubnova-Erlikh praised An-ski, who, having been raised in the realist tradition, "suddenly blaze[d] forth with this dance of invincible, loving magnetism."[108] The review generated controversy as Yiddishists criticized the critic for championing Hebrew. She responded that language is beside the point; Habimah was first and foremost a world-class theater troupe.

While Dubnova-Erlikh's professional life thrived, Erlikh was arrested in the early 1920s. Although he was released within months, the family lived in constant fear that he would be taken from them a second time. Once he returned home, Erlikh took up once again with the Bund, editing *Di folkstsaytung* and participating in socialist international congresses, as well as sitting on the Warsaw city council and the *kehillah* board (local Jewish governing body). For her part, Dubnova-Erlikh, though immersed in Polish culture, continued to "listen to Russian voices," and so began translating the works of Russian authors like Babel, Maiakovskii, and Ehrenburg for her husband's newspaper.[109]

In 1925, Dubnova-Erlikh left Poland with her sons to accept an invitation to conduct research for a year at the Bund archive in Berlin as Erlikh set out for a speaking tour within the United States. Dubnova-Erlikh immediately became associated with the Russian émigré community in her new city, reestablishing ties with people she had known in St. Petersburg and reuniting with her parents, who had arrived in Germany in 1922. Dubnova-Erlikh would, a decade later, turn the fruits of her research into a two-part history of two inter-city Bundist unions in Eastern Europe.[110] The critic-turned-historian penned the book in Russian, but given the Bund's devotion to Yiddish, it was translated into and published in Yiddish in 1937 in order to reach the widest possible audience. That Dubnova-Erlikh chose to write a history relating to the Bund in Russian rather than Yiddish underscores her continuing dependence on and devotion to her mother tongue. Another twenty years would pass before books in Yiddish with her byline would be published—and these, too, were translated from Russian.[111]

When Dubnova-Erlikh returned to Warsaw in the late 1920s, she began to contribute articles to a Bundist journal in Polish, edited by her husband's close colleague Viktor Alter (1890–1941). Her articles on the problems of existence in the changed Polish social context struck a particularly sympathetic chord with young readers, especially students and factory workers. New forms of social intercourse that had been introduced by party work in political circles, summer camps, and the like had brought about the creation of a new moral order. As the conservatism generated by centuries of Catholicism in Poland began to dissolve, young people were banding together to discuss the newly-emerging progressive outlook. Dubnova-Erlikh became a celebrity of sorts at these meetings, though, as she explained it, she came "neither as an essayist, nor as a teacher, but simply as a comrade participating in a discussion of the questions."[112] In essence, she served as a role model to the young adults. And women, especially, would seek her out for practical help or advice.

Dubnova-Erlikh's optimism for a better future in Poland was dampened by worsening political circumstances across Europe and by news from her parents. In 1933, her mother died from cancer, and she remained for a spell with her father who had moved to Riga earlier that same year. Father and daughter continued to see each other in the summers when they vacationed together, and in 1935 they met in Vilna at the second congress of YIVO (*Yidisher Visenshaftlikher Institut*), the institute established for conducting research and preserving documents in Yiddish.[113] In 1939, during what was to become their final summer together, Erlikh summoned his wife home; Poland was under siege. On September 5, 1939 the family decided to leave Warsaw: the city to which "fate had cast [her] in World War I was now casting [her] off in World War II."[114] Following the crowds of refugees and retreating troops to the eastern border, the Erlikhs trudged through woods and across back roads.[115]

While Dubnova-Erlikh and her sons reached Vilna safely and remained there until 1941 before heading to America, Erlikh was arrested
along with his associate, Viktor Alter, by Stalin's secret police.[116] Once released in 1941 under a general amnesty for Polish prisoners, the two immediately went to work organizing a massive Jewish anti-Hitler front
with the aid of the Soviet secret police. Within two months, however,
their plans were frustrated when the police arrested them as alleged Nazi
spies. Until 1992, the only clue to Erlikh's fate was a short letter written
in 1943 by the then-Soviet Ambassador to the United States Maksim Liti-
nov announcing that he had been executed. Erlikh's niece Victoria Dubnova began a battle with the KGB in 1991 to unearth the details surrounding her uncle's death. The following year, she uncovered a
one-and-a-half page graphic description of Erlikh's suicide.[117] Dubnova-
Erlikh went to her grave believing that her husband had been murdered.

Dubnova-Erlikh lived out the latter half of her life in New York City,
involved once again in a Russian émigré community but immersed as
well in the life of her host country as represented by her literary and political activities. As mentioned above, she wrote histories of the Bund.
But she also participated in the civil rights movement and protested
against the Vietnam War. She continued to write poetry into the ninth
decade of her life. In 1973, at the age of eighty-eight, Dubnova-Erlikh
published a collection of her poetry spanning sixty-two years from 1910
to 1972—all penned in her native Russian—entitled *Stikhi raznykh let*
(Poems of Various Years), dedicated to her two sons.[118] She died on May
4, 1986 at the age of 101.

* * * * *

The Symbolists strove to create for their readers a single image that
would provide at a glance a multilayered and intricate reality—in a word,
a symbol, whose meaning went far beyond its appearance. In many ways,
Dubnova-Erlikh's last published work is a symbol. Its various characteristics point out the salient features of her life and literary career.

First, it is noteworthy that Dubnova-Erlikh dedicated *Poems of Various
Years* to her sons. From 1912, when she gave birth to her firstborn, she
devoted herself to the tasks of motherhood and let it dictate the shape
and pace of her career path. Maternity became the central theme of her
best work, and in her lengthy memoirs, Aleksander and Viktor figure

prominently. Mothering, she claimed, illuminated her life, and while she never allowed its light to overshadow her literary ambitions, the latter never came at the expense of her children. Of her own volition, Dubnova-Erlikh seemed to assume the stereotypical roles assigned to women. But, at the same time, she was no enthusiastic housewife. She had no love of domestic chores and, like other middle-class women of the era, employed servants to maintain her household. In addition, her education set her apart from women of her generation by allowing her to forge a career—one supported by her husband but also subordinated to his.

Secondly, the genre of her last published volume is of interest. While, in addition to verse, Dubnova-Erlikh wrote literary and theater criticism, history and biographies, social commentary and translations, her principal love was poetry. From her father she acquired a rich knowledge of verse, which she conveyed to her own children. But unlike him, by adolescence, she began to create her own poetry and did not stop until her death. She often used the poetic muse as a vehicle for reflecting on personal issues, and thus her poetry is saturated with the autobiographical, though not with Jewish themes. In the ongoing discussions of gender and genre in the Jewish context, it has been noted that a preponderance of women writing in the so-called "Jewish languages" of Hebrew and Yiddish were poets rather than prose writers.[119] A similar phenomenon, it has been argued, is not evident in the so-called "European languages" in which women took to writing novels.[120] Until now, participants in this discussion had identified European languages with those of the West. Factoring the Russian poetry of Dubnova-Erlikh (and Feiga Kogan, and the prose of Rashel' Khin) into the equation forces students of literature and history to examine the reality of Jewish women writing in the Eastern European languages as well and the larger implications of that phenomenon.

Thirdly and most significantly, Dubnova-Erlikh penned *Poems of Various Years* in Russian. This, despite the fact that it had been sixty-eight years since she had lived in the Russian Empire (with the exception of 1939–1941 when she lived under duress in Vilna after fleeing Poland). She departed from her homeland in 1918, at the age of thirty-three, and then resided over twenty years in Poland and forty-four years in the United States. Russian was her native tongue, and she employed it in her writing nearly to the exclusion of all the other languages she could speak and/or read, including Polish, Yiddish, Hebrew, German, French, and English. Even her works on the Yiddish-loving Bund were composed in Russian, as were her memoirs. And all known translations by Dubnova-Erlikh were from a foreign language into Russian. Yet, her archives reveal that late in life she was intensely involved in Yiddish culture of New York City. When she died, she was memorialized in the pages of the Yiddish press; and she merited inclusion in the standard work on Yiddish literary history.[121]

Dubnova-Erlikh moved to Russia's interior during her late adolescence, and St. Petersburg suited the woman born and raised on Autonomism. She fell in love with the city, identifying with its cultural offerings of both a Russian and Jewish nature. In effect, the capital afforded her the opportunity to live out Autnomism's ideal existence: to be, at one and the same time, a Russian and a Jew.

According to daughter and father, "Russian Jew" was not a contradiction.[122] For them, Jewishness implied neither faith nor religion; it was an inherited status with its own distinctive culture, which through a dynamic process was constantly being enriched by imports from other civilizations. Thus the Jewish culture in which Dubnova-Erlikh had been cultivated was not the classical one of Rabbinic texts; rather it was the newly-created modern one of secular Hebrew literature influenced by the West. As a girl, she was not familiarized with the former but it was natural that she be familiarized with the latter. After all, Jewish daughters of the middle class were regularly introduced to the riches of Western cultures. At the same time, for them, Russianness implied neither national nor ethnic but cultural distinction, which could be acquired and then combined with one's inherited national birthright. According to daughter and father then, in a multinational empire like Russia, Jews were one of many national minorites who could adopt the Russianness of their homeland while maintaining their autonomy, both political and cultural. A Russian Jew could thrive in the Russian Empire.

It could be said that Dubnova-Erlikh had been training to be a "Russian Jew" since birth. Dubnov had provided her with the necessary tools for co-existing within two cultures: language, grammar and a passion for the products of each. From childhood, she had followed the twists and turns of both cultures as each sought to recreate itself, based largely on Western models. Since Russian was her mother tongue, it was natural that it would capture her poetic talents rather than Hebrew or Yiddish, which she adopted as, at most, secondary and tertiary languages. Her literary achievements were, in effect, also her teacher's. His experiment to produce an enlightened Jew integrated into her native land had proven successful. Indeed, she was his spiritual heir.

As a one-time Symbolist, Dubnova-Erlikh might well have appreciated the title *Bread and Matzah* bestowed upon her memoirs. On the simplest level, the combination represents the anti-religious environment of Dubnova-Erlikh's child- and adulthood. As discussed, she referred to Passover seders in which the forbidden leavened product made its way onto her father's table together with the unleavened cakes. On a much deeper level, though, matzah evokes freedom from slavery, a crucial theme in Dubnova-Erlikh's political identity, which was, given her strong connection to the Bund, cast within a Jewish mold. And bread, in the Russian context, evokes all that is good, secure, and plentiful, thereby symbolizing the cultural nourishment that sustained Dubnova-Erlikh's spirit. As Slavic ethnographers would have it, bread has a reverential, nearly religious, connotation.[123] One could suggest, therefore, that for Dubnova-Erlikh, Russian culture (symbolized by the bread) and Jewish political ties (symbolized by the matzah) functioned as her faith. Be that as it may, the title of her memoirs surely functions as a fitting symbol for Dubnova-Erlikh's hyphenated existence.

Conclusion

A Composite Biography

Eastern Women Typical of the West

It is likely that Hava Shapiro's own life experiences led her to conclude in 1930 that

> "Woman's search for light" . . . predated that of man: She recognized the aspirations and ideals of the *intelligent* long before the Jewish Enlightenment movement. [For] she was schooled in the world of literature—being exempt from the yoke of the Torah—at the same time that the boy was still immersed in the . . . Torah.[1]

The details concerning the lives of Jewish women writers that fill these pages strengthen Shapiro's case considerably. We have discerned how the Jewish tradition's inattention to formal education for girls left daughters of the middle-class—including Markel-Mosessohn, Shapiro, Khin, Kogan, and Dubnova-Erlikh—free to pursue opportunities for study beyond the Jewish purview while their sons were limited theoretically to Jewish learning alone. Even among the Jewish masses, opposition to Russian schools was much less stringent with regard to girls than boys. Daughters of the Jewish bourgeoisie in Eastern Europe became, in effect, a "privileged" class among Jews insofar as cultivation of a broad, refined mind was concerned. Thus, by the time the Haskalah struck deep roots in the Tsarist Empire, a group of secularly educated Jewish women was already looking westward for cultural inspiration and enlightenment.

These enlightened Jewish women formed part of the phenomenon of cultured, urbanized, female professionals emerging in late nineteenth-century Russia. Taking advantage of increased educational opportunities for women at home and abroad, along with the growing acceptance of female professionals among the populace, Russian and Jewish women alike pursued careers as lawyers, midwives, and writers. The literature of pioneering Jewish authors and poets analyzed here provides new evidence of how women functioned in society. Neither housewife par excellence nor political anarchist, the Jewish woman writer represents a different kind of Eastern European Jew, one who challenges sentimental stereotypes engraved in the collective Jewish memory.

While it is impossible to describe *the* Jewish woman writer in Tsarist Russia, the composite biography of their disparate lives yields several shared characteristics.

Socioeconomic background

The majority of Jewish women writers in Tsarist Russia came from the middle class. Markel-Mosessohn's father was an affluent businessman and her husband was a merchant. Shapiro's family had been in the lucrative paper-manufacturing business for generations. Khin's husbands were lawyers. Kogan's father was a furrier and shopkeeper. And Dubnova-Erlikh's maternal ancestry was endowed with some prosperity, while her father's attitudes and occupation, if not his income, resembled those of the bourgeoisie.

As members of the Jewish middle class, each of the Jewish women writers received an excellent secular education. Tutors (all), enrollment in gymnasia (Khin, Kogan and Dubnova-Erlikh), attendance at university courses in Russia (Kogan and Dubnova-Erlikh) or abroad (Shapiro and Khin) provided them with skills that granted them entrée to the expanding literary realm in the Tsarist Empire. In addition to Russian (which was for Shapiro, Khin, Kogan and Dubnova-Erlikh their native tongue), they mastered German, French, and other languages that assured them exposure to European literary traditions, which then influenced their contributions to Russian-Jewish culture.

The Influence and Company of Men

These Jewish women writers remained self-consciously aware of their trailblazing status, and while some (Markel-Mosessohn and Shapiro) suffered self-doubt, all sought the company of literary men both to garner support for their efforts and to assuage the loneliness of the solitary writing life. In fact, men's examples and encouragement proved crucial in their professional development. Markel-Mosessohn relied on Yehudah Leib Gordon, Moses Leib Lilienblum, and Abraham Mapu, as well as her husband, Anshel, to steer the course of her writing career, which was buttressed by the maskilim's desire to translate foreign works into Hebrew. Reuven Brainin, David Frischmann, and Y.L. Peretz, albeit in different ways, provided Hava Shapiro with the assistance necessary to start publishing, and her participation in the latter's literary gatherings remained with her as a fond memory throughout her life. Khin, for her part, turned to Ivan Turgenev, whose advice influenced both her educational choices and her short stories in the realist tradition. Her friendships with the literati at home and abroad were a near-constant preoccupation and a source of self-confidence. Kogan's attachment to the Symbolists Valeri Briusov and Viacheslav Ivanov had a direct impact on the nature of her published poetry, while Menahem Gnessin pushed her to pursue her love of Hebrew through study and theater. Dubnova-Erlikh's relationship to her father is legendary. His desire to make her into his "spiritual heir" met with success, as she forged an independent life from his ideological and intellectual model. Moreover, Jewish women writers received support from literary men who either intervened to get their writings into print (Markel-Mosessohn, Shapiro, Dubnova-Erlikh) or composed favorable reviews once they appeared (Markel-Mosessohn, Shapiro, Khin, Kogan, Dubnova-Erlikh).

Geographic Locale

High culture flourishes in cities. After all, the larger the population the more likely that artistic talents, experimentation, and novelty will be supported and patronized. Not surprisingly then, these Jewish women writers were born in, or eventually moved to, cities where they could express themselves in the printed word. Khin and Kogan were born and raised in Moscow, though in radically different settings. Dubnova-Erlikh spent her childhood in various locales (Mstislavl, Odessa, Vienna) but claimed to find herself most at home in the efflorescent cultural and political activities of St. Petersburg. Though she left the capital by the age of thirty-two, her attachment to it, like Khin's for Moscow, remained constant. While Markel-Mosessohn and Shapiro did not reside in Russia's interior, they resided off and on in major cities within the Russian Empire or Congress

Poland or abroad. City living afforded these women links to cultural activity, both of a Russian and Jewish nature.

Domestic Life

In large measure, these Jewish women writers rejected bourgeois Jewish standards of domesticity that idealized marriage and motherhood and relegated women to the private realm. At the same time, of course, the act of publishing virtually guaranteed that they fell outside the norms established for women by Jewish tradition. Markel-Mosessohn came close to finding and maintaining a marriage based on egalitarianism and friendship—that is, until her husband Anshel met with financial ruin and disgrace. She bore no children. Shapiro's mismatch to Limel Rosenbaum ended in divorce, whereupon she left her only child temporarily to his father's care. She maintained a long-distance romance with Reuven Brainin for a quarter century. Khin converted to Catholicism to dissolve her marriage to Solomon Feld'shtein and then wed another Jew, Osip Gol'dovskii, who confessed Protestantism to marry her. She had a son Mikhail. Kogan appears to have been no man's wife and no child's mother. Dubnova-Erlikh married Genrykh Erlikh, and she raised their two sons Aleksander and Viktor almost single-handedly due to her husband's long absences from home. Except for Dubnova-Erlikh, whose marital separations were necessitated by political instability, the domestic relationships of the writers caused them intermittent or long-term sorrow. One can draw the obvious conclusion that their unusual literary talents and ambitions clashed with the conventional roles assigned to women. The fortunate ones either created new roles for themselves (perhaps, Kogan) or found men who accepted their unconventional ways (Markel-Mosessohn, Khin, Dubnova-Erlikh); while the less fortunate suffered, using the pages of their writing tablet as solace (Shapiro).

It is important to note that the very factors that propelled these Jewish women into the literary arena figured prominently as well in the lives of non-Jewish women writers of the Tsarist Empire. Scholars like Charlotte Rosenthal have shown that success for female authors from 1885 to 1917 depended largely on "being born into a professional family, getting oneself a high-school level education, taking up residence in one of the two capital cities [and] the acquisition of culture and connections through relatives or marriage. . . ."[2] Significantly, the women writers in this study not only fit Rosenthal's paradigm but resemble women writers everywhere in nineteenth-century Europe. As Westernized Eastern Europeans, they resembled their sisters in Berlin and Vienna more than those in the shtetls of the Pale. Characteristics once thought typical only of Jewish women of nineteenth-century Western Europe are evident at the same time among Jewish women in the East.

What the Writings Reveal: Cultural Production and Gender

In contrast to their biographies, which show common features, there is little that connects the writings of the Jewish women writers in our study.[3] Indeed, they are noteworthy for their dissimilarities and share neither genre nor theme. Markel-Mosessohn acted primarily as a translator and published only four original works at her brief stint at *Ha-melitz* as the Viennese correspondent. After Shapiro's preliminary attempts to depict women's inner experience in short sketches, she followed in Markel-Mosessohn's journalistic footsteps, writing frequently for the Hebrew press on culture and politics. Khin acquired a reputation as a playwright and short story writer in the realist tradition, using Russian as her medium and occasionally depicting the lives of middle-class Jews in her works. Kogan published several volumes of Symbolist poetry in Russian, while her archives reveal her attention to Jewish themes incorporated into verse of a personal nature. Dubnova-Erlikh, too, composed Russian poetry during the Silver Age and later turned to history, biography, and journalism. Even the important act of translation, which was undertaken by progenitors of both Russian and Jewish cultures to enhance the status and quality of their respective literature, was carried out by only four of the five women. (There are translations only among Kogan's manuscripts and none in Shapiro's bibliography.)

Perhaps the most significant distinguishing feature of the writings is language. Markel-Mosessohn and Shapiro wrote in Hebrew; Khin, Kogan, and Dubnova-Erlikh in Russian. Focusing on how the Hebraists, on the one hand, and the Russian writers, on the other, portrayed women will shed light on cultural production among Jews in late Tsarist Russia.

The Female Experience in Two Tongues: Failure and Success

Of all the writers, Shapiro offers the most intensive examination of the position of women. Her initial attempt to reveal the inner soul of women to the Hebrew-reading public through an allegorical sketch entitled "The Rose" about a flower that is plucked from the garden and longs to return to its natural environment appeared in 1901. It met with an enthusiastic response from male Hebraists, who sought to invigorate and enhance their language with qualities deemed inherent only to females. Besides Shapiro, they had already showered accolades on Markel-Mosessohn and other women whom they regarded as fonts of emotion and aesthetic refinement, in contrast to most Jewish men, whose literary talents, they argued, had been corrupted by centuries of traditional Jewish study. But for all their praise, their reviews of Shapiro's sketch show that they did not understand it in the way she had intended. Rather than viewing it as an allegory for women who felt restrained by unnatural boundaries dictated by convention, they interpreted it, in keeping with their nationalistic ideology, as an allegory for Jews longing for a homeland in which they could thrive and grow freely.

A series of sketches similar to and including "The Rose" was published in a single volume in 1909, but before long Shapiro's initial ardor for self-revelation faded and she turned to the neutral ground of journalism. Like Markel-Mosessohn before her, she recognized the danger of women trespassing Hebrew's linguistic divide. As the language of Jewish study and worship, it had for centuries been the domain of men. When it was resurrected as a vehicle for secular culture at the end of the nineteenth century, its creators claimed to seek women's participation so as to elevate Hebrew to the level of European languages, which they felt were infused with "female sensibilities." At this stage in the development of secular Hebrew culture, women's contributions as translators were much appreciated, but their revelations concerning the female experience found no audience. The largely male Hebrew reading public had little interest in such disclosures. The ancient tongue remained a vehicle of self-revelation for men only.

Women seeking to express their experience in print made far more progress in languages other than Hebrew. Khin's short stories and plays and Dubnova-Erlikh's poetry in Russian succeeded where Shapiro's sketches had not. Khin's depictions of gentiles and Jews alike show the inner turmoil of ambitious and educated women of the middle-class who broke with convention and forged ahead to actualize ideals promulgated by a segment of Russian society who regarded women's emancipation, at least theoretically, as a good. Since her literary debut in 1883, Khin's works proved popular with the Russian-reading public, who had grown accustomed by then to women exposing the constraints of their situation in vivid terms.[4] The popularity of Khin's works is evident from her large bibliography, which includes two plays performed at the Malyi Theater and two volumes of collected short stories, one of which was printed in three editions over the course of eight years. Through the years, Khin befriended distinguished members of the Russian cultural elite, whom she came to host at her home. Significantly, many of her inner circle expressed a considerable amount of sympathy toward Jews.

A generation after Khin, Dubnova-Erlikh used verse to draw attention to women's lives in general and the experience of motherhood in particular. Her exquisite six-poem cycle "Mother" achieves what the Hebraists desired for their own language. That is to say, Dubnova-Erlikh infused Russian with "feminine sensibilities," if by the latter we mean what they did not—drawing on the unique experiences, and not the so-called innate attributes, of women. "Mother" became a favorite among the public, appearing in three different venues—as a separate volume, in a Russian journal, and in an anthology of poetry by various authors. It was even resurrected two decades ago and republished in Tel Aviv. Although Dubnova-Erlikh's primary attachments were to Jews, she, like Khin, formed associations with important figures in Russian culture.

While it is apparent that Khin and Dubnova-Erlikh passed easily into the Russian cultural milieu, it is important to note that only Khin attempted to present Jewish themes in her writings. Whereas Dubnova-Erlikh, a poet of the Silver Age, muted her Jewish voice, Khin, a Russian realist, occasionally referred to Jewish matters. In several short stories, she depicted the reality she knew well: Jewish men—and women—whose socioeconomic background launched them into a Russian society not yet prepared to live up to its ideals of unity and fraternity. The stories appeared in *Voskhod*, the most important organ of the Russian-Jewish press, where they were reviewed favorably. Apparently, the problems she depicted knew no gender. These stories, unlike Shapiro's sketches, could also be appreciated by Jewish men. Russian-Jewish culture, as well as Russian culture, provided a hospitable environment for Khin's creations.

* * * * *

Creative contributors to both Hebrew and Russian cultures wanted to emulate the offerings of Western European literature and thus embraced women (and men) educated in the ways of the West. Yet Russian culture could tolerate diversity far more easily than the fledgling secular culture of the ancient tongue. At the same time, Jewish women were more likely to gravitate toward creative efforts in non-Jewish languages. After all, Jewish girls were rarely trained in Hebrew, and daughters of the middle class had at best a minimal interest in Yiddish. Moreover, for obvious reasons, those inclined to write are more likely to produce literature in their native tongue, which, in the case of Jewish women writers, was usually Russian. So in the end, it was in Russian rather than secular Hebrew that Jewish women writers in Tsarist Russia best expressed themselves. To succeed as a writer, a Jewish woman needed to venture beyond the Pale—geographically and otherwise—to the interior of Russia's cultural landscape.

Notes

Introduction

1. See Steven Zipperstein's *Imagining Russian Jewry* (Seattle: University of Washington Press, 1999) for a discussion of the Jews' romance with the shtetl.

2. See Naomi Shepherd's collective biography *A Price Below Rubies: Jewish Women as Rebels and Radicals* (Cambridge: Harvard University Press, 1993).

3. There is a mere trio of references to women in Simon Dubnov's classic three-volume *History of the Jews in Russia and Poland* (Philadelphia: Jewish Publication Society of America, 1916), 1:121, 2:113, 3:30. For both separate articles and anthologies of articles on the experiences of Jewish women of Western and Eastern Europe, see the bibliography.

4. For a discussion of the memoirs, see Shulamit Magnes, "Pauline Wengeroff and the Voice of Jewish Modernity," in *Gender and Judaism*, ed. T.M. Rudavsky (New York: New York University Press, 1995), 181–90.

5. Paulina Vengerova, "Iz dalekavo proshlavo," (From the Distant Past) *Voskhod* (October 1902): 28–41 and (November 1902): 70–82 (translated from the German).

6. I am grateful to Mr. Aleksander Leyfell for allowing me to peruse his meticulous, handwritten index of contributors to *Voskhod*.

7. "The Writings of Yetty Wohllerner," *Kokhvei yitzhak* 18 (1853): 39–40.

8. See Maria Saker', "Ob evreiakh v zapadnom krae" (About Jews on the Western Border) *Den'* 7 (1869). The weekly *Den'* (1869–71) was an organ of the Society for the Promotion of Culture among the Jews of Russia, a group established by wealthy Jews of St. Petersburg for overcoming the perceived religious, social, and cultural separatism of Jews.

9. Alice Stone Nakhimovsky, *Russian-Jewish Literature and Identity* (Baltimore: The Johns Hopkins University Press, 1992), 6.

10. Marion A. Kaplan, *The Making of the Jewish Middle Class: Women, Family and Identity in Imperial Germany* (New York and Oxford: Oxford University Press, 1991) and Paula E. Hyman, *Gender and Assimilation in Modern Jewish History: The Roles and Representations of Women* (Seattle and London: University of Washington Press, 1995).

11. Christine Johnson, *Women's Struggle for Higher Education in Russia,*

1855–1900 (Kingston [Ontario]: McGill-Queens University Press, 1987), 31 and Preface.

12. Benjamin Nathans has indicated, for example, that Jewish girls were a disproportionate presence in St. Petersburg's primary and secondary schools. By the 1880s, the percentage of Jewish girls in the city schools was over four times that of the population as a whole. See his "Beyond the Pale: The Jewish Encounter with Russia, 1840–1900," (Ph.D. diss., University of California at Berkeley, 1995), 141.

13. Benjamin Harshav, *Language in Time of Revolution* (Los Angeles, CA: University of California Press, 1993), 27.

14. In his influential work *Prophecy and Politics: Socialism, Nationalism and the Russian Jews, 1862–1917* (Cambridge, England: Cambridge University Press, 1982), Jonathan Frankel deems the events of 1881 as the fire that fueled the rejection of emancipation and assimilation in favor of autonomous national revival. In the time since his work appeared, however, a number of scholars have proposed significant revisions of aspects of Frankel's argument.

CHAPTER ONE: MIRIAM MARKEL-MOSESSOHN

1. Miriam Markel-Mosessohn (hereafter MMM) to Yehudah Leib Gordon (hereafter Yalag), 19 Tammuz 1868, transcript in the hand of MMM. Two copies of MMM's letters to Yalag are housed at the Jewish National and University Library Archive, Hebrew University, Jerusalem. One set is filed in the Schwadron Collection under MMM's name. The other identical set is in the Yalag archive, 40 761. I used the former set and refer to these according to the table of contents fixed and furnished by the archivist of the Schwadron Collection. Other materials found among Markel-Mosessohn's archive in the Schwadron Collection are described later in the chapter. All translations from the Hebrew are my own.

2. Ibid.

3. See Shaul Stampfer, "Gender Differentiation and Education of the Jewish Woman in Nineteenth-Century Eastern Europe," in *From Shtetl to Socialism, Studies in Polin*, ed. Antony Polonsky (London and Washington: Littman Library of Jewish Civilization, 1993), 187–211.

4. See Naomi Seidman, *A Marriage Made in Heaven* (Berkeley, CA: University of California Press), 11–39.

5. For an overview of the creation of modern Hebrew, see Shalom Spiegel, *Hebrew Reborn* (Cleveland: World Publishing Company, 1962).

6. Literally "anchored woman," according to Jewish law, an agunah is a mar-

ried woman who is separated from her husband and cannot remarry either because she cannot obtain a divorce from him or because it is not known whether he is still alive. According to Jewish law, women may initiate divorce proceedings only in certain limited cases, and the husband alone has the power to grant or deny her request.

7. For analyses of "The Tip of the Yud," see Michael Stanislawski, *For Whom Do I Toil?* (New York: Oxford University Press, 1988), 125–29 and Zilla Jane Goodman, "Traced in Ink: Women's Lives in 'Qotzo shel yud' by Yalag and 'Mishpachah' by D. Baron," in *Gender and Judaism*, 191–208.

8. Yalag's letters to each of the other five women appear in *Iggerot Yehudah Leib Gordon*, ed. Isaac Jacob Weissberg, 2 vols. (Warsaw, 1894), 1:312, 2:5–6, 157–58, 330–32, 338–39, 365–66, 375. Their letters to him are not extant.

9. Yalag to MMM, 26 Tammuz 1868, *Tzror iggerot Yalag el Miriam Markel-Mosessohn* (A Collection of Yehudah Leib Gordon's Letters to Miriam Markel-Mosessohn) ed., Avraham Yaari (Jerusalem: Darom, 1936), 5–6 [Hebrew].

10. Sarah Novinsky, "Ḥokhmot Nashim" (Wisdom of Women) [consisting of Novinsky's letter to her father, Aug. 8, 1876], *Ha-boker or* (1877): 153–55. The only biographical data on Novinsky indicates that she was the daughter of Hayim Novinsky, who was the son of Mordecai Lipshitz of Poland. The Hebrew monthly *Ha-boker or* appeared intermittently in Lemberg (Lvov) and later in Warsaw (1876–86).

11. Iris Parush, "Readers in Cameo: Women Readers in Jewish Society of Nineteenth-Century Eastern Europe," *Prooftexts* 14 (1994): 17.

12. For a general discussion of women in the Enlightenment, see Peter Gay, *The Enlightenment: An Interpretation*, 2 vols. (New York: Knopf, 1969), 2: 33–34.

13. Eliezer Ben-Yehudah, as cited by Nurit Govrin in *Devash mi-sela* (Tel Aviv: Misrad ha-bitaḥon), 47.

14. *Iggerot Yehudah Leib Gordon*, letter no. 103 (Nov. 8, 1881), 2: 5–6.

15. For a discussion of the "Woman Question" in the general Russian context, see chapter three.

16. Besides Gordon's "Kotzo shel yud," see Moses Leib Lilienblum's manifesto against the traditional view of Jewish women in *Ketavim avtobiografiim* (Autobiographical Writings), ed. Shlomo Breiman, 3 vols. (Jerusalem: Mosad Bialik, 1970), 2: 89–93.

17. As early as 1835, a girls' branch of the local Jewish community school was

opened in Odessa. See Steven A. Zipperstein, *The Jews of Odessa* (Stanford: Stanford University Press, 1985), 102.

18. See, for example, the protagonist Rachel in R. A. Braudes' *Ha-dat ve-hehayim,* who is modeled on Lopukhov, Chernyshevskii's famous Russian "feminist" in *What is to be Done?* Rachel fights for her independence and refuses to surrender to any kind of imposed marriage. She emancipates herself through books and popular revolutionary doctrines and takes part in maskilic campaigns as an equal with men. See Ben Ami Feingold, "Feminism in Hebrew Nineteenth-Century Fiction," *Jewish Social Studies* (1987): 235–50.

19. The correspondence of Yehudah Leib Gordon, Abraham Mapu, and Moses Leib Lilienblum with women will be discussed below.

20. Abby R. Kleinbaum, "Women in the Age of Light," in *Becoming Visible. Women in European History*, eds. Renate Bridenthal and Claudia Koonz (Boston: Houghton Mifflin, 1977), 219–35.

21. For further discussion, see Marion Kaplan, *The Making of the Jewish Middle Class: Women, Family and Identity in Imperial Germany.* Diana Greene argues that female authors in Russia drew on but adapted Western literary conventions to their needs. See her "Gender and Genre in Pavlova's *A Double Life,*" *Slavic Review* 54 no. 3 (1995): 563–77.

22. *Iggerot Yehudah Leib Gordon,* 2:157–58. For more on Pohazhavski, who emigrated to the land of Israel in 1889, see Nurit Govrin, *Devash mi-sela,* 114–71.

23. David Frischmann, "Mikhtav rishon," *Kol kitvei David Frischmann* (Warsaw: Stybel Publishing Co., 1924), 8 vols., 5:10.

24. Shmuel Feiner, "Ha-ishah ha-yehudiyah ha-modernit: mikrah-mivḥan be-yaḥasei ha-haskalah ve-ha-modernah," *Zion* 58 no. 4 (1993): 453–99. Professor Feiner told me that he is currently working with Professor Tovah Cohen of Bar-Ilan University on an anthology of Hebrew writings composed by women of nineteenth-century Eastern Europe. See also Ben Ami Feingold, "Feminism in Nineteenth-Century Fiction," *Jewish Social Studies* 49 (1987): 235–50. David Biale takes a different tack, emphasizing as he does the maskilim's "neutralization of sexuality within a new [bourgeois] family framework." See his *Eros and the Jews: From Biblical Israel to Contemporary America* (New York: Basic Books, 1992), 148–62.

25. See, for example, the 239-page volume devoted to the correspondence between Yehudah Leib Gordon and Moses Leib Lilienblum, *Iggerot Moshe Leib Lilienblum le-Yehudah Leib Gordon,* ed. Shlomo Breiman (Jerusalem, 1968).

26. See Feiner, "Ha-ishah ha-modernit," 491–97, for an enumeration of women who wrote sporadically to editors of Hebrew newspapers.
27. It is analogous, in our own day, to saying "woman doctor," which points out the exceptional nature of women practicing this professon while arguably undermining those women who do.
28. See below for a discussion of their relationship.
29. See Devorah Efrati's letter of 20 Kislev 1852 to Abraham Mapu published in *Ha-magid* 2 no. 12 (1857): 46.
30. For correspondence, see *Iggerot Yehudah Leib Gordon*, 2: 330–32 and 338–39. Her poem, known both as "Zion" and "Al tal ve-al matar" ("Not dew and not rain") appeared in *Kenesset yisrael* 2 (1887): 107.
31. Yosef Klausner, *Historiyah shel ha-sifrut ha-ivrit ha-ḥadashah*, 4 vols. (Odessa, 1909–25), 4: 279 and Reuven Fohen, "Shir nishkaḥ" (A forgotten poem) *Ha-olam* 46 (June 30, 1938): 835–37.
32. For David Shapira's defense of Gordon, see "Ḅikoret le-bikoret," *Ha-boker or* 1886 (special edition).
33. This movement constituted the intermediate link between the forerunners of Zionism in the middle of the nineteenth century and the beginnings of political Zionism with the appearance of Theodor Herzl and the First Zionist Congress in 1897.
34. The poet adopted an ABAB rhyme scheme throughout in its original, which I did not adhere to in my translation. Her grammatical feat elevates the poem's standing to a certain limited extent.
35. Upon hearing of the deaths of Saul and Jonathan, David laments: "O hills of Gilboa—let there be no dew or rain on you, or bountiful fields, for there the shield of warriors lay rejected, the shield of Saul, polished with oil no more." See II Samuel 1:21.
36. An oblique reference to Psalm 137, alluding to the Babylonian destruction of Jerusalem and subsequent mourning and exile.
37. *Iggerot*, 2: 331.
38. Ibid., 332.
39. Ibid., 339. Gordon told Rivkah Ratner of Shapira's generous gift after Ratner sent a similar frame to him in 1892. See *Iggerot*, 2:375.
40. Poems either to or about Shapira appear in *Kitvei Yehudah Leib Gordon* (Tel Aviv: Dvir, 1960), 298–300.
41. My translation does not preserve the poem's original rhyme scheme, in which the last word of each verse rhymes.
42. An oblique reference to the biblical Sarah to whom Yalag's contemporary Sarah presumably deserves comparison.

43. Reference to citron, one of the four species used for ritual purposes at the autumnal festival of Sukkot.

44. *Shapir* is an Aramaic word for "good."

45. *Ahavat yesharim* (Part I: Vilna, 1881; Part II: Vilna, 1883). A similarly meager entry on Meinkin appears in William Zeitlin, *Kiryat sefer bibliotheca hebraica post-Mendelssohniana*, 2 vols. Second edition (New York: Arno Press, 1980), 1: 235. For more recent revelations regarding Meinkin, see Morris Rosenthal, "A Girl Can't Become a Gaon?" in *Women's League Outlook* (Winter 2000).

46. *Iggerot*, 1: 312.

47. *Mevaker* (Gordon's pseudonymn meaning "the critic"), "Review of *Ahavat yesharim* (Part I)," *Voskhod* (Apr. 1881): 40–43.

48. David Frischmann, "Review of *Ahavat yesharim*," *Ha-boker or* 6 (1881): 387–91.

49. Note that throughout this chapter I refer to the subject by her married name of Markel-Mosessohn even when discussing her life before marriage.

50. *Encyclopedia Judaica*, 1st ed., s.v. "Vilkaviškis."

51. Searches for biographical data on Markel-Mosessohn's relatives yielded no results. Her letters offer only the vaguest clues about them.

52. That Shimon Wierzbolowki was quite affluent is attested by a letter of Lilienblum in which he declared: "The father of our friend Miriam Markel is worth 25,000 rubles." In 1897, when Russia moved to the gold standard, a ruble was worth 50 cents to the dollar. See Letter (14 Nisan 5631 [1871]), *Iggerot Moses Leib Lilienblum le-Yalag*, 224.

53. See Jacob Katz, *Out of the Ghetto* (Cambridge, MA: Harvard University Press, 1973). He coined the useful phrase "(semi-)neutral society" to be applied to this historical context.

54. Without exception, every biographical source on Markel-Mosessohn records that she was born in 1841, and most record that she died in 1921. This is not accurate, as based on her archival holdings, including especially an Austrian travel document of March 15, 1906, which gives her year of birth as 1839. See Markel-Mosessohn, Schwadron Collection, Miscellaneous Document no. 15. Yaari gives the exact date of death as 7 Tevet 5681 (December 18, 1920). See his introduction, *Tzror*, 1.

55. The biblical Miriam was the sister of Aaron and Moses. She was known as a prophet and led the women of Israel at the Sea of Reeds. See Exodus 15: 20–21.

56. Letter of MMM to Unknown, Sunday of week of *parashat vayakhel* [1875].

57. No addressee appears on the letter. However, its contents indicate that it

was being sent to one who would pass the biographical information therein to Meyer Kayserling, who was at that time collecting data for a book on Jewish women. The book appeared four years later. The entry on MMM appears on pages 311–12. See the bibliography for the complete citation.

58. Dan Miron, "Why was There No Women's Poetry in Hebrew before 1920?" in Sokoloff, et. al., eds. *Gender and Text in Modern Hebrew and Yiddish Literature*, 69; Emanuel Etkes, *Lita Biyrushalayim* (Jerusalem: Yitzhak Ben-Zvi, 1991), 208 and 224; Dov Sdan, *Ben din le-ḥeshbon* (Tel Aviv: Dvir, 1963), 367–70.

59. Shaul Stampfer confirms Miriam's contention that coeducation was the norm at Jewish primary schools. See his "Gender Differentiation,"189.

60. Kiddushin 29a stipulates that a father is obligated to teach his son Torah. Berakhot 17a delineates that the role of women in the study of Torah is in encouraging and enabling their husbands and sons to pursue it.

61. MMM described her mother as "my good and compassionate and wise mother."

62. Letter of MMM to Unknown, Sunday of week of *parashat vayakhel* [1875].

63. Ibid.

64. See, for example, the discussion on the early life of Yehudah Leib Gordon in *For Whom Do I Toil?*, 8–24.

65. See the following chapter on Hava Shapiro for such a case. As well, see Paula Hyman, *Gender and Assimilation in Modern Jewish History*, 64–67.

66. Letter of MMM to Yalag, July 17, 1868.

67. A letter in German to her niece Dora indicates that MMM was fluent in the language. See Letter no. 19, Sept 18, 1899. Iris Parush has shown how Jewish women were far more likely than their male counterparts to acquire fluency in foreign languages. See "The Politics of Literacy: Women and Foreign Languages in Nineteenth-Century Eastern Europe."

68. Mapu's three extant letters to MMM are found in *Mikhtevei Avraham Mapu* (The letters of Avraham Mapu), ed., Ben-Zion Dinur (Jerusalem: Mosad Bialik, 1970), 160, 164 and 183–84. See also Yaari, *Tzror*, 40–41. Only rough drafts of MMM's letters to Mapu survive. They are found in her archives as Letters 52 and 53.

69. Letter 98 (18 Marḥeshvan 1861) *Mikhtavei Avraham Mapu*, 160.

70. Conflation of Letters 121 and 102, Ibid., 184 and 164. The reference here is to the biblical Miriam's rousing of the Israelite women in songs and dances of praise to their God in the wake of the parting of the Sea of Reeds.

71. Draft of Letter of MMM to Mapu, no. 53. The reference here is to the patriarch Abraham, who is selected by the Israelite God to be the father of the Israelite nation. Of course, Markel-Mosessohn is punning here on the fact that Mapu himself was a first as well—that is, the progenitor of the Hebrew novel.

72. Asked by Reuven Brainin to articulate the influence Mapu had on her, Markel-Mosessohn consented by writing a letter (July 3, 1899), which appears in full in Brainin's biography of Mapu. The draft of said letter is found in Markel-Mosessohn's archival holdings. See Reuven Brainin, *Avraham Mapu* (Petrokov, 1900), 86–87 and Archives, Letter 73.

73. A letter of July 17, 1868 of MMM to Yalag confirms that the two were wed in 1863. The age gap is noteworthy given that the wife was five years her husband's senior.

74. Letter of MMM to Anshel, May 1, 1864.

75. Letters of MMM to Anshel, May 12, 1864, Suvalk.

76. Letter of MMM to Yalag, July 17, 1868.

77. See for example, Yalag to Anshel, *Tzror*, 27–30. Several of Anshel's letters are contained in the Miriam Markel-Mosessohn archival holding. Note that Yalag sought Anshel's opinon on his writing. See Letter of Yalag to Anshel, Nov. 22, 1870, *Tzror*, 27–30.

78. Letters of MMM to Anshel, Thursday of week of *parashat behar*, 5625 [1865]; Warsaw, Jan. 7–20, 1869; Suvalk, Hanukkah 1880.

79. Letters of MMM to Anshel, Dec. 30, 1868; Jan. 7–20, 1869.

80. Letter of MMM to Anshel, July 27, 1879.

81. Letter of MMM to nephew Ya'akov, Purim 5643 [1883]; MMM to nephew Eliyahu, Feb. 4, 1902; Mar. 30, 1902; no day 1902.

82. Letter of Yalag to MMM, Aug. 14, 1869, *Tzror*, 19–20.

83. Yaari refers to this letter of 1888 and quotes from it at length. I did not uncover it in MMM's archival holdings. The book in question is Meyer Kayserling's.

84. There is a twelve-stanza poem in Hebrew in MMM's hand that survives in her archival holdings. The work is not dated and barely legible.

85. Marina Ledkovsky et. al., eds. *Dictionary of Russian Women Writers*, p. xxix. See as well Catriona Kelly, *A History of Russian Women's Writing*, 1820–1992 (Oxford and New York: Clarendon Press, 1994), 28.

86. Letter of MMM to Unknown, Sunday of week of *parashat vayakhel*, [1875].

87. MMM to Father, June 7, 1863.

88. MMM to Unknown, Sunday of week of *parashat vayakhel* [1875]. Her

archive also contains a manuscript of a Hebrew translation of a German play dated 4 Kislev 5621 [1861], Manuscript no. 1.

89. For discussion of this important development, see Yosef Yerushalmi, *Za-khor* (Seattle: University of Washington Press, 1982), 82–86 and Ismar Schorsch, *From Text to Context: The Turn to History in Modern Judaism* (Hanover, NH: University Press of New England, 1994).

90. Letter of MMM to her brother Yosef, Jan. 4, 1871.

91. Yalag to MMM, 26 Tammuz 1868, *Tzror*, 5.

92. *Ha-yehudim be-angliyah, o ha-yehudim ve-nosei ha-tzlav be-malokh rikard lev-ha-ari* ("The Jews in England, or The Jews and the Crusades under the Reign of Richard the Lionhearted") (Warsaw, 1869). The title was changed in the Hebrew out of concern that some would steer clear of a book on Jews and the Crusades. See Letter of MMM to Gordon, Mar. 27, 1869.

93. The letter appears in its entirety in *Tzror*, 11–13.

94. Prozer was a mutual friend of MMM and Yalag. He often acted as a courier for their correspondence. See *Tzror*, 3.

95. Letter of MMM to Prozer, Jan. 1869, no. 54.

96. Ibid.

97. Letter of MMM to Yalag, Dec. 25–Jan. 6, 1868–69.

98. See Kelly, 233.

99. Letter of MMM to Prozer, Jan. 22, 1879, no. 55.

100. Letter of MMM to Sachs, Mar. 24, 1887, no. 57.

101. Letter of Moses Leib Lilienblum to Prozer, in *Ketavim*, 1:89.

102. See *Iggerot Yalag*, 1:144–46 and 165–68. Letters of Moses Leib Lilienblum to Miriam Markel-Mosessohn appear in the Hebrew weekly *Ketuvim* 7 (29 Elul 5686): 3–4 and 13 (26 Heshvan 5687): 5.

103. For details concerning their relationship, see Shlomo Breiman's introduction to *Ketavim avtobiografiim*, 1: 32–35, as well as index to vols. 1–3; and Klausner, *Historiyah*, 4: 239–42.

104. *Ketavim*, 1:191 (June 16, 1869).

105. The poem appears in *Ha-shaḥar* 3 (5632): 163 and is signed M-M. MLL noted that FN liked the poem and translated it into German, see *Ketavim*, 1: 210 (Aug. 13, 1869).

106. The clever turn of phrase that captures the nature of their relationship is Alan Mintz's in his *Banished from Their Fathers' Table* (Bloomington and Indianapolis: Indiana University Press, 1987), 45. A portion of MLL's letters to FN are found in *Ketavim*. FN's single extant letter to MLL, which is in Yiddish, is stored among the Lilienblum papers A9/59–61 at the Central Zionist Archives, Jerusalem. For MLL's poem to FN, see *Ketavim*, 1: 79.

107. Letter of Yalag to MMM, *Ḥol ha-moed Pesaḥ* [intermediary days of Passover] 1869, *Tzror*, 16. MMM would be working from a German translation of the English novel.

108. Letter of Yalag to MMM, 5 Heshvan 5631 [1870] and Letter of Yalag to Anshel, Nov. 22, 1870, *Tzror*, 27–30.

109. Letter of Yalag to MMM, 26 Tishri 1868, *Tzror*, 6–7.

110. MMM tells Yalag that she has constantly wandered from city to city with her husband in the past year. Letter of MMM to Yalag, May 9, 1871.

111. Letters of MMM to Yalag, Mar. [6?], 1870 and Mar. 30, 1870.

112. For a discussion of Yalag's marriage, see Klausner, *Historiyah*, 4: 370–71.

113. Letter of Yalag to MMM, Aug. 14, 1869, *Tzror*, 19.

114. Letters, Yalag to MMM, *Hoshanah Rabbah* 1870, Tzror, 25–26 and MMM to Yalag, Oct. 11, 1870.

115. Letters of MMM to Yalag, Oct. 11, 1870; May 9, 1871; and Apr. 6, 1877.

116. Letter of MMM to Yalag, May 9, 1871.

117. Letter of MMM to Yalag, Feb. 1, 1877.

118. Ibid.

119. For a discussion of the poems, see *For Whom Do I Toil?*, 62ff.

120. Letter of MMM to Yalag, Apr. 6, 1877.

121. Letter of Yalag to MMM, *Hoshannah Rabbah* 1870, *Tzror*, 25–26.

122. Letter of Yalag to Anshel, Nov. 22, 1870, *Tzror*, 27–30.

123. Letter of MMM to Yalag, Mar. 9, 1887.

124. Letter of Yalag to MMM, 20 Adar 5647 [1887], *Tzror*, 35–37.

125. Introduction, *Ha-yehudim be-angliyah* (Warsaw, 1895).

126. See miscellaneous letters to her relatives, including especially Letter of MMM to her brother Yosef, Oct. 21, 1880.

127. Letter of MMM to Yalag, Apr. 12, 1887.

128. Letter of Yalag to MMM, n.d., *Tzror*, 37.

129. Letter of MMM to Yalag, May 24, 1887.

130. Notably, MMM wrote to her husband about her attempt to publish an article in *Ha-ivri*, a newspaper she claims was published in Brody. I found no such publication. See Letter of MMM to Anshel, Hanukkah 1880.

131. Letter of MMM to Unknown, Sunday of week of *parashat vayakhel*, [1875].

132. For details of the fine exacted upon Anshel's release from prison, see Letter of Shimon Wierzbolowski [MMM's father] to Yalag, Jun. 1–13, 1877 among MMM's archives in the Schwadron Collection.

133. Letter of MMM to A. Tzuckerman, May 31, 1887.

134. Letter of MMM to Yalag, July 19, 1887.

135. Anonymous, [correspondents' column] *Ha-melitz* 97 (May 1, 1887): 1029

and M.M.M, "[Correspondence from] Vienna," *Ha-melitz* 111 (May 21. 1887): 1168–69.

136. M.M.M. "[Correspondence from] Vienna," *Ha-melitz* 122 (June 3, 1887): 1296–98.

137. M.M.M. "From the Summer Heat," *Ha-melitz* 157 (July 14, 1887): 1659–62.

138. Steven Beller, *Vienna and the Jews, 1867–1938: A Cultural History* (Cambridge and New York: Cambridge University Press, 1989).

139. Letter of MMM to Yalag, Mar. 9, 1887.

140. MMM, Schwadron Collection, Manuscript no. 5.

141. Letter of MMM to her brother Yosef, *Rosh Ḥodesh* Nisan [new month of Nisan] [1878?]. Jewish law stipulates that Jews strip their home of all leavened products for Passover.

142. Letter of MMM to Anshel, Hanukkah 1880.

143. Letter of MMM to Yalag, Dec. 25–Jan. 6, 1868–69.

144. A Hebrew translation of Herzl's story "The Left Bell," originally published in German in 1901, is found in her hand among her archives as Manuscript no. 2. Herzl himself was no advocate of reviving Hebrew. He envisioned the creation of a Westernized Jewish homeland with pockets of Europeanized Jews speaking the imported languages of their native countries.

145. Pirkei Avot 4:2.

146. Letter of MMM to Yalag, Jan. 31, 1888.

147. Letter of MMM to her nephew Eliyahu, Feb. 4, 1902, no. 20.

148. See the gravestone inscription penned by MMM for Anshel in her archive, as well as her Austrian passport from 1906.

149. Yaari introduction, *Tzror*, 1.

Chapter Two: Hava Shapiro

1. Hava Shapiro, Diary, Thursday, 5 Av (Aug. 2), 1900. The diary (1899–1941) is housed at Genazim, Tel Aviv. The Hebrew transcript is in her hand. I have listed dates as they appear in the diary, along with the location, when given. All translations are my own.

2. For information on her mother's proficiency in Hebrew, see Hava Shapiro, "The Days of Hanukkah," *Ha-olam* 12 no. 52 (Dec. 26, 1924): 1. Two letters and a postcard written in Hebrew by Menuhah Shapiro are housed in the Reuven Brainin Correspondence, Jewish Public Library, Montreal. For details of Hebrew's centrality in the Shapiro home, see Moshe Shapiro (Hava's brother), Letter of May 13, 1956 in *Kovetz Genazim* (1965): 36.

3. The Ba'al Shem Tov is known as the father of Hasidism, the pietistic move-

ment that emerged in eighteenth-century Russia and transformed the religious practices and leadership of traditional Judaism.

4. See Shapiro's bibliography at the end of the book.

5. Naomi Caruso, "Chava Shapiro: A Woman Before her Time" (Master's thesis, McGill University, 1991); Yosef Klausner, "On a Unique Daughter," *Hadoar* (27 Kislev 1939): 107; M. Ungerfeld, "Dr. Hava Shapiro," in *Ha-poel ha-tza'ir* 25 (1968): 20; Getzel Kressel, ed. *Leksikon ha-sifrut ha-ivrit ba-dorot ha-aharonim*, 2 vols. (Merhavyah: Sifriyat po'alim, 1965–67); Solomon Reisen, *Leksikon fun der yidisher literatur, presse un filologia*, 4 vols. (Vilna: B. Kletzkin, 1926–1930); Yehudit Harari, *Ishah ve-em be-yisrael*; and Eliezer Tash, "Hava Shapiro," in *Enziklopediyah Yizrael*.

6. Note that the famous Hebrew poet Rahel (Bluwstein) got her literary start in the Russian language. See her translations into Hebrew of Russian poems by Pushkin, Essenin and others in *Shirat Rahel* (Tel Aviv: Dvir, 1962/3) and twenty-nine of her poems composed in Russian in *Lakh ve-alayikh: ahavat Rahel u-Mikhael: mikhtavim, shirim, divre hesber* (Tel Aviv: Ha-kibbutz ha-meuhad, 1987).

7. For insightful analyses of the writings of these five women writers, see Nurit Govrin, *Davash mi-sela.*

8. Dr. Hava Shapiro, "Memories of Frischmann's Life," *Ha-toren* 9 no. 11 (1923): 88 and Diary: Feb. 25, 1923 and Feb. 5, 1924.

9. Hava Shapiro, Diary, Mar. 23, 1915, Slavuta. There is some uncertainty as to when exactly Shapiro first met Peretz. In this diary entry, she claims to have been twenty years old when they initially met. If born in 1878, they would have met in 1898. Shapiro first mentions Peretz in her diary on 4 Shevat 1901, Warsaw.

10. Diary, Mar. 27, 1902.

11. Diary, 4 Shevet 1901, Warsaw.

12. Stephen D. Corrsin, *Warsaw before the First World War: Poles and Jews in the Third City of the Russian Empire, 1880–1914* (New York: Columbia University Press, 1989), 1, 2, 31, 55 and 63. According to a childhood friend of Shapiro's son, it was widely known in Slavuta that the Rosenbaum marriage was a failure. See Yisrael Fogel, "Hava Shapiro is 'em kol hai,'" *Davar* 28 (Sept. 19, 1986).

13. Brainin saved Shapiro's letters, despite her repeated requests for him to destroy them. Her letters to him (Aug. 1899–Dec. 1928) are located in the Reuven Brainin Collection, Jewish Public Library, Montreal. All translations from the Hebrew are my own. See the following letters for references to the *shoter* ("policeman"): Nov. 10, 1903; Nov. 17, 1903; Nov. 27, 1903;

Dec. 1, 1903; June 8, 1904; Sept. 10, 1904; Sept. 14, 1904; May 17, 1904; Oct. 9, 1909.

14. Peter Gay, *The Naked Heart: The Bourgeois Experience from Victoria to Freud,* Book 4 (New York: W.W. Norton and Co., 1995), 5.

15. Ivan Turgenev, *On the Eve,* trans. Gilbert Gardiner (New York: Penguin Books, 1950), 197.

16. Gay, 311.

17. For an additional example of how a group of intellectuals turned to writing self-reflective autobiographies in an effort to purge themselves of failures and shattered dreams, see Richard Wortman, *The Crisis of Russian Populism* (London: Cambridge University Press, 1967).

18. On the maskilim's autobiographies, see Alan Mintz *Banished from their Father's Table* (Bloomington and Indianapolis: Indiana University Press, 1987) and Marcus Moseley, "Jewish Autobiography in Eastern Europe: The Prehistory of a Literary Genre" (D.Phil., Trinity College, Oxford, 1990).

19. For background on Pinhas the Younger, see Abraham Joshua Heschel, *The Circle of the Ba'al Shem Tov,* ed. Samuel H. Dresner (Chicago: University of Chicago Press, 1985), 1–11 and Simon Dubnov, *Toldot ha-ḥasidut* (Tel Aviv: Dvir, 1967), 104.

20. H.D. Friedberg, *Toldot ha-defus ha-ivri be-polanyah* (Tel Aviv, 1950), 104.

21. Dr. Hava Shapiro, "The Brothers of Slavuta,"*Ha-shiloaḥ* 30 no. 6 (1914): 541–54.

22. Besides Hava Shapiro's essay, see Friedberg, 108–9 and Alexander Tzederbaum, *Keter kehunah* (Odessa, 1866), 139–41 for details surrounding this incident.

23. Tzederbaum, 140. According to Friedberg, 108, the two witnesses were apostate Jews.

24. Shapiro describes the punishment in Hebrew, but calls it by its Russian name of *skvoz' stroi* (run the gauntlet).

25. Shapiro, "Brothers," 543.

26. Ibid., 548. "Valley of tears" (*emek ha-bakha*) derives from Psalms 84:7.

27. There is no record of Ya'akov Shamia's first wife. He apparently was a widower when he met Menuhah. Except for her children's brief references to her, there is no information on Menuhah, save that her father was Yisrael David Sheinberg of Kishinev.

28. *Encyclopedia Judaica,* 1st ed., s.v. "Slavuta."

29. There is a good deal of controversy over Shapiro's year of birth probably owing to the fact that she was born on the cusp of two years of the secular calendar, coupled with the twelve-day lag of the Russian (Gregorian) cal-

endar and the potential error when converting from the Jewish calendar to the secular one. While Naomi Caruso favors 1876, neither Shapiro's letters and diaries nor bibliographic encyclopedias support this early estimate. Kressel, Reisen, and Harari give 1879 as the year of her birth but furnish incorrect dates for other events in Shapiro's life, which are easily obtainable, such as the copyright of her first book. The entry in *Enziklopediyah Yizrael*, based on a letter of Shapiro's brother and Ungerfeld, a critic of Shapiro's work who is accurate on all other dates, claimed 1878 as the year of her birth. On Dec. 26, 1920, Shapiro wrote in her diary that on this birthday, "I need to take inventory of my soul—especially after forty has passed." If this enigmatic statement means that Shapiro turned forty-one in 1920, then she was born in 1879. In another diary entry, we are informed that Shapiro's son was six on Oct. 25, 1903 (though this was apparently not his birthday). Thus, he was born some time after Oct. 25, 1896 and before Oct. 25, 1897. Her brother maintained that Shapiro married at the age of seventeen and two years later gave birth to a son. So in all probability, Shapiro was nineteen when her son was born (Oct. 1896–Oct. 1897), which would in turn mean that she was born in 1877 or 1878. This assortment of evidence collectively points to a birthdate of Dec. 26, 1878.

30. Eve, of course, was the first woman mentioned in the Bible. Ya'akov Shamai had two daughters from his previous marriage, and he and his second wife would have another daughter after Hava.

31. Shapiro's earliest publications are printed under the name *em kol ḥai*. She later took to signing her published works as Dr. Hava Shapiro, though at times she reverted to the pseudonym.

32. *Em kol ḥai*, "Sanctification of the Moon," *Kovetz tziurim* (Warsaw, 1909), 61.

33. Ibid.

34. Diary, Dec. 26, 1920. A Jewish girl reaches the age of religious maturity at 12 years and a day.

35. "Sanctification of the Moon," in *Kovetz tziurim*, 62.

36. Diary, Dec. 1, 1904 and Letter to RB, Sept. 24, 1901, Yom Kippur, Warsaw.

37. Diary, Mar. 30, 1905.

38. Diary, 4 Shevet 1901.

39. Dr. Hava Shapiro, "The Days of Hanukkah," *Ha-olam*, 2.

40. M. Shapiro, *Genazim*, 36.

41. From allusions throughout her diary and letters (and occasionally in articles and sketches), it is clear that Shapiro's family led a traditional Jewish

life. Shapiro makes direct references to observance of Shabbat, Sukkot, Rosh Hashanah, Yom Kippur, and Hanukkah.

42. It seems that Russian was Hava Shapiro's native tongue from the following eclectic evidence: (a) when HS had difficulty expressing herself in Hebrew, she most often reverted to Russian (see footnote 24 above); (b) HS spoke to her son only in Russian (Diary, Aug. 4, 1903); (c) Shapiro often used Russian syntax when expressing herself in Hebrew (Letter to RB, Apr. 30, 1904, Vienna); and (d) HS's Yiddish, as evidenced by her articles in that language, are poorly written, according to Naomi Caruso (phone conversation on Sept. 20, 1995). I could locate none of her Yiddish articles. I deduced that she was fluent in the languages listed from the letters penned in such. In addition, her articles are replete with footnotes citing foreign publications (Letter to RB, Dec. 2, 1905, Berne and Letter to Sadie Greenwald, Genazim, Tel Aviv).

43. Fogel, 28.

44. For her refusal, see letter to Reuven Brainin, Mar. 6, 1920.

45. Diary, Nov. 15, 1909, Berne.

46. An account of her sister's tragic demise written on the eighth anniversary of the death is found in the Diary, Oct. 7, 1901, Warsaw and Letter to RB, Oct. 7, 1901.

47. I inferred the years of Shapiro's marriage and birth of her son from her diary and letters, as well as from a letter of Shapiro's brother on May 13, 1956. M. Shapiro, 36–37. See n. 29 above.

48. Diary, Thursday, 5 Av 1900.

49. Diary, n.d. first entry.

50. The single extant letter of Brainin to Shapiro was written on July 14, 1899 and is located in the Reuven Brainin Collection, Jewish Public Library, Montreal. This is apparently the second letter he sent; he refers to a first letter sent two days earlier.

51. Diary, Thursday, 4 Shevet 1901, Warsaw.

52. Caruso, "Chava Shapiro," 118.

53. For Kulmos, Letters to RB, June 24, 1910, Berne and July 25, 1910, Wiesbaden. For Hayim Sheinberg, Letter to RB, Dec. 29, 1913.

54. Letter to RB, Mar. 10, 1901

55. Letter to RB, Oct. 30, 1901: "I wanted to show the last manuscript to Peretz, but I remembered your request: don't show them to anyone before [I] read them."

56. See letters to RB: July 29, 1900, Slavuta; June 28, 1904; Mar. 10, 1901; Sept. 18, 1901, Warsaw; Nov. 15, 1901.

57. See letters to RB: Oct. 21, 1901; Warsaw; Oct. 10, 1901; Dec. 1, 1903; June 10, 1903.

58. Diary, Aug. 5, 1908, Slavuta.

59. Letter to RB, Apr. 25, 1901, Goettingen.

60. Letter to RB, Apr. 20, 1904—for an example of Shapiro's attempt to end their affair.

61. Letter to RB, Sept. 24–25, 1901.

62. *Em kol ḥai*, "Ha-shoshanah" (The Rose), *Ha-dor* 48 (Dec. 12, 1901): 13–14.

63. Diary, Wednesday, 15 Tevet 1902.

64. Yosef Klausner, "On a Unique Daughter," and M. Ungerfeld, "Dr. Hava Shapiro."

65. Uprooting and transplantation appear as metaphors in much early Zionist writing, including Leon Pinsker's "Auto-Emancipation" and Theodor Herzl's "The Jewish State."

66. Diary, June 1, [1908], Berne.

67. For more on Peretz, see Ruth S. Wisse, *I.L. Peretz and the Making of Modern Jewish Culture* (Seattle: University of Washington Press, 1991).

68. Diary, Oct. 20, 1922.

69. Diary, Mar. 23, 1915, Slavuta.

70. Shapiro commented parenthetically: "I don't think I was supposed to hear that remark." Diary, Mar. 25, 1915, Slavuta.

71. Shlomo Rubin translated the play into Hebrew in 1856.

72. Diary, Feb. 22, 1903.

73. Caruso estimates that Shapiro and Brainin were together a total of two months over the course of their lives.

74. Letter to RB, June 30, 1903.

75. Letters to RB, Sept. 14, 1903, Slavuta and July 1, 1904, Slavuta.

76. Letter to RB, Sept. 14, 1903, Slavuta.

77. Letter to RB from M. Khelemer', June 15, 1908, Reuven Brainin Archives, Group III, Correspondence. I'm grateful to Naomi Caruso for pointing out this letter to me.

78. In letter after letter, entry after entry, Shapiro expressed pain over the separation from her son: See Letters to RB, Apr. 30, 1904, Vienna; May 7, 1904; June 20, 1904; June 24, 1904. See Diary, Sept. 20, 1903, Slavuta; Oct. 25, 1903, Warsaw; Apr. 14 and 21, 1904; Nov. 14, 1904, Vienna; Aug. 16, 1906, Slavuta; Nov. 23, 1908, Berne; Sept. 14, 1914.

79. Diary, Mar. 20, 1904.

80. Diary, Aug. 26, 1906.

81. Letters to RB, Dec. 8, 1901, Warsaw; Oct. 8, 1903; Apr. 30, 1904, Vienna; Sept. 14, 1904; Dec. 2, 1905, Berne.

82. For more on Berdischevsky, see Alan Mintz, *Banished from their Father's Table*, 91ff. Shapiro mentions meeting Berdishevsky in a letter to RB, Sept. 24, 1901, Warsaw.

83. Letters to RB, Dec. 2, 1905 Berne and Jan. 7, 1907, Paris.

84. Diary, January 24, 1910.

85. Lichtenberg was, besides a philosopher, a satirist and scientist. He had but a modest influence on the development of thought, particularly in the area of lingusitics. He was professor at the University of Goettingen from 1767 until his death.

86. Letters to RB, Apr. 24 and 25, 1909, Goettingen.

87. Diary, Aug. 4, 1910, Slavuta. Note that Shapiro affixed the title of doctor to her name in nearly all subsequent publications and correspondence.

88. Letter to RB, June 24, 1910, Berne.

89. David Frischmann, letter no. 14, *Kol kitvei David Frischmann*, 1:190–95.

90. Sandra Gilbert and Susan Gubar, *The Madwoman in the Attic* (New Haven: Yale University Press, 1979), 73.

91. Carolyn G. Heilbrun, *Writing a Woman's Life* (New York: Norton, 1988) and Nurit Govrin, *Ha-maḥatzit ha-rishonah: Devorah Baron* (Jerusalem: Mosad Bialik, 1988).

92. Letter to RB, Nov. 22, 1903.

93. In another interpretation, the clipped wings and gilded cage might represent the limitations put on women when they seek to soar intellectually. They are restrained, for example, by a lack of education or, in Shapiro's case, by the absence of opportunities to use a hard-won education.

94. The phrase is borrowed from Gilbert and Gubar, 13.

95. The sketch appears in *Kovetz tziurim*, 27–31. "Types of Women" was originally published in *Ha-olam* 27 (July 8, 1908): 359–60.

96. Diary, July 25, 1907.

97. "Old Maid," *Kovetz tziurim*, 23–26. It first appeared in *Ha-olam* 18 (May 6, 1908): 359–60.

98. "The Dreamer" and "The Loner," *Kovetz tziurim*, 40–42 and 17–22.

99. Letter to RB, Mar. 13, 1901.

100. Shapiro redefined male types as well, depicting them as woman's nemesis, wreaking havoc on her emotional well-being and wounding her ego. They spring forth from Shapiro's imagination like so many Reuven Brainins on the printed page. For the most poignant example, see "The Poet of Sorrow"(*Kovetz tziurim*, 43–48), in which a young man woos a nameless hero-

ine with an oath of undying love before venturing abroad to study at a European university. A year later, he reveals to her that it's not her he needs but rather the memory of her love, which will enable him to compose tragic verse. The omniscient narrator criticizes such behavior, sardonically charging: "And in every new poem, . . . he began with charges against the muse who was the first to dash his hopes, . . . against the evil one who betrayed him. And thus he sang about the sorrow that engulfed him."

101. Dr. Hava Shapiro, "The Female Image in our Literature,"*Ha-tekufah* 26–27 (1930): 617–33. Portions of this article appeared in two previously published articles: Dr. Hava Shapiro, "Y.L. Peretz, the Man and the Author" *Ha-shiloah* 34 (1918): 347–54, 501–10 and Dr. Hava Shapiro, "Female Types in Mendele's Stories," *Ha-shiloah* 34 (1918): 92–101.

102. See chapter one for a discussion of Gordon and his colleagues.

103. "The Female Image," 620.

104. Ibid.

105. Ibid., 625.

106. Ibid., 627.

107. See bibliography.

108. Diary, Nov. 2, 1913.

109. Diary, Jan. 24, 1914.

110. Diary, Dec. 27, 1925.

111. Little is known of Shapiro's activities from 1915–1918. During this period, she neither published articles nor wrote to Brainin (i.e. from Apr. 4, 1915 to Oct. 19, 1919). In her diary, she wrote time and again about her travels between Slavuta and Kiev, but offered no details save "my hands are full of work." I have inferred that she was engaged in some sort of revolutionary activity in Kiev, given her frequent travels to this city and her early enthusiasm for the Revolution.

112. Diary, Apr. 21, 1917.

113. Diary, Dec. 15, 1917.

114. Diary, May 20, 1919.

115. Diary, Feb. 19, 1917, Slavuta.

116. Diary, July 7, 1918, Odessa.

117. *Em kol hai*, "You must not Forget," *Ha-olam* (Dec. 19, 1919): 2–4.

118. She claimed to have written the article for an American audience; see letter to RB, Feb. 17, 1920.

119. All such letters are part of the collection housed at Genazim, Tel Aviv.

120. Diary, Apr. 11, 1927.

121. Diary, Dec. 14, 1921, Munkacs. Shapiro does not name her gentile lover, and there is no biographical information on Winternitz.
122. Diary, Apr. 10, 1934; Feb. 27, 1935; Dec. 11, 1937; June 18, 1939.
123. Diary, Sept. 29, 1922.
124. Diary, Mar. 31, 1940. Moshe Shapiro maintains that Pinhas Shapiro was killed in a car accident in St. Louis, Missouri not long after his immigration; M. Shapiro, 37. Hava mentions throughout her diary only one of her three brothers, to whom she was particularly close. He lived with her in Berne, later graduated from the Zhitomir yeshivah, and died on Aug. 16, 1934. See Diary, Oct. 7, 1934.
125. Diary, Oct. 21, 1941.
126. As discussed, while some male reviewers interpreted "The Rose" as something other than depicting the experience of women, its inclusion in *Kovetz tziurim*—a collection of sketches wholly devoted to the female—left no ambuiguity concerning its author's intent.
127. Diary, Feb. 5, 1924; Letters to RB: Dec. 29, 1913, Berlin; June 8, 1914; June 11, 1914.
128. Terrence Doody, *Confession and Community in the Novel* (Baton Rouge: Louisiana State University Press, 1980), 4.
129. Diary, Oct. 20, 1922.

CHAPTER THREE: RASHEL' MIRONOVNA KHIN

1. Khin will be referred to as such throughout the chapter, though she married twice and each time took her husband's name. In most instances, Khin published under her maiden name.
2. For the former distinction see for example Jacob Raisin, *The Haskalah Movement in Russia*, 329, n. 22; Gregor Aronson, "The Jews in Russian Literature, Journalism, Literary Criticism and Political Life" and "Jewish Periodicals in the Russian Language," in *Kniga o Russkom Evreistve* (Book on Russian Jewry) (New York: Union of Russian Jews, 1960), 365 and 568. For the latter see I. Ignatov, ed., *Galereia russkikh pisatelei* (Moscow, 1901), B.P. Koz'min, ed., *Pisateli sovremennoi epokhi* (Moscow, 1928) and Marina Ledkovsky, Charlotte Rosenthal and Mary Zirin, eds. *Dictionary of Russian Women Writers*. Often those small number of Jewish names that are included in these Russian literary encyclopedias belong to apostates or children of mixed marriages who were not raised as Jews.
3. The entry found in *Evreiskaia entsiklopediia* is based on Simon Vengerov, *Entsiklopedicheskii slovar'*, vol. 37 (St. Petersburg, 1903). See the complete bibliography of her works on pp. 245–46.

4. For the history of the rise of the intelligentsia in Russia see Isaiah Berlin, "The Birth of the Russian Intelligentsia (1838–1848)" in *Russian Thinkers*, eds. Henry Hardy and Aileen Kelly (New York: Viking Press, 1978), 114–149 and Martin Malia, "What's the Intelligentsia?" *Daedalus* (Summer 1960): 441–458. A revisionist interpretation is offered by Michael Confino, "On Intellectuals and Intellectual Traditions in 18–19th Century Russia," *Daedalus* 2 (1972): 117–50.

5. Malia attributes the coining of the term to Boborykin.

6. For example, among Khin's archival holdings are a calling card from Emile Zola and letters to Khin from Brandes and France (Zola: RGALI, f. 128, op. 1, d. 76; Brandes: RGALI, f. 128, op. 1, d. 67; France: RGALI, f. 128, op. 1, d. 153). See note 10 below for information on her papers.

7. John Doyle Klier, *Imperial Russia's Jewish Question, 1855–1881* (Cambridge and New York: Cambridge University Press, 1995), 25ff.

8. This fact is mentioned in passing by Mark Vishniak in his memoirs, *Dan' proshlomu* (New York: Chekhov Publishing House, 1954), 73. Vishniak (1883–1977) was born and raised in Moscow in a Jewish family and subsequently became a Socialist Revolutionary and—in exile in Europe after 1918—an editor and non-fiction author of some influence. He knew Khin's second husband. I am grateful to Benjamin Nathans for providing this very important reference.

9. On salon Jewesses, see Deborah Hertz, *Jewish High Society in Old Regime Berlin* (New Haven: Yale University Press, 1988).

10. Khin's papers are located at the Rossiiskii gosudarstvennyi arkhiv literatury i iskusstva (hereafter RGALI) (Russian State Archive of Literature and Art), Moscow, fond 128, opis 1 and 2 (1838–1928). A total of 235 files are found among her letters, including correspondence with forty-three individuals, manuscripts of short stories, a nearly 4,000-page Russian handwritten diary (1891–1917), an approximately 600-page typewritten memoir, newspaper clippings, photographs, and miscellaneous items such as playbills of her performed dramas and invitations to participate in literary evenings. It appears that Khin began to save her letters and papers for posterity in 1890, at the age of twenty-nine. The single exception to this are the two letters from Turgenev, which were penned in 1881. Her papers were donated to the archive in 1941. The standard Russian archival notation will be used hereafter: f. (fond), op. (opis'), d., dd., (delo, dela), l. ll. (list, listy). I have bracketed dates and years when none is given, but can be inferred from the context or chronology. All translations are my own.

11. Her memoirs are found in RGALI, fond 128, opis 1, dd. 34–35 (1891–1906 and 1914–1917).

12. See Benjamin Ira Nathans, "Beyond the Pale: The Jewish Encounter with Russia, 1840–1900," (Ph.D. dissertation, University of California at Berkeley, 1995), 50–63.

13. Khin mentioned that Dekapol'skii was a friend of Kliuchevskii and Aleksei Fedorovich Fortunatov (1856–1925), a Russian statistician. Nothing else is known of her former teacher. Memoirs, Feb. 1,1892.

14. Memoirs, Sept. 8, 1897.

15. Memoirs, Dec. 28, 1899.

16. While traveling abroad in her adulthood, Khin mentioned that she lived in Salzburg in her childhood. See Memoirs, Oct. 4, 1893.

17. Elias Cherikover, *Istoriia obshchestva dlia rasprostraneniia prosveshcheniia mezhdu evreiami v Rossii, 1863–1913* (St. Petersburg, 1913), 124, 129, 151 and Barbara Alpern Engel, *Mothers and Daughters: Women of the Intelligentsia in Nineteenth-Century Russia* (Cambridge and New York: Cambridge University Press, 1983), 159. Professor Engel kindly sent me a copy of "Alfavitnyi spisok zhenshchin-vrachei" (Alphabetical index of female doctors, 1904), 416–31 confirming this assertion.

18. The courses were offered at a military hospital (Nikolievskii). They were closed in 1881 when Minister of War Vanovskii came to power and forbade the existence of such courses at a military hospital. The courses were reopened in 1897. See Alexander Kornilov, *Modern Russian History,* 2 vols. (New York: Knopf, 1912), 2: 171.

19. Koz'min claimed that a short story by Khin appeared in 1881 in *Drug zhenshchin* entitled "Uchitel'nitsa muzyki" ("The Music Teacher"). Searches for such a story proved fruitless, and Khin's archives, which contain manuscripts of a selection of her writings, have none for this story.

20. Rashel' F. . . ein, "Iz storony v storonu," *Drug zhenshchin* 1–3 no. 3 (1883): 1–28, no. 6 (1883): 1–37, 4–6 no. 10 (1883): 1–13, nos. 12–13 (1883): 1–22 and no. 15 (1883): 1–16.

21. For further discussion of the proliferation of such journals, see Kelly, 122–23.

22. "Iz storony," chap. 3.

23. Rashel' F . . . ein, "Neskol'ko slov o Turgeneve," (A few words about Turgenev) *Drug zhenshchin* 2 (1884): 66–70; R. M. Khin, *Glava iz neizdannykh zapisok* (A chapter from unpublished notes) (Moscow, 1901): 1–14; *Pis'ma Turgenevu shchukinskii sbornik* (Turgenev's letters) VIII (1909): 207–210; and RGALI, f. 128, op. 1, d. 107.

24. How Turgenev and Khin came to meet each other and develop a close relationship is a mystery. Yet it is known that Turgenev befriended Baron Horace de Gunzburg (1833–1909), the influential Jewish banker who frequently made his home in Paris when not in his Russian native land. Together the pair founded the "Society for mutual aid and charity for Russian artists in Paris" (1877). Perhaps their joint interest in promoting young Russian artists led Khin to their door. See "Some Letters of Ivan Turgenev to Baron Horace de Gunzburg, 1877–1883," intro. by I. De Vries-Gunzburg, *Oxford Slavonic Papers* 9 (1960): 73–103.

25. "Neskol'ko slov," 66.

26. *Glava*, 2.

27. *Pis'ma*, 209 for indication that he read her works.

28. "Neskol'ko", 67.

29. *Glava*, 3.

30. Ledkovsky, xxxiv. See as well Mary F. Zirin, "Women's Prose Fiction in the Age of Realism," in *Women Writers in Russian Literature*, eds. Toby W. Clyman and Diana Greene (Westport, Connecticut: Prager, 1994), 77–94.

31. Ibid., p. xxxiii.

32. "Neskol'ko," 70.

33. Khin's letters to Turgenev appear in *Pis'ma Turgenevu* (1909): 207–10. The first is dated June 8, 1881, from Paris; the second, July 7, 1881, from Moscow. His very short letters to her are found among her archival holdings: RGALI, f. 128, op.1, d. 107 (Apr. 17–Aug. 19, 1881).

34. This is the single reference to a sister. Nothing else is known of her but this episode. Khin also had a brother, Mark, who wrote an article on the "Woman Question." See *Ukazatel' literatury zhenskago voprosa na russkom iazyke*, entry no. 267.

35. See Michael Stanislawski, "Jewish Apostasy in Russia: A Tentative Typology," in *Jewish Apostasy in the Modern World*, ed. Todd Endelman (New York: Holmes and Meier, 1987), 189–205.

36. Ibid., 190 and 203, n. 4.

37. Ibid., 197.

38. *Pis'ma Turgenevu*, 208.

39. See introduction by Don C. Rawson, in O.O. Gruzenberg, *Yesterday: Memoirs of a Russian-Jewish Lawyer* (Berkeley, CA: University of California Press, 1981).

40. R.K., "Ne ko dvoru," *Voskhod* 8–12 (1886). The story appeared as well in Khin's collection of short stories, *Siluety* (Moscow, 1894): 203–368. It is from this version that I quote.

41. "Ne ko dvoru," 204.

42. Ibid., 209.

43. As one of the outstanding representatives of the German Enlightenment, the playwright Gotthold Ephraim Lessing (1729–1781) frequently incorporated the theme of tolerance into his works. Lessing befriended Moses Mendelssohn, the founder of the Jewish Enlightenment movement in Berlin, and used him as an inspiration for this play.

44. "Ne ko dvoru," 229.

45. Ibid., 233.

46. Ibid., 237.

47. Ibid., 253.

48. Ibid., 283.

49. Ibid., 287.

50. Ibid., 353–54.

51. O.O. Gruzenberg, "Literatura i Zhizn'," (Literature and life) *Voskhod* 10 (1894): 33–50.

52. O.O. Gruzenberg, *Vchera* (Yesterday) (Paris, 1938), 5. The memoirs appeared in English as well, see n. 39 above.

53. The dating of Khin's marriage to Fel'dshtein is surmised by Khin's meager correspondence from these years, as well as her published works. By 1881, letters were being addressed to Rashel' Mironovna Fel'dshtein, indicating that a marriage had taken place. Two pieces appeared in 1883 and 1884 with the byline R. Fel'dshtein. By 1886, she was signing her published works with her maiden name. This could be an indication of a divorce having occurred already by 1886.

54. For a discussion of the use of conversion as a means for dissolving marriage between Jews, see ChaeRan Freeze, "Making and Unmaking the Jewish Family," 258ff.

55. On pogroms: Memoirs, Apr. 19, [1903]; May 1, [1903]; May 7, [1903]; May 16, [1903]; May 16, [1905]; Oct. 20, [1905]; Oct. 22, [1905]. On evacuations: Memoirs, May 22, [1915]. On military restrictions: Memoirs, Mar. 26, [1915]. On quotas: Memoirs, Sept. 26, [1904] and Aug. 11, [1914].

56. Memoirs, Apr. 19, [1903].

57. Memoirs, Mar. 26, [1915].

58. Ibid.

59. For further discussion of privileged Jews returning to Judaism, see Christoph Gassenschmidt, *Jewish Liberal Politics in Tsarist Russia, 1900–1914* (New York: New York University Press, 1995), 6–9.

60. The invitation is found in RGALI, f. 128, op. 1, d. 118.

61. *Sbornik v pol'zu nachal'nykh evreiskikh shkol* (St. Petersburg, 1896) and *Pomoshch' evreiam* (St. Petersburg, 1901).

62. "Mechtatel'" was reprinted in Khin's collection of short stories *Pod goru: rasskazy* (Moscow, 1900): 259–310.

63. "Mechtatel'," 267–69, 275.

64. Zon' is expelled in some unspecified year, though one can safely assume that the author had in mind the expulsion of Jews illegally residing in Moscow in 1891 that affected close to 15,000 Jews. Khin penned the story in the years following the Moscow crisis.

65. Notably, it was "Mechtatel'" that was singled out for lengthy review in the pages of *Voskhod*. Arkadii Gornfel'd, a literary editor at *Russkoe bogatsvo*, penned a positive review of Khin's *Pod goru* in which he highlighted Zon's suicide note, calling on Jews to bring spring about by their own actions. Jews, he argued, must be actors in their future and not wait for it to develop on its own. See *Voskhod* 5 (1900): 125–28. *Pod goru* was reviewed favorably in terms of its felicitous style in *Russkaia mysl'* 9 (1900): 120–21.

66. Memoirs, Dec. [no day given] 1893.

67. RGALI, f. 128, op. 1, dd. 51–61.

68. Memoirs, Aug. 9, 1894. Auer's own memoirs, which contain only passing reference to his wife and no mention of Khin, appeared in English. See Leopold Auer, *My Long Life in Music* (New York, 1923).

69. The Auer-Khin correspondence lasted until 1921.

70. Memoirs, July [no day given] [1895].

71. Memoirs, Aug. 9, 1894.

72. For the impact of da Costa on Hava Shapiro, see chapter 2, p. 66.

73. Memoirs, Oct. 12, [1902]. Khin mentions socializing with celebrities, including Andreev.

74. Memoirs, July [no day given] [1895].

75. Ibid.

76. Memoirs, Nov. 30, [1898].

77. *Jewish Encyclopedia*, s.v. "Bliokh."

78. "Makarka," *Voskhod* 4 (1889) and later published in a separate volume along with Nikolai Ivanovich Naumov's short story, "V glukhom' mestechke" (Moscow, 1895), 75–96. The story also appeared in Khin's collection *Siluety* (Moscow, 1894; 3rd edition, St. Petersburg, 1902), 459–484. My citations are from the latter.

79. "Makarka," 460.

80. Ibid., 462.

81. Ibid., 467 and 465.

82. For further discussion of this triumvirate and the development of Symbolism in Russia, see chapter four.

83. For a discussion of Solov'ev's attitudes toward the Jews, see Judith Deutsch Kornblatt, "Vladimir Solov'ev on Spritual Nationhood, Russia and the Jews," *Russian Review* 56 no. 2 (Apr. 1997): 157–79.

84. Ibid., 157.

85. Salo Baron, *The Russian Jews under Tsars and Soviets* (New York: Schocken Books, 1987), 51. Twenty years later, Khin would express dismay with Tolstoi's changed attitude toward the Jews. Though in the 1880s he willingly protested against the pogroms, by 1903 this man who "advocates that each human being is a messenger of God on earth" reneged on his promise to speak out on Jews' behalf. Memoirs, May 16, [1903], Friday.

86. Memoirs, Sept. 2, [1902].

87. Memoirs, July [no day given but after 23] 1895.

88. Memoirs, Aug. 24, 1894 and July [no day given, but after 23] 1895.

89. Memoirs, Feb. 10, [1896].

90. Memoirs, Feb. 27, 1896.

91. Memoirs, July [no day given, but after 23] 1895.

92. Gets wrote an article on Solov'ev's attitudes toward the Jews. See Feivel' Gets, "Ob otnoshennii Vl. S. Solov'eva k evreiskomu voprosu," *Voprosy filosofii i psikhologii* 56 (1901): 165–68.

93. Memoirs, Thursday, Aug. 7, [1914].

94. Fel'dshtein appears in no known encyclopedia. Repeated searches turned up nothing on his biography.

95. For Gol'dovskii's memories of Urusov, see the commemorative volume edited by Gol'dovskii and A. Andreev, *Prince Aleksandr' Ivanovich Urusov,* vols. 2 and 3 (Moscow, 1907). A short essay by Khin is also included; she praises Urusov as a "true knight of civilization." Sergei Nechaev, a revolutionary active in the student protests of the late 1860s, demanded unquestioning obedience on the part of his followers. When one of his adherents expressed doubts, Nechaev decided that he should be killed and the deed was carried out on November 21, 1869. Police arrested scores of radicals in connection with the case, and while a trial ensued, Nechaev escaped abroad.

96. For further discussion of legal professionalization in Russia, see Richard Wortman, *The Development of a Russian Legal Consciousness* (Chicago: University of Chicago Press, 1976).

97. Memoirs, Nov. 10 and 29, 1904. Additionally see his typed notes on the Judiciary Reforms, RGALI, f. 128, op. 1, d. 158 (October 1904).

98. For his sustained interest in the Jewish people, see Gol'dovskii, *Evrei v Moskve: stranitsy iz istorii sovremennoi* (Jews in Moscow: Pages from contemporary history), (Berlin, 1904).

99. Vishniak, p. 73.

100. Memoirs, Aug. 4, [1903]. Iushkevich met with some success later in life when his stories appeared in *Russkoe Bogatsvo, Voskhod* and the American Yiddish press. Perhaps to his patron's chagrin, in his plays, Iushkevich contrasted poor, but virtuous, Jews with their wealthy, but vulgar, coreligionists.

101. From his extant papers, we know that Gol'dovskii even corresponded with Emile Zola and Oktave Mirbeau, RGALI, f. 128, op. 1, dd. 133 and 135a.

102. For a discussion of Jews in the legal profession, see chapter four of Nathans, "Beyond the Pale: The Jewish Encounter with Russia, 1840–1900."

103. Ibid., 257.

104. For more on censorship in Russia, see Charles A. Ruud, *Fighting Words: Imperial Censorship and the Russian Press, 1804–1906* (Toronto: University of Toronto Press, 1982).

105. Khin mentioned that Koni was visiting *daily* in Memoirs, Apr. 8, [1902]. For correspondence, see RGALI, f. 128, op. 1, dd. 79–85 (Mar. 25, 1890–Jan. 21, 1927) and Koni archive at Pushkin Dom in St. Petersburg, as listed in appendix to *Pamiati A.I. Koni* (Leningrad-Moscow, 1929). Note as well Khin's essay "Pamiati starogo drug" (Memories of an old friend) in the same volume, 55–78.

106. "Pamiati starogo druga," 58 and 70.

107. Wortman, 282.

108. See Memoirs, Dec. 31, 1898 and Jan. 1, 1904.

109. Memoirs, Jan. 4, 1891, Moscow.

110. Memoirs, Aug. 17, 1895, Thursday.

111. See respectively, Memoirs, Moscow, Jan. 21, [1900] and Katino, Sept. 25, [1899].

112. Memoirs, June 8, [1897].

113. Khin briefly mentions her father's short illness and subsequent death in Memoirs, Mar. 26, 1896. Her mother's death is referred to on Sept. 11, [1903]. These are the only references to her parents.

114. Memoirs, Dec. 31, [1898] and Apr. 14, [1900].

115. Memoirs, Feb. 11, [1902] and Katino, Feb. 18, [1902], Monday.

116. Memoirs, Mar. 15, [1902], Friday.
117. Baron, 48 and 53.
118. Memoirs, Moscow, Sept. 26, [1904], Sunday and Monday, Aug. 11, 1914.
119. Jewish historiography, with few exceptions, has focused, on the one hand, on Jewish political movements like the Bund or, on the other, on Jews' participation in Russian revolutionary parties. Christoph Gassenschmidt has recently sought to correct this imbalance by studying the less visible and less spectacular Jews who were either members of the liberal Russian Constitutional Democrats (Kadets) or at least supported their political programs. See his *Jewish Liberal Politics in Tsarist Russia, 1900–1914*. His proposition, however, that Jewish liberals emerged as the successors to the maskilim, while provocative, is ill-founded. Erich Haberer makes a similar claim but in a different context when he asserts that the Haskalah was the cradle of Jewish radicalism. See his *Jews and Revolution in Nineteenth-Century Russia* (Cambridge: Cambridge University Press, 1995).
120. Gassenschmidt, 38.
121. Memoirs, Nov. 10, [1904].
122. Memoirs, Oct. 4, [1905]; Oct. 13, [1905], Thursday; Oct. 15, [1905].
123. Hans Rogger, *Russia in the Age of Modernisation and Revolution, 1881–1917* (London and New York: Longman, 1983), 6.
124. Memoirs, Aug. 4, [1905], Thursday.
125. Memoirs, Tuesday, Oct. 18, [1905].
126. Memoirs, Aug. 4, [1905], Thursday. This fairy tale is very popular among Russian children. At this particular juncture in the story, the queen gives birth to a son while the king is away. Relatives send a message to the king that his wife gave birth "not to a little mouse nor to a little frog, but to some unknown beast." The king replies that the queen should wait for his return to set things right. The cruel relatives distort his message, resulting in the queen and her son being cast into the ocean. The boy eventually grows up to become the prince of an island.
127. Memoirs, Aug. 9, [1905], Tuesday.
128. Memoirs, Tuesday, Oct. 18, [1905].
129. Memoirs, Friday, Dec. 22, [1905].
130. *Great Soviet Encyclopedia*, transl. from 3rd ed. *Bolshaia sovetskaia entsiklopediia*, s.v. "Malyi Theater."
131. Khin mentioned that she went to see *Volki i ovtsy* (Wolves and Sheep) at the Malyi Theater. This satirical play by the prominent playwright Aleksandr Nikolaevich Ostrovskii (1822–1886) denounced the new breed of businessmen emerging in Russia, whom he called "moneybags and Euro-

peanized merchants." See Memoirs, Feb. 2, 1894. Khin also mentioned
that Boborykin's play was showing at the Malyi. See Memoirs, Oct. 31,
[1904].

132. Respectively, Memoirs, July [before 10], [1895] and Feb. 2, 1892.

133. Respectively, Memoirs, Feb. 2, 1892; Katino, Sept. 1, [1897]; Mar. 16,
[1903], Monday.

134. *Okhota smertnaia*, in *Prizyv'* (Moscow, 1897), 435–46. The collection included as well works by Anton Chekhov, Tatiana Shepkina-Kupernik,
Konstantin Dmitrievich Bal'mont and other illustrious literary figures.

135. For further discussion, see Richard Stites, *The Women's Liberation Movement
in Russia* (Princeton, New Jersey: Princeton University Press, 1978); Jane
Costlow, "Love, Work, and the Woman Question in Mid-Nineteenth Century Women's Writing" in *Women Writers in Russian Literature*, 61–75; and
Kelly, 152 ff.

136. The "Woman Question" entered public discourse with the appearance of
M.L. Mikhailov's essays on the subject. Publicists Dmitirii Pisarev and
Nikolai Chernyshevskii contributed in fundamental ways to articulation of
the "Question" for educated Russia.

137. Memoirs, Feb. 21, 1892.

138. Memoirs, Feb. 1, 1892.

139. "Sud'by russkoi devushki" (The Fate of Russian Young Women"), *Drug
zhenshchin* 2 (1883): 56–68.

140. *Sbornik na pomoshch' uchashchimsiia zhenshchinam* (Moscow, 1901), 80–83.

141. At the same time, of course, Russia was, so to speak, coming of age as well.
Khin, however, penned this play in 1904 or earlier, as the censors' notices
indicate, and so could not have known what was about to unfold in 1905
when she situated her play. See n. 143 below.

142. On the role played by sexual ideology in the struggle for cultural and po-
litical influence, see Laura Engelstein, *The Keys to Happiness. Sex and the
Search for Modernity in Fin-de-Siècle Russia* (Ithaca: Cornell University
Press, 1992). On revolutionary behavior, see Engel, *Mothers and Daughters*.

143. The censors' notices granting permission for *Budding Sprouts* to be staged
are found in RGIA, f. 497, op. 10, d. 797, l. 15 (Aug. 24, 1904) and f. 497,
op. 14, d. 298, ll. 57–59 (Aug. 24, 1904). An invitation addressed to Khin
to attend the rehearsals of *Budding Sprouts* from Jan. 24–Feb. 6, 1905 is
found among her papers, RGALI, f. 128, op. 1, d. 125.

144. *Pod sen'iu Penatov'* (Moscow, 1907). According to Roman mythology, Penates are the gods of the household.

145. For the censor's notice, see RGIA, f. 776, op. 26, d. 26, l. 139 (June 5, 1907).
146. For the playbill for *Nasledniki*, see RGALI, f. 128, op. 1, d. 126. Unfortunately, the play itself was not recovered after searching Moscow and Petersburg libraries.
147. *Ledokhod'* (Moscow, 1917).
148. Memoirs, prologue to part II.
149. Memoirs, Saturday, July 19, [1914].
150. Memoirs, Monday, Jan. 12, [1915].
151. Memoirs, Wednesday, Mar. 26, [1914].
152. Memoirs, [Summer, 1915].
153. Memoirs, Saturday, Oct. 17, [1915].
154. Memoirs, Saturday, Dec. 19, [1915].
155. Memoirs, 5:00 a.m., Friday, Mar. 17, [1917].
156. On the salon and salonière of Russia, see Lina Bernstein, "Women on the Verge of a New Language: Russian Salon Hostesses in the First Half of the Nineteenth Century," and Beth Holmgren, "Stepping Out/Going Under: Women in Russia's Twentieth-Century Salons," in *Russia Women Culture*, eds. Helena Goscilo and Beth Holmgren (Bloomington and Indianapolis: Indiana University Press, 1996), 209–24 and 225–46.
157. Deborah Hertz examines this oft-repeated generalization in chap. 7 of *Jewish High Society in Old Regime Berlin*.

CHAPTER FOUR: FEIGA IZRAILEVNA KOGAN

1. Historians generally agree that the beginnings of Symbolism in Russia can be dated from the lectures delivered by Dmitry Merezhkovskii (1865–1941) in 1892 when he attacked positivism and praised the French Symbolists for their mysticism, symbolism, and impressionism. For an overview of the movement, see Ronald E. Peterson, *A History of Russian Symbolism, 1892–1917* (Amsterdam and Philadelphia: J. Benjamin Publishing, 1993).
2. For a full study of Ivanov's world view, see Pamela Davidson, *The Poetic Imagination of Viacheslav Ivanov, A Russian Symbolist's Perception of Dante* (Cambridge and New York: Cambridge University Press, 1989).
3. Ivanov to M.O. Gershenzon, "Perepiska iz dvukh uglov" (A Corner-to-Corner Correspondence) 15 July 1920, translated in Marc Raeff, *Russian Intellectual History: An Anthology* (New Jersey: Humanities Press, 1988), 398.
4. The lecture appears as "Zavety simvolizma" in *Apollon* 8 (1910): 5–20.

5. See, for example, recent biographies such as Charlotte Rosenthal's entry in *Dictionary of Russian Women Writers,* where the only hint of Kogan's Judaism is the mention of her "unique conception of the divine." In contrast, Ruth Rischin has recently demonstrated a link between Kogan's study of classical Hebrew (as attested by her masterful translation of the Book of Psalms) and her important theoretical findings on the concept of rhythm. As in this chapter, Rischin suggests that Kogan's unpublished writings are "examples of the persistence of [the poet's] religious sensitivity in an aesthetic climate. . . ." See Rischin, "F.I. Kogan (1891–1974): Translator of the Psalms," in *Jews and Slavs* 2 (1994): 193–222.

6. Note that the Russian language contains no sound akin to the English "h." Oftentimes when English would use an "h," Russian substitutes a "g." Thus "Cohen" in English becomes "Kogan" in Russian.

7. Feiga Izrailevna Kogan's papers are housed at Rossiskii gosudarstvennyi arkhiv literatury i iskusstva (RGALI) (Russian State Archive of Literature and Art), Moscow, f. 2272, op. 1 and 2 (1908–1968). A total of 120 files are found among her letters. She donated her papers to the archive in 1964. All translations are my own.

8. Hand-written autobiography, RGALI, f. 2272, op. 2, d. 3 and typed autobiography, f. 2272, op. 1, d. 32. Hereafter, the former is referred to as "Autobiography I," the latter as "Autobiography II." Note that Autobiography II is a 2-page distillation of Autobiography I, along with 2 additional pages called a "Supplement to the Autobiography." Following the archivist's lead, I have grouped all four pages as "Autobiography II."

9. Kogan, Autobiography, f. 2272, op. 2, d. 3, l. 1

10. Kornei Chukovskii, *From Two to Five*, trans. Miriam Morton (Berkeley, CA: University of California Press, 1963), 7. The book was originally published uner the title *Malen'kie deti* (Little children) in 1925.

11. Autobiography I, 5.

12. The papers of Ita Izrailevna Kogan, a historian, are housed at Gosudarstvennyi istoricheskii muzei (GIM) (State Historical Museum), Moscow, fond 494 (1905–1964).

13. *Bolshaia sovetskaia entsiklopediia,* s.v. "Mariinskie Zhenskie Gimnasii" and "Marinskie Zhenskie Uchilishcha."

14. Kogan's father was previously married, and he fathered children during his first marriage.

15. See chapter 5 for information on Simon Dubnov.

16. *Evreiskaia entsiklopediia,* s.v. "Yakov Isaevich Maze."

17. Autobiography I, 9.

18. See RGALI, f. 2272, op. 1, d. 73 for Kogan's diploma.
19. See RGALI, f. 2272, op. 1, d. 75 for a notice from the Moscow *meshchan-skii uprav* (bourgeois authority) summoning Kogan to appear before the St. Petersburg police (September 21, 1915).
20. See Autobiography I, 11 for the reference to "free lessons." Feiga Kogan, *Moia dusha* (Moscow, 1912).
21. Autobiography II, 1.
22. Ibid.
23. B. Sergeev, "F.K.—*Moia dusha*" *Zhatva* 3 (1912): 273–74.
24. Autobiography I, 12.
25. Autobiography I, 13.
26. The translation is my own. I have attempted to be as literal as possible and have omitted the rhyme scheme altogether. *Moia dusha*, 11.
27. Michael Green, *The Russian Symbolist Theater: An Anthology of Plays and Critical Texts* (Ann Arbor, Michigan: Ardis Publishers, 1986), 31.
28. See RGALI, f. 2272, op. 1, d. 1 for a hand-written draft of "Adonai." It is undated.
29. It should be noted that in 1917, Kogan published a short book of verse entitled *Pesnia gusliara* (Songs of a Psaltery Player) (Moscow, 1917) under the pseudonym Talin.
30. Autobiography II, 3.
31. There are no records to suggest what this meant.
32. Autobiography I, 2.
33. Autobiography I, 11.
34. Autobiography I, 12.
35. *Moia dusha*, 19.
36. The same verse appears in the Hebrew Bible in Psalms 22:2, though rather than *sabahtani, azavtani* appears.
37. *Evreiskaia entsiklopediia*, s.v. "Obshchestvo liubitelei evreiskogo iazika."
38. Kogan complimented her friend in her Autobiography I, 15. For more on Zhirkova, see entries in Reisen's *Leksikon* and in *Encyclopedia Judaica*, as well as correspondence between Zhirkova and M. Noviaski published in *Genazim* (1961): 151–162 and Hayim Weiner, *Pirkei hayim ve-sifrut* (Jerusalem, 1960), 74–5. See also Dan Miron, *Imahot meyasot, ahayot horgot* (Founding Mothers, Step Sisters).
39. The article on Blok appears in *Ha-tekufah* 21 (1924).
40. Her first Hebrew poem appears in *Ha-tekufah* 13 (1921).
41. Letter to Noviaski (June 15, 1919) in *Genazim* (1961), 152.
42. Letter to Noviaski (Oct. 5, 1919), in *Genazim* (1961), 155.

43. Feiga Kogan, "Review of Elisheva's *Tainye pesni* (Secret Songs)," in *Khronika Evreiskoi Zhizni* 6–7 (Feb. 28, 1919), 32.

44. Autobiography I, 15.

45. See RGALI, f. 2272, op. 1, d. 13.

46. Autobiography I, 15.

47. Autobiography II, 4.

48. Mendel Kohansky, *The Hebrew Theatre, Its First Fifty Years* (New York: Ktav, 1969), 1.

49. Kohansky, p. 10. Lilienblum's *Zerubavel,* or *The Return to Zion,* as translated by David Yellin, was performed during Sukkot in 1890 at the Laemel Secondary School in Jerusalem. Yehudah Leib Gordon's *The Hebrew Tongue* was performed in the back yard of a teacher at the secondary school in Rishon Lezion. See chapter one for more on Lilienblum and Gordon.

50. *Encyclopedia Judaica,* s.v. "Theater."

51. For more on Gnessin, see his memoirs *Darki im ha-teatron ha-ivri, 1905–1926* (Ha-kibbuz ha-meuchad, 1946).

52. For further information on this play, see chapter 2.

53. Shoshanah Avivit, "When the Guest Came," in *Bereshit habimah,* ed. Benjamin Vest (Jerusalem, 1966), 60.

54. Autobiography I, 16.

55. Autobiography II, 3.

56. Autobiography I, 11 and Autobiography II, 4. The archival overview provided among Kogan's papers indicates that she enrolled in the courses from 1918 to 1919.

57. Alla Sosnovskaya, "Was Habimah a Jewish Theater or a Russian Theater in Hebrew?" *Jews in Eastern Europe* 3 no. 22 (1993): 26.

58. Autobiography I, 16.

59. Feiga Kogan, "Gadybbuk," *Evreiskii vestnik* 6 (1922). Given Kogan's interests, it is notable that *The Dybbuk* has been interpreted as a Symbolist drama.

60. RGALI, f. 2272, op. 1, d. 21.

61. As quoted in Kohansky, 26.

62. Ibid.

63. Green, 110 and 15.

64. Feiga Kogan, "Zapisi" (Notes), Institut mirovoi literatury im Gorkogo (IMLI), Moscow, f. 55, op. 1, d. 6.

65. Among her papers is a 116-page memoir recounting her experiences in Ivanov's poetry circle, RGALI, f. 2272, op. 1, d. 33 (1953). Rischin notes a special rapport between Kogan and Ivanov. See "F.I. Kogan," p. 209.

66. The scholar Simon Markish placed Ivanov in the same camp as tolerant Christians like Solov'ev (see chapter three on the latter). See Simon Markish, "Vjaceslav Ivanov et les juifs," *Cahiers du Monde russe et sovietique* 25 no. 1 (Jan.–Mar. 1984): 35–47.
67. Autobiography I, 16.
68. Bible stories, RGALI, f. 2272, op. 1, d. 12 (1917).
69. Kogan testified to her reliance on *Sefer ha-aggadah* in the epilogue to the Bible stories.
70. See David Stern, "Introduction," *The Book of Legends*, transl. William Braude (New York: Schocken Books, 1992), xviii–xxii.
71. Feiga Kogan, *Plamennik* (Moscow, 1923).
72. Valerii Briusov, "Sredi stikhov," *Pechat' i revoliutsiia* 6 (1923): 67.
73. Autobiography II, 2.
74. Viacheslav Ivanov, *Eros* (St. Petersburg, 1907).
75. *Plamennik*, 52–53.
76. I am grateful to Gregory Krukov for this insight.
77. RGALI, f. 2272, op. 1, d. 1. Apparently the version I discovered in Kogan's archive is the middle section of a three-part poem.
78. Kogan quoted Pascal in her diary as well. See RGALI, f. 2272, op. 1, d. 30.
79. Autobiography II, 2.
80. Zvi Gitelman, *A Century of Ambivalence. The Jews of Russia and the Soviet Union, 1881 to the Present* (New York: Schocken Books in cooperation with YIVO, 1988), 110–15.
81. See Exodus 15: 20–21.
82. Autobiography II, 4.
83. Autobiography I, 28–29.
84. Archival inventory, RGALI, f. 2272, op 1.
85. Autobiography I, 28.
86. Ibid., 33.
87. *Kak nuzhno deklamirovat' stikhi* (Moscow, 1927), *Tekhnika ispolneniia stikha* (Moscow, 1935) and *Khudozhestvennoe chtennie. Ispolnenie stikhov* (vol. 1, Moscow, 1936 and vol. 2, Moscow, 1940).
88. See Letter to Stalin (Dec. 19, 1946), RGALI, f. 2272, op. 1, d. 43.
89. Ibid.
90. RGALI, f. 2272, op. 1, d. 16.
91. Davidson, p. 4.
92. Autobiography II, 4.
93. For an informed discussion of Ilya Ehrenburg's Jewish attachments, see

chapter 13 of Joshua Rubenstein, *Tangled Loyalties: The Life and Times of Ilya Ehrenburg* (New York: Basic Books, 1995).

94. Letter of Kogan to Ehrenburg (some time after January 29, 1962), RGALI, f. 2272, op. 1, d.. 45.

95. RGALI, f. 2272, op. 1, d. 72 (May 16, 1963 and Nov. 12, 1964).

96. After her death, a second group of papers was donated.

97. See chaps. 1 and 2.

98. Autobiography II, 2.

99. Ibid.

100. Baron, 243. Marrano (medieval Castillean for "swine") is the term adopted retroactively to describe the Jews of the Iberian Peninsula who converted to Catholicism but privately retained ties to their former faith.

CHAPTER FIVE: SOFIIA DUBNOVA-ERLIKH

1. Sofiia Dubnova-Erlikh, *Khleb i matsa. Vospominaniia* (Bread and Matzah, Memoirs) (St. Petersburg: Maksim, 1994), 134. The subject of the chapter will be referred to as Dubnova-Erlikh (D-E), even in her youth. The name is transliterated according to its Russian spelling.

2. Ibid., 20.

3. Ibid., 16. For the relationship between D-E and her father, see Kristi Groberg, "Dubnov and Dubnova: Rapport between Father and Daughter," in *A Missionary for History: Essays in Honor of Simon Dubnov*, eds. Avraham Greenbaum and Kristi Groberg (Minneapolis: University of Minnesota, 1998).

4. The term "Silver" implicitly compares the period to the Golden Age of Russian poetry: the 1820s and 1830s, dominated by Alexander Pushkin.

5. For D-E's confession of Russian as her mother tongue, see "Shotns fun der fargangenheyt," *Di tsukunft* (Dec. 1934), 694. See the appendix for her bibliography.

6. D-E mistakenly claimed that the poem was to appear in the journal *Budushchnost* (The Future). See *Khleb*, 103 and n. 86, 280. At the same time, a search of *Voskhod* turned up no such poem, indicating the censor's success.

7. Avraham Feinzilber, Obituary, *Unzer tsayt* 5 (1986): 38.

8. S. Dubnov-Erlikh, "Bagegenishn, a bletl zikhronos," *Unzer tsayt* 5 (1966): 57.

9. *Khleb*, 158.

10. D-E recalled her participation in civil rights rallies, and even translated the song "We Shall Overcome" into Russian. Ibid., 81.

11. As her son Victor informed me, D-E wrote primarily in Russian and composed a couple essays in Polish. Her writings that appeared in Yiddish and English were translations from Russian originals.

12. Sofiia Dubnova-Erlikh, *Zhizn' i tvorchestvo S.M. Dubnova* (New York, 1950). It was translated into Yiddish in 1952 and into English as *The Life and Work of S.M. Dubnova*, transl. Judith Vowles, ed. Jeffrey Shandler, introduction by Jonathan Frankel (Bloomington and Indianapolis: Indiana University Press, 1991). Dubnova-Erlikh wrote a condensed version of the biography in Russian, which was subsequently translated into French, Spanish and Hebrew. See bibliography.

13. A copy of the untitled original is housed at YIVO, RG108. The entire memoir was published as *Khleb i matsa*. I am grateful to Dr. Victor Erlich for sending me an advance copy of the book. All translations are my own.

14. *Khleb*, 175.

15. See, for example, Robert M. Seltzer, "Simon Dubnow: A Critical Biography of his Early Years," (Ph.D. diss., Columbia University, 1970) and Koppel Pinson's "Simon Dubnow: Historian and Political Philosopher," in Dubnow, *Nationalism and History: Essays on Old and New Judaism* (Philadelphia, 1958).

16. Simon Dubnov, *Kniga zhizni* (The Book of My Life), 3 vols. (vols. 1–2, Riga, 1934–1935; vol. 3, Riga, 1940, New York, 1957). At the time of writing, D-E had no access to the third volume, whose recovery in Australia postdated the biography's publication.

17. *Khleb*, 9–10. The same account on Mera Freidlin appears in *Life and Work*, 54.

18. See chapter one on this.

19. *Life and Work*, 53ff.

20. *Kniga zhizni* as quoted in *Life and Work*, 72.

21. *Life and Work*, 73 and 75.

22. Ida's self-denial would earn her daughter Sofiia's respect only years after the fact when D-E had herself undergone a somewhat similar process for the sake of her own husband. See *Life and Work*, 77 for a description of the ceremony and *Khleb*, 15 for D-E's musings on her mother's fate.

23. *Kniga zhizni*, 1:90 as quoted in Jonathan Frankel's introduction to *Life and Work*.

24. *Khleb*, 10 and *Life and Work*, 77.

25. *Khleb*, 16.

26. Ibid., 40.

27. Ibid., 36.

28. Ibid., 38–9.

29. Ibid., 20.

30. Ibid, 39. On female poets of the Silver Age using the male voice, see Jane A. Taubman, "Women Poets of the Silver Age, in *Women Writers in Russian Literature*, 172.

31. D-E claimed that her father expressed his religion through pantheism. See *Khleb*, 47.

32. *Kniga zhizni*, 1: 364–65.

33. Ibid., 40. D-E claimed that her father had sent "Visions" to Frug who heaped praise upon it.

34. Frankel, *Life and Work*, 4.

35. *Khleb*, 40.

36. Ibid.

37. The poem is based on a *midrash* in which God weeps over the misfortunes that beset the Jewish people as the tears are collected into a skin-bottle (*nod dema'ot*). For the poem, see *Shirei Frug*, ed. Yakov Kaplan (Warsaw, 1898), 85–86.

38. *Khleb*, 47–48.

39. See chapter four for an overview of Symbolism and chapter three for a discussion of Solov'ev.

40. *Khleb*, 79.

41. Ibid., 81.

42. Ibid., 53.

43. D-E does refer to the involvement of one anonymous woman in the Odessa Circle, whom she met in Geneva in 1912. See *Khleb*, 56. This is probably Maria Saker' who is mentioned as participating in the Odessa Circle in Steven J. Zipperstein, *Elusive Prophet: Ahad Ha'am and the Origins of Zionism* (Berkeley, CA: University of California Press, 1993), 182. Saker' was the first Jewish woman to publish an article in the Russian language. See introduction, n. 8.

44. Ibid., 20, 108–110 and n. 1, 206. Of course, it does not take a good deal of psychological insight to suggest that Ol'ga was probably deeply jealous of the relationship between her older sister and father.

45. Ibid., 21ff. D-E devotes a full fourteen pages to her relationship to her beloved brother.

46. Ibid., 64.

47. *Encyclopedia Judaica*, s.v. "Odessa" and Steven J. Zipperstein, *The Jews of Odessa: A Cultural History, 1794–1881* (Stanford: Stanford University Press, 1986).

48. Christine Johanson, *Women's Struggle for Higher Education in Russia, 1855–1900* , 62.

49. Ibid., 73.

50. *Khleb,* 64–66.

51. Ibid., 58.

52. S. Dubnova-Erlikh, Introduction, "Obshchestvennyi oblik zhurnala *Letopis'*," (Paper No. 14 of the Inter-University Project on the History of the Menshevik Movement) (New York, 1963), 2.

53. *Khleb,* 81.

54. Ibid., 86.

55. Ibid., 89.

56. Ibid., 90.

57. Ibid., 94.

58. Ibid., 71.

59. Ibid., 72.

60. Ibid., 104 and 114. Her memories of her experience in Grodno can be found in Sofiia Dubnov-Erlikh, "Shotns fun der Fargangenheyt."

61. *Khleb,* 113.

62. Sofiia D., "Pevets' stradaniia," *Nashe slovo* 7 (July 29, 1906): 9–16 and 7 (Aug. 3, 1906): 20–26.

63. For more on Iushkevich, see chapter 3.

64. For more on Orzheshko, especially her interest in the Jews, see Gabriella Safran, *Rewriting the Jew: Acculturation Narratives in the Russian Empire* (forthcoming, Stanford University Press).

65. Orzheshko's stories appeared in *Voskhod* with more regularity than those of any other woman.

66. S. Mstislavskaia, "Eliza Ozheshko (sic)," *Evreiskoe obozrenie* (Jewish Review) 2 (June 3, 1910): 9–15. For a time, *Evreiskii mir* was published under the name *Evreiskoe obozrenie.*

67. See her bibliography for a complete listing of D-E's contributons to *Evreiskii mir.*

68. Eliza Orzheshko, "Ob evreiakh i evreiskom voprose," *Russkii evrei* 26–32, 34, 37–41 (1882).

69. "Proshchanie" (Farewell) appeared as well in two of D-E's collections: *Osenniaia svirel'* (Petersburg, 1911) and *Stikhi raznikh let* (New York, 1973).

70. *Khleb,* 126.

71. RGIA (Russian State Historical Archive), St. Petersburg, f. 1328, op. 2, d. 38.

72. See chapter four for discussion of Chukovskii and Ivanov.
73. S. Dubnova-Erlikh, "Obshchestvennii oblik zhurnala *Letopis'*," 3.
74. D-E recorded her reminiscences of Vinaver in "Mikhail Vinaver," *Chronicle of Human Rights in the USSR* 27 (Apr.–June 1977): 90–95.
75. *Khleb*, 135.
76. Ibid., 34.
77. S. Mstislavskaia, Bibliography Column (Review of Bialik's *Pesni i poemy*), *Evreiskii mir* 12 (Mar. 25, 1911): 12–15. In passing, she chastised her old friend Jabotinsky, the translator and editor of the volume, for interjecting his politics into his otherwise useful introduction. Sofiia Dubnova, *Osenniaia svirel': stikhi* (St. Petersburg, 1911).
78. *Khleb*, 150.
79. *Life and Work*, 142. Presumably, D-E's documentation for such an intimate portrayal of her father was his own autobiography.
80. In my translation, I do not attempt to replicate the ABAB ryhme scheme. Note that the translation is based on the version of the poem that appears in *Stikhi raznykh let*.
81. *Khleb*, 152 and 151.
82. Ibid., 152. Ivanov called it "music"; Briusov mentioned the book in a review about young poets; Blok noted its musicality even while criticizing D-E for not yet "finding [her] own words."
83. The great Russian poet Marina Tsvetaeva also wrote poems on women, including Ariadne.
84. *Osenniaia svirel'*, 13–14.
85. *Khleb*, 140.
86. Ibid., 142.
87. Ibid., 148.
88. Ibid., 153.
89. Ibid.
90. Ibid.
91. Kristi Groberg, "Dubnov and Dubnova: Rapport between Father and Daughter."
92. *Khleb*, 158.
93. Ibid., 156.
94. Ibid., 158.
95. Ibid., 159.
96. Ibid., 161.
97. My translation is based on the version published in *Stikhi raznykh let*. No attempt has been made to retain the rhyme scheme in the translation.

98. *Khleb*, 136.
99. *Letopis'* 3 and 12 (1916).
100. Sofiia Dubnova-Erlikh, *Mat'* (Petrograd, 1919, 2nd ed. Tel Aviv, 1969). The cycle was published as well in *Poeziia revoliutsionnoi Moskvy* (Berlin, 1922), a separate edition of *Kniga dlia vsekh*, ed. Ilya Ehrenburg, 57–58.
101. Dubnova-Erlikh, "Obshchestvennyi," 2.
102. *Khleb*, 162.
103. Ibid., 175.
104. Ibid., 182.
105. Ibid., 198.
106. Ibid.
107. See chapter four for more on Habimah and the Hebrew theater in the Russian Empire.
108. *Khleb*, 192.
109. Ibid., 194.
110. *Garber-bund un bershter-bund, bletlekh fun der yidisher arbeyter-bavegung.* Hayim Shmuel Kazdan and Leyvik Hodes, translators. (Warsaw, 1937).
111. Sophie Dubnow-Erlich and Leon Oler, eds. *Khmurner-bukh* (New York, 1958), Sophie Dubnov-Erlikh, ed. *Biografye un shriftn, Leyvik Hodes* (New York, 1962) and Sophie Dubnow-Erlich, Jacob S. Hertz, Gregor Aronson, et. al., eds. *Di geshikhte fun 'bund'* 5 vols. (New York, 1960–81).
112. *Khleb*, 207.
113. Groberg, "Dubnov and Dubnova."
114. *Khleb*, 229.
115. *Life and Work*, 276.
116. D-E's entrance visa to the United States dated May 23, 1942 is among her papers at YIVO in the Bund Archives ME 16–103, RG 1400, Box 405.
117. Lucan Way, "Exhuming the Buried Past," *The Nation* (Mar. 1, 1993): 267–68.
118. Sofiia Dubnova-Erlikh, *Stikhi raznykh let* (New York, 1973).
119. See for instance, Anita Norich, "Jewish Literature and Feminist Criticism: An Introduction to Gender and Text," in *Gender and Text in Modern Hebrew and Yiddish Literature*, 11–12. She rejects the typical explanations for why women turned first to poetry, including the theory that Eastern European life did not allow women the time or the space or the resources to write novels. "The image that comes to mind is of a woman with little bits of paper coming out of apron pockets, jotting down another short line of po-etry between the soup and *tsimmes* (carrot stew)." Surely, she argues, no poet would proffer the argument that poetry takes less time or concentra-

tion than prose. Another view holds that Jewish women could not write novels because the expansive social worldview implicit in that genre was inaccessible to them.

120. This has been documented insofar as English is concerned by Michael Galchinsky, *The Origin of the Modern Jewish Woman Writer*.

121. See D-E's obituary in *Unzer tsayt* 5 (1986), the memorial to D-E in *Unzer tsayt* 11–12 (1987) on the occasion of her gravestone unveiling, and Zalman Reisin, ed. *Leksikon fun der yidisher literatur, prese un filologi*, 4 vols. (Vilna, 1926–29).

122. Note that Dubnova-Erlikh translated Julian Tuvim's famous poem "We, Polish Jews" into Russian for the journal *Novosel'e*. Tuvim had before the war rejected a specifically Jewish identity. When in 1944 he heard about the decimation of Jews, he identified with Jewish suffering for the first time. But he was still a Pole, too. His poem is a response to those for whom the phrase "We, Polish Jews" is a contradiction.

123. *Entsiklopedicheskii slovar'. Slavianskaia mifologiia* (Moscow, 1995), s.v. "Khleb."

CONCLUSION

1. Hava Shapiro, "The Female Image in Our Literature," *Ha-tekufah* 26–27 (1930): 627.

2. Charlotte Rosenthal, "Carving Out a Career: Women Prose Writers, 1885–1917, The Biographical Background," in *Gender and Russian Literature*, ed. Rosalind Marsh (Cambridge University Press, 1996), 137.

3. The single link I found between any two of these writers was in an article by Dubnova-Erlikh on Jewish literature in the Russian language. In it, she describes Khin as displaying "compassion for the disinherited Jewish people" in her short stories. See S. Dubnow-Erlich, "Jewish Literature in Russian," vol. 3, *The Jewish People Past and Present* (New York: Central Yiddish Culture Organization, 1952), 261.

4. Mary F. Zirin, "Women's Prose Fiction in the Age of Realism," in *Women Writers in Russian Literature*, 77.

Bibliographies of the Writers
(includes all published writings, in chronological order)

MIRIAM MARKEL-MOSESSOHN
(Other bylines: M.M.M.)

Ha-yehudim be-angliyah, o ha-yehudim ve-nosei ha-tzlav be-malokh ricard lev-ha-ari (The Jews in England, or The Jews and the Crusades under the Reign of Richard the Lionhearted). Part I. Warsaw, 1869.

[Correspondents' Column]. *Ha-melitz* 97 (May 1 (13), 1887): 1029.

"[Correspondence from] Vienna." *Ha-melitz* 111 (May 21 (June 2), 1887): 1168–69.

"[Correspondence from] Vienna." *Ha-melitz* 122 (June 3 (15). 1887): 1296–98.

"From the Summer Heat." *Ha-melitz* 157 (July 14 (26), 1887): 1659–62.

Ha-yehudim be-angliyah, o ha-yehudim ve-nosei ha-tzlav be-malokh ricard lev-ha-ari (The Jews in England, or The Jews and the Crusades under the Reign of Richard the Lionhearted). Part II. Warsaw, 1895.

HAVA SHAPIRO
(Other bylines: *em kol ḥai*, EKH, H.S.)

"The Rose." *Ha-dor* 48 (December 12, 1901): 13–14.

"Wilting Roses." *Ha-dor* (October 21, 1904): 27–28.

"Old Maid." *Ha-olam* 2 no. 18 (May 6, 1908).

"Young Poet." *Ha-olam* 2 no. 22 (June 3, 1908).

"Typical Women." *Ha-olam* 2 no. 27 (July 8, 1908).

"Broken Tablets." *Ha-olam* 2 no. 37 (September 18, 1908).

"The Days of Awe." *Hed ha-zeman* 209 (September 20 and October 3, 1908): 1.

"On Literature." *Ha-olam* 39 (October 2, 1908) and 40 (October 9, 1908): 506–8 and 518–20.

Kovetz tziurim. Warsaw, 1909.

"Hauptmann's New Novel." *Ha-shiloaḥ* 28 (1913): 563–68.

"Aphorisms and Typical Principles." *Ha-toren* 2 no. 4 (May 1914): 135–40.

"False Prophets in Israel and among the Nations." *Ha-shiloaḥ* 31 (1914): 317–31.

"The Brothers of Slavuta." *Ha-shiloaḥ* 30 no. 1 (1914): 541–54.

"From General Literature." *Ha-shiloaḥ* 31 (1914): 90–6, 267–73, 317–31 and 549–55.

"On Death." *Ha-shiloaḥ* 32 (1915): 63–9.

"Female Types in Mendele's Stories." *Ha-shiloaḥ* 34 (1918): 92–101.

"Y.L. Peretz, the Man and the Author." *Ha-shiloaḥ* 34 (1918): 347–54 and 501–10.

"Notes from Ukraine." *Ha-olam* 9 (October 6–7 and November 1919): 3–4.

"You Must not Forget!" *Ha-olam* 9 no. 10 (December 19, 1919): 2–4.

"Love in the Poems of Tchernichovsky." *Ha-shiloaḥ* 35 (1919):151–57.

"Letter from Prague." *Ha-toren* 7 no. 6 (March 27, 1920): 11–13.

"Arguments." *Ha-olam* 9 no. 25 (April 2, 1920): 2–4.

"Meeting of *ha-po'el ha-tza'ir.*" *Ha-olam* 9 no. 29 (July 15, 1920): 7–8.

"Letter from Switzerland." *Ha-olam* 9 no. 50 (October 15, 1920):4–5.

"Preparation." *Ha-olam* 9 no. 34 (November 6, 1920): 6–8.

"Letters from Prague." *Ha-olam* 10 nos. 4 and 8 (November 11 and December 9, 1920).

"Meeting of *ha-poel ha-tza'ir* and *tze'irei tzion.*" *Ha-toren* 7 nos. 8–9 (1920): 10–12 and 14–16.

"Letter from Czechoslavakia." *Ha-toren* 7 no. 39 (1920): 6–9.

"Letter from Prague." *Ha-toren* 7 no. 49 (1920): 9–10.

"The Jewish Movement." *Ha-olam* 10 nos. 19–20 (February 24, 1921 and March 3, 1921).

"Notes." *Ha-olam* 10 no. 27 (April 21, 1921).

"Letter from Czechoslavakia." *Ha-olam* 10 no. 31 (May 21, 1921).

"Letter from Prague." *Ha-toren* 10 no. 33 (June 9, 1921).

"Zionist Customs in Prague." *Ha-olam* 10 nos. 40–41 (July 28, 1921 and August 4, 1921).

"Meetings of the Congress." *Ha-olam* 10 no. 46 (September 8, 1921).

"World Meeting." *Ha-olam* 10 nos. 46–47 (September 8 and 15, 1921).

"Around the Congress." *Ha-olam* 10 no. 47 (September 15, 1921).

"Theodor Gomperz." *Ha-olam* 11 no. 45 (November 30, 1921).

"Letters from a Tuberculosis Patient." *Ha-shiloaḥ* 38 (1921): 122–31.

"Notes from the Congress." *Ha-toren* 8 no. 5 (1921): 38–40.

"Martin Buber." *Ha-toren* 9 nos. 2–3 (1922): 45–49 and 42–52.

"Reuven Brainin, His Spiritual Persona." *Eyn ha-kore* 2–3 (April-September 1923): 73–82.

"Memories of Frischmann's Life." *Ha-toren* 9 no. 11 (1923): 84–89.

"Young Literature." *Ha-toren* 10 nos. 4–5 (1923): 74–83.

"From Czechoslavakia to Romania." *Ha-olam* (May 9, 1924).

"From Carpathian Russia." *Ha-olam* 12 no. 25 (June 20, 1924).

"Jewish Education in the Russian Carpathians." *Ha-olam* 12 no. 38 (September 19, 1924).

"Meshut in the Lands." *Ha-olam* 12 no. 46 (November 14, 1924).

"What is Hanukkah?" *Ha-olam* 12 no. 52 (December 26, 1924).

"Two Stories" (criticism of Wasserman and Buber). *Ha-toren* 10 no. 11 (1924): 72–79.

"Paganism, Christianity and Judaism" (review of Max Brod). *Ha-toren* 11 nos. 8–9 (1924): 47–57.

"Contemporary Russian Literature." *Ha-shiloaḥ* 43 (1925): 76–87.

"President-Philosopher" (on Masaryk). *Ha-shiloaḥ* 44 (1925): 159–67.

"The Female Image in our Literature." *Ha-tekufaḥ* 26–27 (1930): 617–33.

T.G. Masaryk. Prague, 1935.

RASHEL' KHIN
(Other bylines: R. F___shtein)

"Iz storony v storonu." *Drug zhenshchin* 2–3, 4–6 (1883).

"Sud'by russkoi devushki. Ocherk po narodnym svadebnym pesniam i obriadam." *Drug zhenshchin* 2 (1883).

"Neskol'ko slov o Turgeneve." *Drug zhenshchin* 2 (1884).

"Siluety." *Russkaia mysl'* 8–9 (1886).

"Ne ko dvoru." *Voskhod* (1886).

"Makarka." *Voskhod* 4 (1889).

"Na staruiu temu." *Severnyi vestnik* 1 (1890).

"Natasha Krinitskaia." *Russkoe obozrienie* 6 (1891).

"Antoinette" (from French of L. Halevi). *Russkie vedomosti* 146 (1891).

"In Defense of Jews" (from French of Emile Zola) and "Russia" (from French of Georg Brandes) *Pomoshch' evreiam.* St. Petersburg, 1891.

"Makarka." With Nikolai Ivanovich Naumov's "V glukhom' mestechke." Moscow, 1895.

"Ustroilas'." *Vestnik Evropy* (1896).

"Tifena." *Russkie vedomosti* 356 (1896).

"Mechtatel'." *Sbornik v pol'zu nachal'nykh evreiskikh shkol.* St. Petersburg, 1896.

"Okhota smertnaia." *Prizyv.* Moscow, 1897.

"Elka." *Russkie vedomosti* 295 (1898).

"Odinochestvo." *Vestnik Evropy* (1899).

Pod goru: rasskazy. Moscow, 1900.

Glava iz neizdannykh zapisok. Moscow, 1901.

"Hamlet" (from French of George Sand). *Sbornik na pomoshch' uchashchimsiia zhenshchinam.* Moscow, 1901.

Siluety. Moscow, 1894, 3rd edition St. Petersburg, 1902.

"Fenomen." *Mir bozhii* (1903).

Porosl'. Moscow, 1905.

Pod sen'iu Penatov'. Moscow, 1907.

"Pamiati kniazia A.I. Urusova." *Kniaz' Aleksandr Ivanovich Urusov.* Vols. 2 and 3. Moscow, 1907.

"Poslednie gody N.I. Storozhenko," *Pamiati N.I. Storozhenko.* Moscow, 1909.

Nasledniki. 1911?.

"Frantsuzskie pisateli v franko-prusskuiu voinu" *Golos minuvshego* 11 (1914).

Ledokhod. Moscow, 1917.

"Pamiati starogo druga," *Pamiati A.F. Koni.* Leningrad-Moscow, 1929.

FEIGA KOGAN
(Other bylines: F.K., A. Talin)
(Based on her autobibliography, RGALI, f. 2272, op. 1, d. 35)

Moia dusha. Moscow, 1912.

Poetry in *Novom zhurnale dlia vsekh.* 1916.

(Talin, A.) *Pesnia gusliara.* Moscow, 1917.

(Talin, A.) "Pesni truda i goria." *Rabochaia zhizn'* 10, 18 (1918).

"Ogarev." *Put'* 5 (1919).

"E. Lisheva (*sic*) 'Tainye pesni.'" *Khronika evreiskoi zhizni* (February 28, 1919).

"V lunnuiu noch'." *Put'* 6 (1919).

"Gadibuk." *Evreiskii vestnik* 6 (1922).

Two poems in *Lirika.* Moscow, 1922.

Plamennik. Moscow, 1923.

"Zhizhn' i znanie." In *Sbornik stikhotvorenii dlia sol'noi i kollektivnoi dekla-matsii*. Moscow, 1923.

Article in *Vestnik prosveshcheniia* 5–6 (1926).

Poetry in *Novye stikhi*. 2 (1927).

Kak nuzhno deklamirovat' stikhi. Moscow, 1927 and 1934.

Article in *Klubnaia stsena* 1 (1928).

"Khitrov rynok." *Klubnaia stsena* 6 (1928).

Poetry translations in *Krasnaia niva* (January 13, 1929).

"Proletariat - stroitel' novoi zhizni." *Derevenskii samouchka* 1 (1929).

Material on the life and work of Gorkii (without her permission). Moscow, 1930 and 1940.

"Kruzhok chteniia khudozhestvennoi literatury." *Klub* 3 (1934).

"Kak nuzhno deklamirovat' stikhi." *Kolkhoznyi aktivist* 12 (November 1934): 35–39.

"Uchites' u klassikov rabotat' nad slovom." *Kolkoznyi aktivist* 1 (January 1935): 31–33.

"Chto takoe iskusstvo khudozhestvennogo chteniia i v chem ego znache-nie." *Kolkoznyi aktivist* 3–4 (February 1935): 76–78.

Tekhnika ispolneniia stikha. Moscow, 1935.

Khudozhestvennoe chtenie. Ispolnenie stikhov. Vol. 1, Moscow, 1936 and vol. 2, Moscow, 1940.

"Mastera khudozhestvennogo slova po forme." *Moskovskii bol'shevik* (February 4, 1942).

"Kak chitat' stikhi Maiakovskogo." *Literatura v shkole* 5–6 (1946).

Two articles on art in *Kul'turno-prosvetitel'naia rabota* 1–2 (1949).

SOFIIA DUBNOVA-ERLIKH
(Other bylines: Sofiia D., Sofiia Dubnova, Sofiia Mstislavskaia,
Mstislavskaia, S. Mstislavskaia, S.M.)
(Based on bibliography compiled by Kristi Groberg)

"Pevets stradaniia." *Nashe slovo* 7 (July 29, 1906): 9–16 and 7 (August 3, 1906): 20–26.

"Iz Bialika; stikhotvorenie S. Dubnovoi." *Evreiskii mir* 1 (March 1909): 19–20.

"Iz evreiskikh narodnykh pesen." *Evreiskii mir* 1 (October 1909): 13–14.

"Iz evreiskikh narodnykh pesen." *Evreiskii mir* 2 (January-March, 1910): 17–18 (translation from Yiddish to Russian).

I.L. Peretz, "Tri shvei." *Evreiskii mir* 2 (January-March 1910): 71–72 (translation from Yiddish to Russian).

"Molodye pobegi." *Evreiskii mir* 3 (January-March 1910): 121–24.

Review of Sagalowitsz's *Stille Traumen*. *Evreiskii mir* 6 (February 11, 1910): 47–48.

Review of Zaidel's *Vykhody iz cherti osedlosti*. *Evreiskii mir* 10 (March 11, 1910): 65.

"Eliza Ozheshko (*sic*)." *Evreiskoe obozrenie* 2 (June 3, 1910): 9–15.

Review of Osipovich's *Povesti*. *Evreiskii mir* 4 (June 17, 1910): 47–48.

"Mariia Konopnitskaia." *Evreiskii mir* 23–24 (October 7, 1910): 56–57.

Review of *Sobranie sochinnenii Sholom Alekhem*. *Evreiskii mir* 29 (November 11, 1910): 46–48.

Review of Bialik's work. *Evreiskii mir* 34 (December 17, 1910): 57–58.

Review of Bialik's *Pesni i poemi*. *Evreiskii mir* 12 (March 25, 1911): 12–15.

Osenniaia svirel': stikhi. St. Petersburg, 1911.

"Mat'." *Letopis'* 3 (1916) and 12 (1916): 137–38 and 93–95.

Leopold Staff, "Iz knigi *Dzien duszy*." *Otechestvo*. Petrograd, 1916 (translation from Polish to Russian).

Leopold Staff, "Zakat." *Otechestvo* (Petrograd, 1916) (translation from Polish to Russian).

Mat'. Petrograd, 1918; Tel Aviv, 1969.

"V chernye dni." In *Evreiskii mir*, eds. A. Sobol' and E.B. Loiter. Moscow, 1918.

Tomas Mann, *Sila i chelovek*, ed. Vladimir Kossovskii (Berlin, 1921) (translation from French to Russian).

"Iz knigi *Mat'*." *Kniga dlia vsekh* 57–58 [under the title *Poeziia revoliutsionnoi Moskvy*] ed. Il'ia Ehrenburg. Berlin, 1922.

"Shotns fun der Fargangenheyt," *Di tsukunft* (December 1934): 694–700.

Garber-bund un bershter-bund, bletlekh fun der yidisher arbeyter-bavegung. Translated from the Russian by Hayim Shmuel Kazdan and Leyvik Hodes. Warsaw, 1937.

"Snimki na letu." *Novosel'e* 7 (1942): 39–43.

"Sovetskomu poetu." *Novosel'e* 16 (1942): 36.

"Partizan." *Novosel'e* 16 (1942): 37.

"Rasput'e." *Novosel'e* 16 (1942): 30.

"Dos lebn fun Vladimir Medem." In *Vladimir Medem, tsum tsvantsikstn yortsayt*. New York, 1943.

"Dve vstrechi." *Novosel'e* 1 (1943): 40–46.

"Mestechko." *Novosesl'e* 3 (May-June, 1943): 64–67.

"V put'i." *Novosel'e* 4–5 (1943): 45.

"Vozvrashchenie v Evropu." *Novosel'e* 4–5 (1943): 45–46.

"Na rubezhe." *Novosel'e* 4–5 (1943): 46.

"Poezd smerti." *Novosel'e* 7–8 (1943–44): 42.

"Rodina." *Novosel'e* 7–8 (1943–44): 42.

Annali Vitmor Dzhakobi (Annalee Whitmore Jacoby), "Kitai zhivet." *Novosel'e* 9–10 (1944): 44–48 (translation from English to Russian).

"Na pepelishche." *Novosel'e* 11 (1944): 70–73.

"Sovremenniku." *Novosel'e* 12–13 (1944): 33.

Iulian Tuvim, "My, pol'skie evrei." *Novosel'e* 14–15 (1944): 39–45 (translation from Polish to Russian).

Iosif Opatoshu (Joseph Opatoshu), "Smert' Meira Balabana." *Novosel'e* 16 (1944): 39–44 (translation from Polish to Russian).

Kei Boil (Kay Boyle), "V gornoi derevne." *Novosel'e* 17–18 (1945): 4–12 (translation from English to Russian).

Sholom Ash (Sholem Asch), "Iz ognennoi pechi." *Novosel'e* 19 (1945): 4–9 (translation from Yiddish to Russian).

"Rebenku." *Novosel'e* 19 (1945): 33.

"Pol'she." *Novosel'e* 22–23 (1945): 49.

"Iz vospominanii o Gor'kom." *Novosel'e* 24–25 (1946): 46–53.

"Renessans romantiki." *Novosel'e* 24–25 (1946): 93–100.

"Podvizhniki getto. *Novosel'e* 27–28 (1946): 103ff.

"V sozvuchii s epokhoi." *Novosel'e* 35–36 (1947): 83–90.

"Pepelishche." *Novosel'e* 37–38 (1948): 65–66.

"Geroicheskaia epopeia." *Novosel'e* 37–38 (1948): 42–44.

"V galere." *Novosel'e* 37–38 (1948): 66.

Zhizn' i tvorchestvo S. M. Dubnova. New York, 1950.

———. In Yiddish. Translated by Moyshe Ferdman. Mexico City, 1952.

———. In English as *The Life and Work of S.M. Dubnov*. Translated by Judith Vowles. With introduction by Jonathan Frankel, ed. Jeffrey Shandler. Bloomington and Indianapolis: Indiana University Press, 1991.

"Jewish Literature in Russian." In *The Jewish People: Past and Present,* vol. 3, 257–67, ed.Rafael Abramovich. New York, 1952.

"Ha-kerem be-odesah." In *Sefer Shimon Dubnov*, 61–66, ed. Simon Rawidowicz. Jerusalem, London, Waltham, MA, 1953.

"Predislovie." In S.M. Dubnov, *Kniga zhizni*, vol. 3. New York, 1957.

———— and Leon Oler, eds. *Khmurner-bukh*. New York, 1958.

Biografye un shriftn, Leyvik Hodes.New York, 1962.

Obshchestvennyi oblik zhurnala Letopis'. New York: Inter-University Project on the History of the Menshevik Movement, 1963.

"La Vie de Simon Dubnov." In *Simon Dubnow, The Man and His Work: A Memorial Volume on the Occasion of the Centennary of of his Birth*, 1–25, ed. Aaron S. Steinberg. Paris, 1963 (written in Russian and published in French).

"Bagegenishn." in *Unzer tsayt* 5 (1966): 57–59.

[other articles in *Unzer tsayt* 3–4 (1949), 10 (1959), 7–8, 9 (1979), 12 (1942)]

Simon Dubnow. Buenos Aires, 1967 (translation of her article "La vie de Simon Dubnow") and in Hebrew as *Shimon Dubnov*. Jerusalem, 1968.

————, Jacob S. Hertz, Gregor Aronson, et. al., eds. *Di geshikhte fun Bund*. 5 vols. New York, 1960–81.

Stikhi raznykh let. New York, 1973.

"Mikhail Vinaver." *Chronicle of Human Rights in the USSR* 27 (April-June 1977): 90–95.

Khleb i matsa. St. Petersburg: Maksim, 1994. [Selections of the memoirs appeared in *Vremia i my* 96 and 97 (1987).]

Bibliography

ARCHIVAL SOURCES

Central Zionist Archive, Jerusalem
A9/59–61   Moshe Leib Lilienblum.

Genazim, Tel Aviv
Hava Shapiro. Diary (1899–1941), handwritten in Hebrew.

Jewish National and University Archive, Hebrew University, Jerusalem
40 761   Yehudah Leib Gordon.
Schwadron Collection. Miriam Markel-Mosessohn.

Jewish Public Library, Montreal
Reuven Brainin Collection.

Rossiiskii gosudarstvennyi arkhiv literatury i iskusstva (RGALI), Moscow
f. 128   Rashel' Mironovana Khin
f. 2272   Feiga Izraelivna Kogan

Rossiiskii gosudarstvennyi istoricheskii arkhiv (RGIA), St. Petersburg
f. 497   Censor's notice
f. 776   Censor's notice
f. 1328   Censor's notice

YIVO, New York
RG108   Dubnov

UNPUBLISHED MASTER'S THESES AND DOCTORAL DISSERTATIONS

Caruso, Naomi. "Chava Shapiro: A Woman Before Her Time." Master's thesis, McGill University, 1991.

Freeze, ChaeRan Y. "Making and Unmaking the Jewish Family: Marriage and Divorce in Imperial Russia, 1850–1914." Ph.D. diss., Brandeis University, 1997.

Moseley, Marcus. "Jewish Autobiography in Eastern Europe: The Prehistory of a Literary Genre." D.Phil., Trinity College, Oxford, 1990.

Nathans, Benjamin Ira. "Beyond the Pale: The Jewish Encounter with Russia, 1840–1900." Ph.D. diss., University of California at Berkeley, 1995 (forthcoming, University of California Press).

CONTEMPORARY NEWSPAPERS, JOURNALS AND PERIODICALS

Apollon

Budushchnost

Den'

Drug zhenshchin

Evreiskii mir (*Evreiskoe obozrenie*)

Evreiskii vestnik

Eyn ha-kore

Ha-boker or

Ha-doar

Ha-dor

Ha-magid

Ha-melitz

Ha-olam

Ha-poel ha-tza'ir

Ha-shahar

Ha-shiloah

Ha-tekufah

Ha-toren

Hed ha-zeman

Kenesset yisrael

Ketuvim

Khronika evreiskoi zhizni

Letopis'

Nashe slovo

Russkaia mysl'

Russkii evrei

Russkoe bogatsvo

Di tsukunft

Unzer tsayt

Voskhod

ENCYCLOPEDIAS AND PUBLISHED GUIDES

Deych, G.M., comp. and Benjamin Nathans, ed. *Arkhivnye dokumenty po istorii evreev v Rossii v XIX - nachale XX vv.: Putevoditel'.* Moscow, 1994.

Encyclopedia Judaica.

Entsiklopedicheskii slovar'. Slavianskaia mifologiia.

Enziklopediayah Yizrael.

Evreiskaia entsiklopediia.

Great Soviet Encyclopedia.

Harari, Yehudit. *Ishah ve-em be-yisrael.* Tel Aviv: Masada, 1959.

Ignatov, I. ed. *Galereia russkikh pisatelei.* Moscow, 1901.

Jewish Encyclopedia.

Kayserling, Mayer. *Die judischen Frauen in der Geschichte, Literatur und Kunst.* Leipzig: F.A. Brockhaus, 1879.

Kelner, Viktor E. and Dmitri A. Elyashevich, eds. *Literatura o evreiakh na russkom iazyke, 1890–1947.* St. Peterburg: Gumanitarnoe agentstvo "Akademicheskii proekt," 1995.

Klausner, Yosef. *Historiyah shel ha-sifrut ha-ivrit ha-hadashah.* 4 vols. Odessa: 1909–25.

Koz'min, B.P. ed. *Pisateli sovremennoi epokhi.* Moscow, 1928.

Kressel, Getzel, ed. *Leksikon ha-sifrut ha-ivrit ba-dorot ha-aḥaronim.* 2 vols. Merhavyah: Sifriyat po'alim, 1965–67.

Ledkovsky, Marina, Charlotte Rosenthal and Mary Zirin, eds. *Dictionary of Russian Women Writers.* Westport, CT. Greenwood Press, 1994.

Reisen, Solomon, ed. *Leksikon fun der Yiddisher literatur, presse un filologia.* 4 vols. Vilna: B. Kletzkin, 1926–30.

Sistematicheskii ukazatel' literatury o evreiakh na russkom iazyke so vremeni vvedeniia grazhdanskago shrifta (1708g) do dekabr' 1889 g. 2nd edition. Cambridge, England, 1973.

Vengerov, Simon, ed. *Entsiklopedicheskii slovar'.* St. Petersburg, 1903.

Zeitlin, William. *Kiryat sefer bibliotheca hebraica post-Mendelssohniana.* 2 vols. 2nd edition. New York: Arno Press, 1980.

PRINTED PRIMARY SOURCES

Auer, Leopold. *My Long Life in Music.* New York, 1923.

Avivit, Shoshanah. "When the Guest Came." In *Bereshit ha-bimah,* ed. Benjamin Vest. Jerusalem, 1966.

Brainin, Reuven. *Avraham Mapu.* Petrokov, 1900.

Breiman, Shlomo, ed. *Iggerot Moshe Leib Lilienblum le-Yehudah Leib Gordon.* Jerusalem, 1968.

———, ed. *Ketavim avtobiografiim Moshe Leib Lilienblum.* 3 vols. Jerusalem: Mosad Bialik, 1970.

DeVries-Gunzburg, I. "Some Letters of Ivan Turgenev to Baron Horace de Gunzburg." *Oxford Slavonic Papers* 9 (1960): 73–103.

Dinur, Ben-Zion, ed. *Mikhtevei Avraham Mapu.* Jerusalem: Mosad Bialik, 1970.

Dubnov, Simon. *Kniga zhizni.* 3 vols. Riga, 1934–35; Riga, 1940; New York, 1957.

Frischmann, David. *Kol kitvei David Frischmann*. 8 vols. Warsaw: Stybel Publishing Company, 1924.

Frug, Shimon. *Shirei Frug*. Edited by Yakov Kaplan. Warsaw, 1898.

Gol'dovskii, O.B. *Evrei v Moskve: stranitsy iz istorii sovremennoi*. Berlin, 1904.

———— and A. Andreev, eds. *Prince Aleksandr' Ivanovich Urusov*. 2 vols. Moscow, 1907.

Gordon, Yehudah Leib. *Kitvei Yehudah Leib Gordon*. Tel Aviv: Dvir, 1960.

Green, Michael. *The Russian Symbolist Theater: An Anthology of Plays and Critical Texts*. Ann Arbor, MI: Ardis Publishers, 1986.

Gruezenberg, O.O. *Vchera*. Paris, 1938. Translated into English as *Yesterday: Memoirs of a Russian-Jewish Lawyer*. Berkeley, CA: University of California Press, 1981.

Koni, A.I. *Pamiati A.I. Koni*. Leningrad-Moscow, 1929.

Turgenev, Ivan. *On the Eve*. Translated by Gilbert Gardiner. New York: Penguin Books, 1950.

————, *Pis'ma Turgenevu shchukinskii sbornik*.

Tzederbaum, Alexander. *Keter kehunah*. Odessa, 1866.

Vishniak, Mark. *Dan' proshlomu*. New York: Chekhov Publishing House, 1954.

Weissberg, Isaac Jacob, ed. *Iggerot Yehudah Leib Gordon*. 2 vols. Warsaw, 1894.

Wengeroff, Pauline. *Memoiren einer Grossmutter*. Berlin: M. Poppelauer, vol. 1, 1908; vol. 2, 1910.

Yaari, Avraham, ed. *Tzror iggerot Yalag el Miriam Markel-Mosessohn*. Jerusalem: Darom, 1936.

SECONDARY SOURCES

Aaronson, Gregor. "The Jews in Russian Literature, Journalism, Literary Criticism and Political Life" and "Jewish Periodicals in the Russian Language." In *Kniga o russkom evreistve*, 361–99 and 548–73. New York: Union of Russian Jews, 1960.

Baron, Salo. *The Russian Jews under Tsars and Soviets*. New York: Schocken Books, 1987.

Baskin, Judith R., ed. *Jewish Women in Historical Perspective*. Detroit: Wayne State University Press, 1991.

_____. *Women of the Word: Jewish Women and Jewish Writings*. Detroit: Wayne State University Press, 1994.

Beller, Steven. *Vienna and the Jews, 1867–1938: A Cultural History*. Cambridge and New York: Cambridge University Press, 1989.

Berlin, Isaiah. "The Birth of the Russian Intelligentsia (1838–1848)." In *Russian Thinkers*, eds. Henry Hardy and Aileen Kelly, 114–49. New York: Viking Press, 1978.

Bernstein, Deborah, ed. *Pioneers and Homemakers: Jewish Women in Pre-State Israel*. Albany, NY: State University of New York, 1992.

Biale, David. *Eros and the Jews: From Biblical Israel to Contemporary America*. New York: Basic Books, 1992.

Biale, Rachel. *Women and Jewish Law*. New York: Schocken Books, 1984.

Carlebach, Julius. "Family Structure and the Position of Jewish Women." In *Revolution and Evolution, 1848 in German-Jewish History*, eds. Werner E. Mosse et. al., 157–85. Tuebingen: Mohr, 1981.

Cherikover, Elias. *Istoriia obshchestva dlia rasprostraneniia prosveshcheniia mezhdu evreiami v Rossii, 1863–1913*. St. Petersburg, 1913.

Cohen, Stephen M. and Paula E. Hyman, eds. *The Jewish Family: Myths and Reality*. New York: Holmes and Meier, 1986.

"Conference Proceedings of *Di froyen*: Women and Yiddish." New York: National Council of Jewish Women, 1997.

Confino, Michael. "On Intellectuals and Intellectual Traditions in 18–19th Century Russia." *Daedalus* 2 (1972): 117–50.

Corrsin, Stephen D. *Warsaw before the First World War: Poles and Jews in the Third City of the Russian Empire, 1880–1914*. New York: Columbia University Press, 1989.

Davidson, Pamela. *The Poetic Imagination of Viacheslav Ivanov. A Russian Symbolist's Perception of Dante*. Cambridge and New York: Cambridge University Press, 1989.

Dawidowicz, Lucy, ed. *The Golden Tradition*. New York: Holt, Rinehart and Winston, 1967.

Doody, Terrence. *Confessions and Community in the Novel*. Baton Rouge: Louisiana State University Press, 1980.

Dubnov, Simon. *History of the Jews in Russia and Poland*. 3 vols. Philadelphia: Jewish Publication Society of America, 1916.

Engel, Barbara Alpern. *Mothers and Daughters: Women of the Intelligentsia in Nineteenth-Century Russia.* Cambridge and New York: Cambridge University Press, 1983.

Engelstein, Laura. *The Keys to Happiness: Sex and the Search for Modernity in Fin-de-siècle Russia.* Ithaca: Cornell University Press, 1992.

Etkes, Emanuel. *Lita Biyrushalayim.* Jerusalem: Yizhak Ben-Zvi, 1991.

Feiner, Shmuel. "Ha-ishah ha-yehudiyah ha-modernit: mikrah-mivḥan be-yaḥasei ha-haskalah ve-ha-modernah." *Zion* 58 no. 4 (1993): 453–499.

Feingold, Ben Ami. "Feminism in Hebrew Nineteenth-Century Fiction." *Jewish Social Studies* (1987): 235–50.

Fohen, Reuven. "Shir nishkaḥ." *Ha-olam* 46 (June 30, 1938): 835–37.

Frankel, Jonathan. *Prophecy and Politics: Socialism, Nationalism and the Russian Jews, 1862–1917.* Cambridge, England: Cambridge University Press, 1982.

Friedberg, H.D. *Toldot ha-defus ha-ivri be-polanyah.* Tel Aviv, 1950.

Galchinsky, Michael. *The Origin of the Modern Jewish Woman Writer: Romance and Reform in Victorian England.* Detroit: Wayne State University Press, 1996.

Gassenschmidt, Christoph. *Jewish Liberal Politics in Tsarist Russia, 1900–1914.* New York: New York University Press, 1995.

Gay, Peter. *The Enlightenment: An Interpretation.* 2 vols. New York: Knopf, 1969.

_____. *The Naked Heart. The Bourgeois Experience from Victoria to Freud.* Book 4. New York: W.W. Norton and Company, 1995.

Gilbert, Sandra and Susan Gubar. *The Madwoman in the Attic.* New Haven: Yale University Press, 1979.

Gitelman, Zvi. *A Century of Ambivalence. The Jews of Russia and the Soviet Union, 1881 to the Present.* New York: Schocken Books, 1988.

Goscilo, Helena and Beth Holmgren, eds. *Russia Women Culture.* Bloomington and Indianapolis: Indiana University Press, 1996.

Govrin, Nurit. *Devash mi-sela.* Tel Aviv: Misrad ha-bitaḥon, 1989.

_____. *Ha-maḥatzit ha-rishonah: Devorah Baron.* Jerusalem: Mosad Bialik, 1988.

Greene, Diana. "Gender and Genre in Pavlova's *A Double Life.*" *Slavic Review* 54 no. 3 (Fall 1995): 563–77.

Groberg, Kristi A. "Dubnov and Dubnova: Rapport between Father and Daughter." In *A Missionary for History: Essays in Honor of Simon Dub-*

nov, eds. Avraham Greenbaum and Kristi A. Groberg. Minneapolis: University of Minnesota Press, 1998.

Haberer, Erich. *Jews and Revolution in Nineteenth-Century Russia*. Cambridge: Cambridge University Press, 1995.

Harshav, Benjamin. *Language in Time of Revolution*. Los Angeles, CA: University of California Press, 1993.

Heilbrun, Carolyn G. *Writing a Woman's Life*. New York: Norton, 1988.

Henry, Sondra and Emily Taitz. *Written Out of History: Our Jewish Foremothers*. New York: Biblio Press, 1990.

Hertz, Deborah. *Jewish High Society in Old Regime Berlin*. New Haven: Yale University Press, 1988.

———. "Work, Love and Jewishnesss in the Life of Fanny Lewald." In *From East to West, Jews in a Changing Europe, 1750–1870*, eds. Frances Malino and David Sorkin, 202–20. Cambridge, MA: Basil Blackwell, 1991.

Herzog, Elizabeth and Mark Zborowski. *Life is with People: The Jewish Little Town of Eastern Europe*. New York: International University Press, 1952.

Heschel, Abraham Joshua. *The Circle of the Ba'al Shem Tov*. Edited by Samuel H. Dresner. Chicago: University of Chicago Press, 1985.

Hyman, Paula E. *Gender and Assimilation in Modern Jewish History: The Roles and Representations of Women*. Seattle and London: University of Washington Press, 1995.

Johanson, Christine. *Women's Struggle for Higher Education in Russia, 1855–1900*. Kingston [Ontario]: McGill-Queens University Press, 1987.

Kaplan, Marion A. *The Making of the Jewish Middle Class: Women, Family and Identity in Imperial Germany*. New York and Oxford: Oxford University Press, 1991.

Katz, Jacob. *Out of the Ghetto*. Cambridge, MA: Harvard University Press, 1973.

———. *Tradition and Crisis: Jewish Society at the End of the Middle Ages*. Translated by Bernard Dov Cooperman. New York: New York University Press, 1993.

Kelly, Catriona. *A History of Russian Women's Writing, 1820–1992*. Oxford and New York: Clarendon Press, 1994.

Kelly, Joan. "Did Women Have a Renaissance?" In *Women, History and*

Theory: The Essays of Joan Kelly, 19–50. Chicago: University of Chicago Press, 1984.

Kleinbaum, Abby R. "Women in the Age of Light." In *Becoming Visible. Women in European History*, eds. Renate Bridenthal and Claudia Koonz, 219–35. Boston: Houghton, Mifflin, 1977.

Klepfisz, Irena. "Queens of Contradiction: A Feminist Introduction to Yiddish Women Writers." In *Found Treasures: Stories by Yiddish Women Writers*, eds. Frieda Forman, et. al., 21–58. Toronto: Second Story Press, 1994.

Klier, John Doyle. *Imperial Russia's Jewish Question, 1855–1881*. Cambridge and New York: Cambridge University Press, 1995.

Kohansky, Mendel. *The Hebrew Theatre, Its First Fifty Years*. New York: Ktav, 1969.

Kornblatt, Judith Deutsch. "Vladimir Solov'ev on Spiritual Nationhood, Russia and the Jews." *Russian Review* 56 no. 2 (April 1997): 157–79.

Kornilov, Alexander. *Modern Russian History*. 2 vols. New York: Knopf, 1912.

Kraemer, David, ed. *The Jewish Family: Metaphor and Memory*. New York: Oxford University Press, 1989.

Magnes, Shulamit. "Pauline Wengeroff and the Voice of Jewish Modernity." In *Gender and Judaism*, ed. T.M. Rudavsky, 181–90. New York: New York University Press, 1995.

Malia, Martin. "What's the Intelligentsia?" *Daedalus* (Summer 1960): 441–58.

Marsh, Rosalind, ed. *Gender and Russian Literature*. Cambridge: Cambridge University Press, 1996.

Mintz, Alan. *Banished from their Father's Table*. Bloomington and Indianapolis: Indiana University Press, 1987.

Miron, Dan. *Imahot meyasdot, ahayot horgot*. Tel Aviv: ha-kibbuz ha-meuhad, 1991.

———. "Why Was There No Women's Poetry in Hebrew before 1920?" In *Gender and Text in Modern Hebrew and Yiddish Literature*, eds. Naomi B. Sokoloff, et. al, 65–91. New York: Jewish Theological Seminary of America, 1992.

Nakhimovsky, Alice Stone. *Russian-Jewish Literature and Identity*. Baltimore: Johns Hopkins University Press, 1992.

Norich, Anita. "Jewish Literature and Feminist Criticism: An Introduction to Gender and Text." In *Gender and Text in Modern Hebrew and Yiddish Literature*, eds. Naomi B. Sokoloff, et. al. 1–15. New York: Jewish Publication Society of America, 1992.

Parush, Iris. "The Politics of Literacy: Women and Foreign Languages in Jewish Society of Nineteenth-Century Eastern Europe." *Modern Judaism* 15 (1995): 183–206.

———. "Readers in Cameo: Women Readers in Jewish Society of Nineteenth-Century Eastern Europe." *Prooftexts* 14 (1994): 1–23.

Peskowitz, Miriam and Laura Levitt, eds. *Judaism Since Gender*. New York: Routledge, 1997.

Peterson, Ronald E. *A History of Russian Symbolism, 1892–1917*. Amsterdam and Philadelphia: J. Benjamin Publishing, 1993.

Raisin, Jacob S. *The Haskalah Movement in Russia*. Philadelphia: Jewish Publication Society of America, 1913.

Rischin, Ruth. "F.I. Kogan (1891–1974): Translator of the Psalms," *Jews and Slavs* 2 (1994): 193–222.

Rogger, Hans. *Russia in the Age of Modernisation and Revolution, 1881–1917*. London and New York: Longman, 1983.

Rosenthal, Charlotte. "Carving Out a Career: Women Prose Writers, 1885-1917: The Biographical Background." In *Gender and Russian Literature*, ed. Rosalind Marsh. Cambridge: Cambridge University Press, 1996.

Rudavsky, Tamar, ed. *Gender and Judaism*. New York: New York University Press, 1995.

Schorsch, Ismar. *From Text to Context: The Turn to History in Modern Judaism*. Hanover, NH: University Press of New England, 1994.

Sdan, Dov. *Ben din le-ḥeshbon*. Tel Aviv: Dvir, 1963.

Seidman, Naomi. *A Marriage Made in Heaven: The Sexual Politics of Hebrew and Yiddish*. Berkeley, CA: University of California Press, 1997.

Shapiro, M. "From Her Brother's Letter (May 13, 1956)." *Genazaim* (1965): 36–37.

Shepherd, Naomi. *A Price Below Rubies: Jewish Women as Rebels and Radicals*. Cambridge: Harvard University press, 1993.

Sokoloff, Naomi B., Anne Lapidus Lerner and Anita Norich, eds. *Gender and Text in Modern Hebrew and Yiddish Literature*. New York: Jewish Theological Seminary of America, 1992.

Sosnovskaya, Alla. "Was Habimah a Jewish Theater or a Russian Theater in Hebrew?" *Jews in Eastern Europe* 3 no. 22 (1993): 23–30.

Spiegel, Shalom. *Hebrew Reborn*. Cleveland: World Publishing Company, 1962.

Stampfer, Shaul. "Gender Differentiation and Education of the Jewish Woman in Nineteenth-Century Eastern Europe." In *From Shtetl to Socialism, Studies from Polin*, ed. Antony Polonsky, 187–211. London and Washington: Littman Library of Jewish Civilization, 1993.

Stanislawski, Michael. *For Whom Do I Toil?* New York: Oxford University Press, 1988.

––––––. "Jewish Apostasy in Russia: A Tentative Typology." In *Jewish Apostasy in the Modern World*, ed. Todd Endelman, 189–205. New York: Holmes and Meier, 1987.

––––––. "Russian Jewry, the Russian State and the Dynamics of Jewish Emancipation." In *Paths of Emancipation*, eds. Pierre Birnbaum and Ira Katznelson, 262–83. Princeton, NJ: Princeton University Press, 1995.

––––––. *Tsar Nicholas I and the Jews* Philadelphia: Jewish Publication Society, 1983.

Stites, Richard. *The Women's Liberation Movement in Russia*. Princeton, NJ: Princeton University Press, 1978.

Taubman, Jane A. "Women Poets of the Silver Age." In *Women Writers in Russian Literature*, eds. Toby W. Clyman and Diana Greene, 171–88. Westport, CT: Praeger, 1994.

Weissler, Chava. "For Women and for Men Who are Like Women: The Construction of Gender in Yiddish Devotional Literature." *Journal of Feminist Studies in Religion* 5 no. 2 (1989): 7–24.

Weissman, Deborah. "Education of Jewish Women." In *Encyclopedia Judaica Yearbook*, 1986–87.

Wisse, Ruth S. *I.L. Peretz and the Making of Modern Jewish Culture*. Seattle: University of Washington Press, 1991.

Wortman, Richard. *The Crisis of Russian Populism*. London: Cambridge University Press, 1967.

––––––. *The Development of a Russian Legal Consciousness*. Chicago: University of Chicago Press, 1976.

Yerushalmi, Yosef Hayim. *Zakhor*. Seattle: University of Washington Press, 1982.

Zipperstein, Steven A. *Imagining Russian Jewry*. Seattle: University of Washington Press, 1999.

_____. *The Jews of Odessa*. Stanford: Stanford University Press, 1985.

Zirin, Mary F. "Women's Prose Fiction in the Age of Realism." In *Women Writers in Russian Literature*, eds. Toby W. Clyman and Diana Greene, 77–94. Westport, CT: Prager, 1994.

Index

Acmeism, 152
Aguilar, Grace, 37
Agunah, 14–15, 39
Ahad Ha'am, 3, 157, 167
Alexander II, 9–10, 22, 58, 85, 111, 113, 114, 168
Alexander III, 85, 107, 113, 169
Allgemeine Zeitung des Judentums, 33
Alter, Viktor, 190
Am olam movement, 45
Andreev, Leonid, 86, 105
An-ski, S., 186, 189
Apollon, 177
Apostasy, 95–96, 101, 110
Auer, Leopold, 86, 104, 105
Auer, Nadine, 104–5, 108, 112
Autonomism, 165, 170–71, 193
Avivit, Shoshanah, 140–41

Ba'al Shem Tov, 56
Baron, Devorah, 52, 71, 80
Baron, Salo W., 155
Beilis, Mendel, 100
Beller, Steven, 43
Belyi, Andrei, 107, 125, 175
Ben-Yehudah, Hemdah, 52, 80
Berdieva, Elena, 3
Berdischevsky, Micah Yosef, 54, 55, 68, 76
Bernshtein, Berta and Esfir', 168–69
Biale, David, 18
Bialik, Hayim Nahman, 55, 78, 137,144, 177, as actor and playwright in Odessa, 169
Bikhovskii, Elizaveta Zhirkova, 126, 136–38, 154
Bliokh, Ivan Stanislavovich, 106
Blok, Aleksandr, 107, 125, 133, 137, 175, 179

Bluwstein, Rahel, 52, 80
Boborykin, Petr Dmitrievich, 85, 108, 117
Brainin, Reuven, 53, 63, 76, 80
Brandes, Georg, 86
Brenner, Joseph Hayim, 76
Breslau, 33
Briusov, Valeri, 154, 197
Brod, Max, 82
Buber, Martin, 76, 82
Bund, 114, 157, 158, 170, 171, 172, 173, 175, 181, 186, 187, 188, 189, 190, 191, 194

Chmielnicki massacre, 56
Chukovskii, Kornei, 129, 175

Da Costa, Uriel, 66, 105, 140
Damascus Affair, 99
Dawidowicz, Lucy, 2
Dekapol'skii, Filadel'f Petrovich, 91
De Maupassant, Guy, 84
Di folkstsaytung, 188, 189
Dimanstein, Simon, 142–43
Doody, Terrence, 81
Dostoevsky, Feodor, 107
Dubnov, Simon, 130, 157, as member of the Odessa circle, 3; murder of, by Nazis, 158; and Autonomism, 165; disapproval of Jabotinsky, 172; distaste for modern poetry, 178
Dubnov, Yakov (brother of Sofiia), 167–68
Dubnova, Olga (sister of Sofiia), 167
Dubnova-Erlikh, Sofiia and men, 156; birth, 157; education, 157; "Haman," 157; and censors, 157; expelled from university, 157; as

anti-militarist propagandist, 157; universities attended, 157; move to Vilna, 157; marriage, 157; as husband's speechwriter, 158; move to Warsaw, 158; move to U.S., 158; biography of Simon Dubnov, 158, 160; *Bread and Matzah* (memoirs), 158, 195; insider status of, 159; motherhood and, 159; grandmother of, 160–61; ancestors of, 160; mother (Ida), 162; liberalism of parents, 163; educated by father, 163–64; move to Odessa, 164; early poetry, 164; and pantheistic beliefs, 164; "Visions," 165; and Autonomism, 165; and Ussishkin, 165; and plans to emigrate to Palestine, 165; and synagogue attendance, 166; and Symbolism, 166; sister's intermarriage, 167; siblings, 167; move to St. Petersburg, 169; political activities of, 169, 170, 171, 172, 175; expelled from St. Petersburg, 169; political differences with father, 170–71; and Jabotinsky, 171–72; and Vladimir Medem, 173; literary debut, 173; and Eliza Orzheshko, 173–74; pseudonym, 174; "Farewell" (poem), 174; *Autumnal Reed Pipe* (poems), 178–80, 182; "Mother" (cycle of poems), 179–80, 182–87; and Lenin, 181; sons Aleksander and Viktor, 182, 188, 189; and S. An-ski, 186; and Maksim Gorki, 187; position at *Letopis'*, 187; move to Warsaw, 188; move to Berlin, 189; escape from Warsaw, 190; death of mother, 190; articles in Polish, 190; in N.Y., 191; death, 191; *Poems of Various Years*, 191–93

Ehrenburg, Ilya, 153
Elisheva, *see* Elizaveta Zhirkova Bikhovskii
Enlightenment, in Russia, 26; confessional literature of, 54
Ephrati, Devorah, 23; letter to Abraham Mapu, 19
Erlikh, Aleksander, 158, 182, 189
Erlikh, Genrikh, 181, 182, 187, 188, 189; murder by Nazis, 158, 191
Erlikh, Viktor, 158, 182, 189
Etkes, Emanuel, 27
Evreiskii mir, 177
Evsektsiia (Jewish section of the Communist Party), 142, 149

Feiner, Shmuel, 18
Feingold, Ben Ami, 18
Feinstein, Nehamah, 17, 23, 52, 80
Fel'dshtein, Solomon, 88, 101, 109
Foner, Sarah Feiga, *see* Meinkin, Sarah Feiga
Francolm, Isaac Asher, 33, 36, 39
Frederick II, King of Prussia, 26
Frischmann, David, 17, 23, 55, 64, 69–70, 76, 80
Frug, Shimon Shmuel, 144, 166

Gapon, Georgii, 115
Gay, Peter, 54
Gets, Feivel', 107, 108
Gilbert, Sandra, 70
Gnessin, Uri Nissim, 126, 138
Gnessin, Menahem, 76, 138–39, 140, 141, 142
Goldman, Emma, 2
Gol'dovskii, Osip Borisovich, 88, 109–13, and formation of Kadets, 114
Gordon, Bella (wife of Yehudah Leib), 38
Gordon, Yehudah Leib, 43, 75; "The Tip of the Yud," 14–15, 24, 39; as

an advocate for women, 14;
Markel-Mosessohn writes to, 15;
letter to Sheine Wolf, 16; letter to
Nehamah Feinstein, 17; defended
by David Shapira against
Lilienblum's accusations, 19–20;
and Sarah Shapira, 20–22; and
Sarah Feiga Meinkin, 22–23;
correspondence with Markel-
Mosessohn, 24; and Anshel
Markel-Mosessohn, 32; assists
Markel-Mosessohn in publication
of *Jews of England,* 35; attitude
toward woman writers, 35;
decline, 46–47
Gorki, Maksim, 173, 187
Govrim, Nurit, 71
Graetz, Heinrich, 34
Gruzenberg, Oskar Osipovich,
100–101
Gubar, Susan, 70
Gunzburg, Baron, 36
Gumilov, Nikolai, 174, 175, 177
Gutzkow, Karl Ferdinand, 66

Habimah Theater, 126, 189;
founding of, 140; effect on Jewish
culture, 139, 141; conflict
between Ivanov and Dimanstein
over, 143; as religious rite, 143;
and Dubnova-Erlikh's review, 189
Ha-dor, 80
Ha-meassef, 26
Ha-melitz, 40, 42, 46, 64, 130
Hararit, Yehudit, 52
Ha-shaḥar, 37–38, 45–46
Ha-shiloaḥ, 64
Haskalah, in Russia, 9; goals of, 33;
and Jewish historiography, 34;
confessional literary efforts of,
54–55; and rationalization of
Jewish education, 14; and women,

48–49; and Hava Shapiro's family
printing press, 58–59
Ha-toren, 78
Hebrew language, revival of, for
secular literature, 14, 81; and the
Haskalah, 14; and gender, 14, 23;
women's role in revival of, 48,
55–56; use of theater to draw
attention to, 139; Sephardic
pronunciation of, 139; as a
"bourgeois language," 149
Heilbrun, Carolyn, 71
Heine, Heinrich, 99
Hibbat Zion movement, 20
Horodetzky, Samuel, 68, 77
Husserl, Edmund, 68

Intelligentsia, Russian, 85–87
Iushkevich, Semon Solomonovich,
173
Ivanov, Mikhail, 167
Ivanov, Viacheslav Ivanovich, 107,
124, 125, 142, 145–46, 148, 154

Jabotinsky, Vladimir, 171–72
Jewish converts to Christianity,
95–96, 110
Jewish Historical-Ethnographic
Society, 176
Jewish literature, importance of
secular, 5
"Jewish Question," 86, 106, 114, 174
Jews, *balibatishe* (merchants and
professionals), 8
Jews, distinctions between East
European and West European, 7, 8
Judiciary Reforms of 1864, 110

Kadets, 85, 115, 121, 187, 114, 121,
176
Kameneva, Olga Davidovna (Trotsky's
sister), 181
Katino (Khin's country estate), 112

Kayserling, Meyer, 32
Khin, Rashel' Mironovna, inclusion
  in Russian Jewish Encyclopedia,
  84; literary accomplishments,
  84–85; and Russian intelligentsia,
  85–87; and Kadets, 85; and Ivan
  Turgenev, 86, 93–95; conversion
  to Catholicism, 88, 101; and
  Salon Jewesses of Berlin, 88, 122;
  mother, 89; birth, 89; father, 89,
  91, 95, 108; childhood, 89, 91;
  fluency in languages, 91;
  enrollment in "Women's Medical
  Course," 92–93; "From Side to
  Side" (novella), 92–93; as student
  in France, 93; and other Russian
  women writers, 94; Silhouettes, 94,
  100; Downhill, 94; sister's apostasy,
  95; encounters employment
  discrimination, 96; "The Misfit"
  (novella), 97–101, 109, 123; as
  Jewish activist, 101, 102, 121;
  "The Dreamer" (novella), 102–3,
  109, 123; opinions about Jews,
  103–4, 109; and Nadine Auer,
  104; and Leopold Auer, 105;
  "Makarka," 106–7; and Vladimir
  Solov'ev, 107; marriages, 109; son,
  Mikhail, 109; and Anatolii Koni,
  111; friends in the legal
  profession, 111–12; country estate
  of (Katino), 112; financial status
  of, 112; political opinions, 113;
  nephew Maks, 113; opinions
  about Duma, 115; move to Paris,
  115; and Anatole France, 115; as
  dramatist, 116; and Malyi Theater,
  116; "Desire to Die" (play), 116;
  "Budding Sprouts" (play), 117–20;
  translation of George Sands'
  Hamlet, 117; "Under the
  Protection of Penates" (play), 120;
  "Generations" (play), 120;

"Drifting Ice" (play), 120;
  self-imposed exile 1905–1914,
  121; death, 122
Klier, John, 86–87
Kliuchevskii, Vasili Osipovich, 91,
  117
Koenigsberg, 26, 33, 38
Kogan, Faiga Izrailevna, as a
  Symbolist Poet, 124; archives of,
  126; and Habimah, 126, 141–43;
  Jewish content of her poetry, 126;
  autobiography of, 127; birth, 127;
  mother, 127, 135; father, 127,
  130, 135; childhood, 129; sister,
  Ita, 129–30; education of, 130;
  Jewish awareness, 130, 133, 135;
  revolutionary activities of, 131;
  My Soul (poetry anthology), 131,
  135; "Prayer" (poem), 131;
  "Prophet" (poem), 132–33, 155;
  "Adonai" (poem), 133–35, 138,
  155; and Hebrew language, 136,
  137–39; "On the Cross" (poem),
  136–37; and Society for Lovers of
  the Hebrew Language, 137; and
  Menahem Gnessin, 138, 141; and
  Elisheva, 138, 154; studies
  rhetoric and elocution, 141;
  review of "The Dybbuk," 142; and
  Viacheslav Ivanov, 143, 153;
  nervous disorder, 143; conceals
  Jewish works, 143; and Sefer
  ha-aggadah, 144; Bible stories for
  children, 144; The Torch
  (collection of poetry), 145–49; "To
  God" (poem), 145; "I am God's
  Orphan" (poem), 146–47; "God"
  (poem), 147, 155; theological
  views of, 148–49; censorship of
  her 1923 volume, 149, 150; and
  State Institute of the Word, 151;
  and State Institute of Dramatic
  Art, 151; as theorist of poetry,

152; *The Art of Performing Verse*, 152; and Stalin, 152; monograph on Vladimir Maiakovskii, 152; translation of Book of Psalms, 153; and Ilya Ehrenburg, 153; death, 153; Jewishness analyzed, 154; and Hebrew language revival, 154; as an "inverted Marrano," 155

Koni, Anatolii Federovich, 86, 111

Kovno, 31, 37

Levinson, Isaac Baer, 109

Lichtenberg, Georg Christoph, 68

Lilienblum, Moses Leib, 19, 36, 37, 54, 140

Luxemburg, Rosa, 2

Malia, Martin, 85

Malyi Theater, 116, 120

Mapu, Avraham, 19, 30–31, 75

Markel-Mosessohn, Anshel, 31–32, 37, 39, 40

Markel-Mosessohn, Miriam, feelings about being a woman writer, 13, 35–36, 49; and Moses Leib Lilienblum 23; and Abraham Mapu, 23, 30–31; and Yehudah Leib Gordon, 23, 33, 37–40, 46, 47; as confidante of maskilim, 24; birth, 24; siblings, 26; education, 27; mother, 28; move to Congress Poland, 28; formal tutoring in Hebrew, 28; self-education in Hebrew literature, 29–30; marriage, 31–32; childlessness of, 32; and translation efforts, 32–36; and Heinrich Graetz, 34; *The Jews of England*, 35–36, 40, 41; interruption in publications, 37; illness, 38; husband's shady business dealings, 39; Gordon's "The Tip of the Yud" dedicated to her, 39; moves to Danzig and Vienna, 40; as Vienna correspondent for *Ha-melitz*, 40–47; financial burdens, 41–42; articles in *Ha-melitz*, 42–44; on Vienna, 44; on antisemitism, 44; and Jewish observance, 45; attitude toward Hasidim, 45; and Herzl, 46; regrets publications, 46; betrayal by Gordon, 47; death, 47, as "maskilah," 49–50

Masaryk, Tomas, 62, 82, 76

"maskilah," 19

maskilim, and attempts to infuse Hebrew language with feminine qualities, 15–16; and women's roles, 16–17; and principles of Enlightenment, 17–18; and encouragement of women as readers of Hebrew literature, 15; education of, in Hebrew language, 29; "old" vs. "young" maskilim, 86–87

Maze, Yakov, 130, 137, 142

Medem, Vladimir, 172

Meinkin, Sarah Feiga, 22–23

Mendele Mokher Seforim, 75, 167, 170

Mendelssohn, Moses, 34, 86

Mirbeau, Oktave, 86

Miron, Dan, 27

Mogilev, 89

Moscow, expulsion order for Jews of, 127

Nicholas I, 9

Nicholas II, 114, 115

Novakhovitz, Feige, 19, 36–37

Novinsky, Sarah, 15

Odessa, Jewish education in, 168

Odessa Circle, 78, 167

Orzheshko, Eliza, 173–74

Paradiesthal, Yehudah Leib, 28
Parush, Iris, 15
Pascal, Blaise, 148
Peretz, Y.L., 10, 52, 65, 75, 76, 80
Philippson, Ludwig, 33
Plehve, V.K., 157
pogroms, 130, 133, 169
Pohazhavski, Nehamah *see* Feinstein, Nehamah
Populism movement, 85

Rahel, *see* Rahel Bluwstein
Ravnitsky, Yehoshua Hana, 144
Rispart, Eugen, *see* Francolm, Isaac Asher
Rosenbaum, Limel, 53, 62, 67
Rosenbaum, Pinhas, 53, 79
Rosenthal, Charlotte, 198
Rovinah, Hannah, 140
Russian political turmoil, 113–15
Russian intelligentsia, antisemitic attitudes of the, 101
Russian Jewish women, stereotypes of, 1–2, 7, 12; first publications of, in Russian-Jewish press, 3; writers unaware of one another, 5, 18; venturing beyond the Pale, 7; and Western European Jewish women, 7, 8, 17, 88; education of, 13, 27–28, 29–30, 48; and maskilim, 17, 18–19, 48–49; and skills in Hebrew language, 18–19, 23, 70–71; alienation from society, 51–52, 82; image of in literature, 75, 75–76; and apostasy, 96; as a privileged class, 195
Russian Jews, and Yiddish, 9; and secular culture, 9; and the Jewish press, 10; languages of, 10; and Zionism, 11; and Autonomism, 11; and revolutionary movements, 11; and immigration to America,

11; and the Russian intellectual elite, 11; and the legal profession, 110

Sachs, Senior, 36
Saker, Maria, 3
Salon Jewesses of Berlin, 88, 122
Saltykov-Shchedrin, Mikhail Evgrafovich, 111
Sand, George, 84
Sdan, Dov, 27
Shapira, Sarah, 19–22
Shapiro, Hava, ancestors, 51, 56–59; family business, 57–59; literary productivity of, 52; trip to Palestine, 52; and Y.L. Peretz, 52, 65; marriage to Limel Rosenbaum, 53, 62; and Reuven Brainin, 53–54, 63–64, 66, 76; diary of, 54; father, 59, 61; mother, 59, 61, 79; birth, 59; and siblings, 60; "Sanctification of the Moon," 60; dissatisfaction with being female, 60; Jewish observance of, 60–61; education of, in modern languages, 61; and Lovers of the Hebrew Language, 62; birth of son Pinhas, 62; dissatisfaction with marriage to Rosenbaum, 62; "The Rose," 65, 80; and Uriel Da Costa, 66; divorce, 67; as student in Berne, 68–69; and Samuel Horodetzky, 68; doctoral dissertation of, 68–69; *Kovetz tziurim*, 69–70, 71–75, 80; "Clipping of Wings," 71; "The Loner," 74; "The Female Image in Our Literature," 75; on male writers, 75; as a literary critic, 76; as Czech correspondent for *Ha-olam*, 76; during World War I, 77; and Hayim Nahman Bialik, 78; escape to Prague, 78; reports

atrocities in Ukraine, 78; regrets about writing career, 79; lives with gentiles, 79; marriage to Dr. J. Winternitz, 79; death, 80; as perpetual wanderer, 80–81; as part of the revival of Hebrew, 82
Sheremetev family, 95–96
Sholem Aleichem, 10
Silver Age Poetry, 156, 158, 176
Slavuta, Volhynia, 56, 58–59
Smolenskin, Peretz, 37, 45, 75
Society for Lovers of the Hebrew Language, 137, 139
Society for the Spread of Enlightenment among the Jews, 102
Society of Lovers of the Russian Word, 93
Sokolov, Nahum, 55, 66, 69
Solov'ev, Vladimir Sergeevich, 85–86, 107
Stampfer, Shaul, 27
Stanislavskii, Konstantin, 141–42
Stanislawski, Michael, 95
Stein, Ludwig, 68
Strakhov, Nikolai Nikolaevich, 108
Suvalk, 28
Symbolist poetry in Russia, 124, 152

Taneev, Vladimir Ivanovich, 111
Thibault, Jacques Anatole, 86
Turgenev, Ivan, 54, 85, 86, 93–95, 118, 120
Tzukerman, A., 42

Unkovskii, Alexei Mikhailovich, 111
Urusov, Aleksandr Ivanovich, 86, 110, 111
Ussishkin, Abraham Menahem Mendel, 165

Vengerov, Simon, 84
Vengerova, Zinaida, 3
Verein für Cultur und Wissenschaft der Juden, 34
Vienna, position of Jews in cultural elite of, 43
Volkovyshki, 24, 26, 28
Voskhod, 2–3, 23, 84, 109, 157

Wengeroff, Pauline, 2,3
Weiss, Isaac Hirsch, 61
Winternitz, Dr. J., 79
Wolf, Sheine, 16, 23
"Woman Question," 117

Yellin, Itta, 52
Yiddish, linked to women, common folk, and daily routine, 13; Communist attitude toward, 149, 151
YIVO, 190

Zasulich, Vera, 86, 111
Zemah, Nahum, 140–41
Zhirkova, Elizabeta Ivanova, *see* Bikhovskii, Elizaveta Zhirkova
Zola, Emile, 84, 86